# Prime-Time Parenting

*Books by Kay Kuzma*

Nursery School and Day Care Center Management Guide
(co-authored with Clare Cherry and
Barbara Harkness)
My Unforgettable Parents
Understanding Children
Understanding Children Study Guide
Child Study Through Observation and Participation
Guidelines for Child Care Centers
Don't Step on the Pansies
Building Character (co-authored with Jan Kuzma)
The Kim, Kari, and Kevin Storybook
Teaching Your Own Preschool Children

# Prime-Time Parenting

Kay Kuzma

Rawson, Wade Publishers, Inc.
New York

Library of Congress Cataloging in Publication Data
    Kuzma, Kay.
    Prime-time parenting.
    Includes index.
    1. Parenting—United States.    2. Parent and
child.   3. Time allocation.   I. Title.
HQ755.8.K89        649'.1          79-67637
ISBN  0-89256-122-X

Published simultaneously in Canada by McClelland
    and Stewart, Ltd.

        Composition by American–Stratford Graphic Services, Inc.,
            Brattleboro, Vermont
        Printed and bound by R. R. Donnelley & Sons Co.,
            Crawfordsville, Indiana

    *Designed by Gene Siegel*
    First Edition

Dedicated to my three *K*'s  . . .
Kimberly,
Karlene, and
Kevin  . . .
who taught me that the secret of
successful Prime-Time Parenting is found in the initials
Q.T.T.
meaning "Quality Time Together" and not as
some might think  . . .
"Quick to Trounce!"

# Acknowledgments

To my husband, Jan, who encouraged me to write, offered creative suggestions, and made the entire project possible by spending prime time with our children. To Kim, Kari, and Kevin for their cooperation, resourcefulness, and prayers for "Mommy's book." *Prime-Time Parenting* has been a family project.

To my students who leave their imprint on my thinking and their spirit of enthusiasm in my soul.

To my colleagues, friends, and fellow working parents —Marilyn Beach, Lyn Behrens, Esther Glaser, Raylene Phillips, Annie Rathbun, Paul Roesel, Darilee and Elmar Sakala, and Elisabeth Ann Wear—for their professional and technical expertise.

To Faith Bosley and Bonnie Koncz for helping me with the typing and to Sandee Kromminga who brought my children home from school so I would have a few more minutes for writing.

To the many busy parents who shared their personal experiences and suggestions—Leslie Brant, Dorothy Comm, Marilyn Crane, Diane Garrett, Marilyn Herber, Janice Mace, Elaine Macknet, Melba Olmstead, Rosemarie Osmunson, Shari Preszler, Gail Rice, Kay Sutton, Nancy Testerman, and Jean Wise—and to those whose names I have forgotten.

To Eleanor Rawson who gave me the title, the focus, and the opportunity to write this book; to Sharon Morgan who helped me polish the rough drafts; and to Maryanne Colas who never gave up hope.

# Contents

# Introduction

I'm a working mother. My husband, Jan, is a working father. But we are striving to be more than working parents. Our goal is to be prime-time parents—parents who are vitally interested in maintaining positive relationships with our children even though our work schedules permit less than a twenty-four-hour-a-day vigil. Prime-time parents are parents who consider every minute with their children prime time to communicate the message of parental love, interest, and care.

Jan and I are among a growing number of couples who aren't concerned about whether our children receive enough "mothering" or "fathering" per se. We *are* concerned that they receive enough effective parenting to assure their continual development as healthy, happy, and competent individuals. Who fills the parenting function (Mom or Dad) is not as critical as the assurance that the job is well done.

Although the working father has been honored and upheld as an ideal parent, the working mother has long been cast in negative shadows. A woman's place was at home— to care for and nurture children, to keep the home fires burning. The ideal mother did not "work"—at least not for money.

However, as a result of many changes in our society during the last decade, the picture of a woman's role has begun to change. And today, many families find it difficult to achieve economic security on one income. The fact is, *women with children are working*—over fifteen million of them! That is approximately half of all the mothers in the country! Many of these mothers are single parents who must work. Others who have a choice have exercised it and chosen to work.

Two positive factors have emerged from this growing influx of working mothers. First, as more mothers join the work force, more fathers are becoming actively involved in child rearing. Second, since parents have fewer hours to teach, nurture, and influence their children, they are becoming more interested in using this prime time efficiently and constructively.

It's a new day, and it's time for us to do away with the somewhat maligned concept of the "working mother" and speak to the generation of busy, yet concerned working parents—prime-time parents.

*Prime-Time Parenting* is a comprehensive sourcebook for *all* busy parents. It will teach you how to get the biggest benefits from the limited time you have to spend with your children. You can work *and* be a successful parent. It is possible to combine a paying job—even a demanding career—with the job of parenting, and raise healthy, happy, competent children. *But it isn't easy*. It doesn't come naturally. And there are no magic formulas that produce immediate success. Just as you must study and strive to become more skilled at your "job-for-pay," you must be willing to study and strive to become more skilled at your prime-time parenting job. This book is an essential starting place. It not only offers practical solutions to such problems as finding time to parent, child care, guilt, illness, and work/

family conflicts, but more importantly, it is a complete parenting guide for the busy working parent. I share my model for developing a prime-time parenting personality, ideas on how to discipline so your child will become self-disciplined, and innovative ways to shape your family into a winning team.

For years I've been in the business of helping moms and dads become more effective parents. Most of the mistakes that parents make stem from ignorance. Parents have good intentions. They want to do what is right. They want to have good kids. But they often don't know how to go about it. Given appropriate information, they can and do transform ineffective and harmful practices into positive parenting skills.

My preparation for this career began as I delved into the study of child development at Michigan State University. At UCLA I obtained a doctorate in early childhood education. Before and during the first years of my own personal child-rearing experience, I worked with parents and taught university students as a vital part of my job teaching in, and directing, nursery schools (The University Elementary School at UCLA, the Preschool Laboratory at California State University at Northridge, the Loma Linda University Child Development Center on the Riverside Campus, and the Children's Center in Loma Linda, California).

After Kim, Kari, and Kevin were born, I realized that I needed to simplify my life if I were to continue being a prime-time parent. I decided to accept a position close to my home and to my children's school. As an added attraction, it was in the same school of the university where my husband taught. Jan is the chairman of the Department of Biostatistics and Epidemiology at Loma Linda University's School of Health, and my office is right down the hall where I'm an associate professor in health sciences (maternal and child health), training public health students in the field of family health and parent education. Under the auspices of Loma Linda University's School of Health, I also design and present a series of instructional programs for parents called Parenting Seminars, and I am now developing a Prime-Time Parenting seminar based on the material in this book. I love my work, I love my students, but most of all I love my own children and don't want them to suffer because I have chosen to combine a career with parenting.

Kim is now eleven years old, Kari is nine, and Kevin is seven. A few weeks ago, at Kevin's classroom open house, I noticed a picture that he drew of our family. Underneath, he had dictated these words, "My daddy is a bionic statistician and my mother teaches other mommies and daddies how to be good to their children." I'm glad Kevin has this image of his working parents.

During a decade of prime-time parenting experience I have learned many valuable lessons about effectively combining a career with parenting. I know there are over fifteen million other mothers out there who are experiencing similar frustrations and pressures as they try to juggle two important responsibilities. Therefore, I have combined my professional experience with my personal experience to offer you ideas and suggestions about how you can become more than just a working parent. My aspiration for you is to become an effective prime-time parent.

Kay Kuzma, Ed.D.
Loma Linda University, 1980.

# Prime-Time Parenting

# 1

## Quality Time Together: The Key to Success

Time is a precious commodity in which we have all been served an equal portion. How we choose to spend that time is our decision. Time can be wasted or invested. As I see it, there are two ways to invest our time. One is in the building of things—better jobs, a good reputation, a clean house, professional competence, a new home, a gourmet meal, a vacation by the lake, a summer cottage, or an extra TV set. The other is in the building of relationships—with oneself, a spouse, children, family, and friends.

Time is the most important ingredient in the building of a relationship. You cannot convince a child of your love unless you spend time with the child. You cannot effectively discipline and guide a child unless you spend time with the child. You cannot even effectively communicate unless time is involved.

Although the importance of time is undeniable, it is an extremely limited commodity for the working parent. There is often precious little left for the family after one tends to job, community, and church responsibilities.

You may have a lifetime to build and accumulate things. You may have a lifetime to build relationships with

3

friends, neighbors, or even a spouse. But the critical time to build meaningful relationships with your children is limited to the few short years they are growing up in your home.

The diagram that follows represents the family life cycle from the time of marriage until the death of the parents. Note that the amount of time children spend in the home, from the birth of the first child until the last child is launched, does not even fill one entire half of the circle.

In the average family, therefore, children are only home for about one half of the time a parent spends as part of the family unit. And this amount of time decreases even further in families with fewer children.

How much time should parents spend with their children? It is impossible to give an answer that would be meaningful for all families since it depends upon the child, the family situation, and the quality of the time given to the parent-child relationship. But in too many cases, children are not receiving their fair share. This point was emphatically made in two studies reported by Urie Bronfenbrenner.* He found that middle-class fathers thought they spent an average of fifteen to twenty minutes per day with their one-year-old infants. This might sound like a ridiculously low figure, but this is only what the fathers "thought." To test the accuracy of this assumption, researchers placed tiny microphones on the babies' shirts, without the fathers' knowledge. The microphones picked up the fathers' voices when they interacted with their babies. That time was recorded and averaged out for all the fathers who participated in the study. The findings were startling: even though fathers thought they spent about fifteen to twenty minutes per day with their infants, they actually averaged 2.7 interactions per day totaling 37.7 seconds!

* Urie Bronfenbrenner, "The Origins of Alienation," *Scientific American*, Vol. 231 (August 1974): 54.

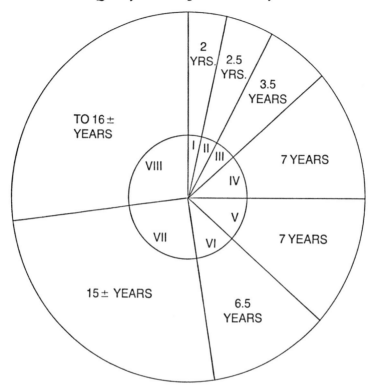

CHART 1. The Family Life Cycle by Length of Time in Each of Eight Stages[1]

I BEGINNING FAMILIES (Married couple without children).
II CHILDBEARING FAMILIES (Oldest child birth–30 months).
III FAMILIES WITH PRESCHOOL CHILDREN (Oldest child 30 months–6 years).
IV FAMILIES WITH SCHOOL CHILDREN (Oldest child 6–13 years).
V FAMILIES WITH TEENAGERS (Oldest child 13–20 years).
VI FAMILIES AS LAUNCHING CENTERS (First child gone to last child leaving home).
VII FAMILIES IN THE MIDDLE YEARS (Empty nest to retirement).
VIII AGING FAMILIES (Retirement to death of both spouses).

[1]Data from U. S. Bureau of the Census.

From: Evelyn M. Duvall, *Family Development,* 3rd ed. (Philadelphia: J. B. Lippincott Company, 1967), p. 13; used by permission.

The amount of time a child needs to develop to his optimum capacity cannot be measured in minutes and hours. It can only be measured in the child's total physical and psychological well-being. If you were to err in the amount of time you give your child, err on the side of too much time rather than too little.

Here is the dilemma. The ideal child-bearing time is between the ages of twenty-one and twenty-nine when the female body is at the peak of its performance to insure a healthy, normal baby. However, this is also the very worst time period for most young parents to find the extra hours needed to care for and nurture their offspring. This is the time to finish school, to establish a career, to mortgage a house, to keep up with the Joneses, and to buy everything it took their parents a lifetime to accumulate.

Children need Mom and Dad most during the first five to ten years of their life. From then on they require less parental time as they go to school and become involved in peer group activities. Ironically, however, in most families Mom and Dad find themselves the busiest during the very years that their children's needs are the greatest.

During these critical child-rearing years, parents who choose to invest some of their time in responsibilities outside the home must commit themselves to quality time together with their children if they wish to build a solid parent-child relationship. Such a commitment involves two key ingredients: 1) parents must carve out as much time as possible for the family; and 2) they must use that time as effectively as possible.

**Quality Time Together versus Negative and
Nothing Time Together**

Listen a moment. The "scene" is next door. (Or is it?)

"Lisa, breakfast's ready. Quit your dilly-dallying and come."

(Silence.)

"Lisa, if you don't come this minute, I'm going to give you a spanking you'll never forget."

(Lisa wanders in slowly with her shoes in her hand.)

"Can't you ever come when you're first called? You are going to make me late for my meeting and it's all going to be your fault. Why do you have your shoes in your hands? Shoes are to be put on your feet.

"Drink your milk quickly. . . . I said drink your milk, not spill it! How can you be so clumsy?"

Time together? Well, yes. At least Mom or Dad felt it was important to stay home long enough to attempt to get poor Lisa dressed and fed. What did Lisa learn from this short encounter with her parent? She may have learned that her parent gets frustrated and angry easily; that her parent threatens her and is impatient. She may even have learned how her parent feels about her—she is clumsy; she doesn't obey; she is responsible for making her parent late. From an accumulation of similar incidents she may even begin to feel that she isn't loved.

Every minute that you spend with your children is prime time. You're on stage, so to speak, influencing and teaching them by your words and behavior—whether you want to or not. So, in parent-child relationships, spending time together is not enough. To make that time meaningful, it must be quality time. Careful thought and planning must be a prerequisite for successful parenting.

There are three ways in which parents and children can use time together. Q.T.T.—quality time together—is the key to success. The other two types are N.T.T.s—negative time together and nothing time together. The N.T.T.s must be avoided if parents are interested in giving their children an "I love you" message.

N.T.T. #1—negative time together—is deadly to parent-child relationships. The pitiful Lisa story is a prime example. Such time is filled with discord, dissension, and conflict. The home, the car, or anyplace where the family assembles can become a battleground. Although the primary weapons are usually words, it is not uncommon for "fists" to follow. The message of negative time together is a message of hostility rather than love.

N.T.T. #2 refers to nothing time together. Although the family is "together," or least in close proximity, and there is no outward conflict, the TV is blaring, the dog is barking, and Dad has barricaded himself in the study to do the income tax. Mom has been gossiping on the phone for an hour. Her message to Junior is, "Go outside and play and don't bother me today!" Nothing time together may not destroy relationships as quickly as negative time together, but it does eventually tear them down, and certainly does nothing to build or repair them. The end result of this type of neglect is the same. The message of nothing time together is a message of indifference and rejection rather than love.

Q.T.T. is the most important factor in building healthy and wholesome parent-child relationships. Quality time together is characterized by more than constant interaction; the key factor is continuing interest. Q.T.T. may be a noisy family celebration; a quiet evening at home listening to daughter practice for her recital—correcting her when necessary; a sleepless night nursing a fevered child; a holiday spent cleaning out the garage; or an hour spent in animated discussion of a family problem. Whatever the activity, quality time together should convey several all-important messages: "I love you," "I want to be close to you," "I enjoy you," "You're fun to be with." Time spent this way fosters a child's self-esteem and encourages a healthy family bond.

### Putting Quality Time Together into Practice

The importance of quality time together can hardly be disputed, yet agreeing with the concept is much easier than consistently putting it into practice. It is easier to know what you should do than to take the time to do it. For example, a number of years ago when I was writing an article on this subject, my son Kevin put in a "timely" appearance and volunteered, "Mommy, can't I help you type?"

Well, my typing was poor enough—at times hardly legible, and the last thing I needed was the help of a three-year-old. So to avoid a conflict I began trying to interest him in leaving me alone. "Kevin," I began, trying to point out the reality of the situation, "I am very busy. I am trying to write a very important article to tell Mommies and Daddies how to spend more time with their children, and I don't have time to let you type now."

But that didn't work, so I tried distraction. "Kevin, why don't you go outside and play with your sisters?" But he didn't want to do that. Next I tried a more understanding approach. "Kevin, I know you want to type. You like to type when I type, don't you."

"Yes, Mommy," he answered as he reached over and put an 83 klp-3 on the page.

"Oh, Kevin. No! No!" I moaned. Finally, I decided to try a contract. "Kevin, if you leave me alone now and do something else, like build a road for your cars, then I'll let you type or I'll read you a story or I'll do anything you want (I was getting desperate) when I'm finished with this article."

"But Mommy, I want to type now and I don't know how to build a road." So I stopped typing, told him to put a couple of blocks together, and reached down and showed him what I meant, then turned back to my work. "That's a yucky road," he sulked. Then with one or two well-placed kicks the blocks were strewn around the room. Dejected, Kevin retreated to the other room.

To reorient my thinking, I read over the last few sentences of my article. Then the light dawned—*Quality Time Together!!!* That's what Kevin needed immediately, not when my article was finished!

I jerked out my half-typed page and inserted a clean one. "Okay, Kevin. It's your turn to type." As he wiggled into a comfortable position on my lap and his fingers began to fly over the electric keys, he smiled and said, "I'm Mommy's big helper, huh?" Forgetting my schedule I sat back to enjoy my son. After about three minutes he hopped off my lap, announced, "I'm finished," and disappeared. I realized that his desire to type was his way of saying, "Mommy, I need some attention." Once his little love cup was full, he was ready to move on to other activities.

How do you determine whether a child is receiving enough parental time? If he is old enough, ask him. In a recent survey eleven-year-olds were asked this very question. Over 50 percent of the children with working mothers said they wished their mothers would spend more time with them. But the surprising finding was that approximately 30 percent of the children whose mothers were classified as "nonworking" wished the same thing! Apparently this is not just a working parent's problem!

Not all children are able to verbalize their need for parental time and attention. When this is true you must interpret a child's behavior. Kevin communicated his need by behaving in a disruptive manner. Sending him off to an isolation room would have only increased his need and would have probably resulted in more negative behavior. But after a few minutes of my undivided attention, he was satisfied and ready to move on.

Negative behavior is often a sign of parental time deficiency. Young children equate love with parental attention. If they do not receive their fill of positive attention, they sometimes resort to behavior that will, without question, bring negative attention. In their way of thinking, even negative attention is better than no attention at all. Therefore, parents must learn to distinguish the hidden meaning behind a child's actions.

Not all children need the same amount of parental time. Needs may fluctuate from day to day. When a child feels feverish or down in the dumps, he may need a triple decker portion of Q.T.T. The very next day he may announce, "Mommy, go away."

Preschoolers generally thrive on parental time. A ten-year-old, on the other hand, may be happy with an audience for her memorized tuba solo, a fifteen-minute rough-and-tumble session, and a good-night kiss. Then, just when you thought you were finally going to have time to read the magazines that have been accumulating over the last ten years, your child becomes a teenager with a new set of problems that demand parental time.

There is no single pattern that all children follow. To fill a child's need for parental time successfully, you must tune in to your child and fill a need as it surfaces. There is one important rule to remember: ignoring a need for parental time will only increase the intensity of that need.

Although long leisurely periods when parents are readily accessible are occasionally important, don't expect a summer vacation on the beach to fill your child's need for parental time for the next nine months. Q.T.T. is like an ice cream cone. It tastes better when consumed lick by lick rather than in one giant gulp. And, if you try to make a big hunk of Q.T.T. last too long, the effect will slowly melt away.

How does your family measure up when it comes to Q.T.T. versus N.T.T.? Take time now to describe an

N.T.T. #1 (negative time together) incident that occurred in your family last week. How could this have been prevented or turned into Q.T.T.? If you have difficulty answering this question, refer to the chart "How to Turn N.T.T. #1 into Q.T.T."

Now think about N.T.T. #2 (nothing time together). Describe a recent N.T.T. #2 incident. How could this have been prevented or turned into Q.T.T.? If you have difficulty answering this question, refer to the chart "How to Turn N.T.T. #2 into Q.T.T.

Now, think positively. Describe a Q.T.T. incident that you had with your family recently. How can you make sure that your family will experience Q.T.T. more often in the future? There are three significant ways: 1) by making parenting an equal-status career; 2) by taking advantage of "wasted" time; 3) by scheduling time together.

The remainder of the chapter will focus on some of the ways you can put these ideas into practice in your busy life to achieve a greater amount of Q.T.T.

### Make Parenting an Equal-status Career

Parenting is the most important career a mother or father can pursue. It has critical, deep-seated, and long-term effects. In this one career no one else can substitute for you with the same degree of meaning. No one can ever really take your place. Yet, in our society, parenting has been relegated to a rather low-status position because it doesn't measure up on those variables that usually determine status. Consider salary for example; there is none. Training required? None—not even basic training. Decent working hours? It's a twenty-four-hour-a-day job with no sick leave or vacations. What about stability? It's seasonal, so to speak, for only about twenty years. The advancement possibilities are limited to grandparent status. Authority? Yes, there is some authority attached to the job, but it only

## How to Turn N.T.T. #1 into Q.T.T.

| *Typical negative time together behavior* | *Prescription for quality time together* |
| --- | --- |
| Quarreling | Be positive. |
| Fighting | Listen carefully to words and |
| Yelling | behavior. |
| Calling names | Never let the little sores fester. |
| Picking on each other | Make peace as soon as |
| Teasing with the aim to hurt | possible—at least by bed- |
| Putting another person down | time. |
| Demeaning others (Belittling) | Don't jump on the defensive |
| Showing jealousy | when attacked. |
| Pestering | Be quick to say, "I'm sorry." |
| Rebelling | Use this phrase when you are |
| Spanking indiscriminately | tempted to argue, "You |
| Hurting another's feelings | have a good point." |
| Demanding your own way | Always make the other person |
| Throwing temper tantrums | feel good about himself. |
| Criticizing | Show unconditional accep- |
| | tance. |
| | Allow others to make a choice |
| | whenever you feel they are |
| | capable. |
| | Forgive and forget. |
| | Clarify the discussion topic. |
| | Be willing to compromise. |
| | Be firm when appropriate. |
| | Settle differences without |
| | excessive anger. |
| | Solve problems as they arise. |
| | Calmly discipline for the first |
| | signs of misbehavior. |
| | Accept your own faults and |
| | mistakes rather than trying |
| | to justify yourself by blam- |
| | ing others. |
| | Treat others as you would like |
| | to be treated. |

# How to Turn N.T.T. #2 into Q.T.T.

| Typical nothing time together behavior | Prescription for quality time together |
|---|---|
| Pouting | Don't punish others by not speaking. |
| Giving others the silent treatment | Don't bottle up your feelings. |
| Doing your own thing and excluding family participation | Be willing to have a confrontation to solve a problem. |
| Ignoring others | Look into the other person's eyes when speaking. |
| Using a minimum of eye contact | Focus on other's needs rather than your own. |
| Seldom touching a family member | Invite others to be with you. |
| Talking only when spoken to | Don't let one person dominate your time to the exclusion of others who need it. |
| Shutting yourself in a room alone | Make special occasions special. |
| Playing the radio or TV so loud that it is impossible to hear others | When you must have private uninterrupted time tell the family why and how long and then do something together when finished. |
| Excessive watching of TV | |
| Halfhearted listening | Spend time with family before becoming involved in your own projects. |
| Talking on the phone to the exclusion of the family | Respect others' feelings. |
| Forgetting birthdays and special occasions | Have an appropriate touch experience with each person daily. |
| Meeting your own needs at the expense of others | Set aside at least fifteen minutes a day for each child. |
| | Limit TV viewing. |
| | If you have difficulty hearing get a hearing aid! |
| | Let the family know, that no matter what, they come first—even though you must sometimes ask them to wait so you can finish a deadline and then give them your full attention. |

applies to minors. Finally, there is not even any guarantee of old-age assistance.

A low status career often negatively affects the attitude of the worker. In turn, his attitude will determine his effectiveness. A positive attitude is a prime prerequisite for a successful parenting career and a healthy amount of family Q.T.T. If you view parenting with a who-cares, laissez-faire attitude you are doomed to failure. If you have a superior, know-it-all attitude you are headed for problems. If you feel parenting is a second-rate job and therefore unworthy of your time, your best efforts, and your full attention, you will do a second-rate job.

The only answer to the problem is to give parenting equal status with other careers. This can be easily justified by the immeasurable importance of two things. First, the product—a child. Nothing can equal the value of a child's life. Second, the personal benefits—benefits above and beyond anything money can buy. Like a good-night bear hug; the present of wilted flowers held up to you by a little hand; or the words, "Mommy, you're the bestest mommy in the whole wide world," when you are tired, weary, and wondering if it's all really worth it. What other career can provide such delightful and spontaneous rewards?

If you view parenting as an equal-status career, you will approach it with a greater sense of dedication. This attitude will, in turn, affect your behavior in a positive way. You will perform your responsibilities as a parent with the same prepartion, time commitment, and professionalism that you would bring to any other important career. The result will be more Q.T.T. for the family.

Specifically, if you view parenting as an equal-status career, you will:

1. *Prepare for your employment.* If it is too late for preemployment training, take advantage of in-service training and workshops. Watch for advertisements in your local paper or call your school district office, the YMCA, the

Red Cross, churches, colleges, counseling centers, or the child services office of your county Health and Welfare Department. Be open and willing to learn from your mistakes. When in doubt don't hesitate to call upon an experienced parent you admire and ask for advice. Become familiar with a good child-care manual. There are a variety of excellent parenting books available. Learn all you can about child development, discipline, and methods of effective parenting. When you prepare for your parenting career thoughtfully, you will do a better job and enjoy it more. In addition, your family will benefit from a greater amount of Q.T.T.

2. *Devote adequate time to the career to assure success.* Don't just rely on the few minutes of leftover time from another career. Special times should be planned when you are freshest, most vibrant, and most creative. Your spouse and children should have an equal chance to see you at your best—as your professional colleagues do.

3. *Perform as a professional.* When you accept a job that you hope to keep, your behavior must be professional, efficient, and conducive to a good working relationship with others. Plan and organize the job of parenting as you would execute your professional career. It will make the job easier and it will also help to insure Q.T.T.

Parenting actually involves many jobs: teaching, cooking, housekeeping, chauffeuring, gardening, and sewing, to name just a few. How would you perform these jobs if you were employed to do them for pay outside the home on a very limited time schedule? Apply some of these same ideas to your job at home.

For example, consider the major task of parenting—teaching. A parent is the child's first teacher and remains the child's most important teacher throughout life. Parents are primarily responsible for teaching children moral values, good health habits, standards of conduct, social behavior, self-discipline, and skills in interpersonal relationships. And in their capacity as homework helpers, they are often expected to be well versed in reading, math, science, history, and other school-related subjects as well!

The professional teacher must know enough about child development to understand the characteristics of his students, and he must know his subject matter well enough to apply it in a way that meets the children's needs. He must establish himself as an authority in certain areas, and maintain discipline while helping his students learn self-discipline. He must set objectives for his students and provide learning opportunities in a way that will motivate the students to learn.

Since teaching is such an important part of parenting, how can you bring more Q.T.T. into your child's life by approaching this job as a professional? Record your ideas, and turn to the following chart for other helpful suggestions.

### Ideas for Making an Equal-Status Career out of the Parenting Job of Teaching

1. Study child development and be well acquainted with the age-characteristics of your children.
2. Teach your children what they are capable of learning.
3. Study methods of parenting.
4. Study subject matter and methods of teaching.
5. Read books on how to teach various areas of knowledge, such as reading, character development, music, etc.
6. Design a curriculum (what you want to teach and what the children need).
7. Write specific objectives.
8. Provide a variety of learning opportunities.
9. Take advantage of the teachable moment—when a child is interested in learning.
10. Learn how to motivate children.
11. Continue to experiment with more effective methods of discipline.
12. Keep current with what the professionals are saying. *Psychology Today, Parents Magazine,* and the education sections of weekly news magazines are a good place to begin.

13. Organize the home environment to be a more effective learning environment: provide a good encyclopedia appropriate for your child's age, craft materials, puzzles, table games, basketball net, and a quiet place to study.
14. Use your community's resources: library, YMCA, tennis courts, concerts, etc.
15. Take field trips. Many places are open evenings and weekends.
16. When your child shows a particular interest in something, provide him with resources for further study. Learn something about it yourself.
17. Teach your child your areas of expertise: basketball, tennis, crocheting, clothing construction, gourmet cooking, etc.
18. "Subcontract" out those teaching areas that need a professional and/or special equipment: music lessons, gymnastics, horseback riding, etc.
19. Keep in touch with your child's classroom teacher (work as partners or co-teachers).
20. Be willing to tutor your child if necessary.
21. Observe your children. Note their strengths and weaknesses and build on these.
22. Be willing to individualize instruction.
23. Seek to make travel time, or other seemingly wasted minutes, teaching time.
24. Periodically evaluate what your child has learned.
25. Evaluate your teaching.
26. Encourage, encourage, encourage. A discouraged child is a child who is headed for learning and behavior problems.

### Other Parenting Jobs

1. Plan routine activities.
2. Write down schedules.
3. Organize materials needed.
4. Continue to work on efficiency.
5. Make sure equipment is in good repair.
6. Train an apprentice (your children).
7. Seek expert advice when needed.
8. Take advantage of in-service training to increase your skills.

9. Subcontract as many of the jobs as possible (what you can afford); especially those jobs you find least enjoyable and least capable of performing.

If other aspects of the parenting career were elevated to an equal-status basis with professional jobs, parents would perform these jobs with more interest, planning, and efficiency than they might if they continued to consider them as menial tasks that had to be done. If children were encouraged to participate in these jobs as an apprentice might, as soon as they showed an interest (which is usually a couple of years before they are really "able"), the parent would again function as a teacher, transforming a previously menial "homework" session into a Q.T.T. learning experience.

The benefits of the parenting career—the reward for a job well done—is the product parents are producing: a happy, healthy child. If you, as a prime-time parent, consider your parenting job as an equal-status career, then you would more readily see that the time you spend with your children is time put to the highest use.

### Take Advantage of "Wasted" Time

A prime-time parent can create more Q.T.T. by utilizing time that *must* be spent with children to the fullest advantage. Young children must be washed, diapered, clothed, and cuddled. Older children have to be chauffeured, chaperoned, and disciplined. Parents who are eager to use their skills to reach above and beyond the fulfillment of these basic needs sometimes feel that these common daily chores are a waste of time. But are they really?

The answer is found in the following words from Antoine De Saint-Exupery's delightful book, *The Little Prince:* "It is the time you have wasted for your rose that makes your rose so important." The story is about the Little Prince who lived up on Asteroid B-612 and took care of a little rose who had led him to believe that she was the only rose in the world. She demanded constant care and attention. He spent his time shading her from the sun, covering her at night, and pulling up the weeds around her. Finally, with much reluctance, he decided that he had to leave her and move on to explore the earth. After meeting a variety of people, the Little Prince finds a large rose garden filled with thousands of roses that look just like his rose. He is heartbroken because he had believed for years that his rose was the only one of its kind. Then a wise fox comforts him with these words, "It is the time you have wasted for your rose that makes your rose so important."

Boswell, the biographer of Samuel Johnson, often talked about the day his father took him fishing and how meaningful this was to him as a young lad. One curious researcher decided to check Boswell's father's diary to see if his father had a similar reaction to that particular event. And there opposite that date these words were penned, "Gone fishing today with my son; a day wasted."

It is the time we "waste" with (and for) our children that will assure a good relationship with them and convince them of our love. This time has to be given joyfully with our wholehearted interest in their affairs. Never let your child think that you would *rather* be doing something else (although you may *need* to do something else), or that you feel you are wasting your time when you are with him.

One evening my friend Marilyn was in the midst of preparing gravy for dinner when her teenage son rushed into the kitchen shouting, "Mom, come outside quickly. I've got something to show you."

There is a critical point in the preparation of gravy when it must be stirred in order to have a smooth consistency. Marilyn, who is a gourmet cook and relishes the thought of a perfect dinner, was at that critical preparation point and almost said, "Can't you wait a minute? I've got to finish stirring the gravy." But an inner sense said, "Go." After all, it had been weeks since her son had asked her anything—or even wanted to be with the family. So she turned off the stove, removed the gravy, and went outside. Her son pointed to the western horizon and exclaimed, "Mom, look at that sunset. Isn't that the most beautiful thing you have ever seen?" They both watched until the last rays disappeared.

A wasted moment? It may have seemed so, if smooth gravy is the thing you value most in your life. But as this mother said, "I'd eat lumpy gravy every night of the week to have that kind of daily experience with my teenager. After all, gravy soon disappears, but the relationship I establish with my son can last a lifetime."

There are only two ways that time can be wasted: N.T.T. #1 (negative time together) with its message of hostility; and N.T.T. #2 (nothing time together) with its message of indifference and neglect. Any other time spent with a child should never be considered "wasted" time. However, even Q.T.T. can vary in terms of quality, so prime-time parents must strive to get as much as possible from the time spent with their child. And with a little effort, you *can* get "more" from your time. To help you achieve this goal, remember these basic principles for redeeming low quality time.

1. Encourage communication, but don't talk all the time.

2. Show a genuine interest in the child.

3. Give focused attention—lots of eye contact and a touch or two.

4. Maintain a positive attitude.

5. Be willing to help.

With this approach, previously "wasted" time can be transformed into high-quality time. The parenting job will become a privilege to look forward to. Parents will learn how to truly enjoy the time they *must* spend with their children and it will become the best investment they ever made.

Start to make better use of your time with your children immediately by listing examples of what you may have considered "wasted" time. Then think about how you can make this time high-quality time with a little effort. Use the following chart to supplement your ideas.

## How to Redeem Low-Quality Time

*Diapering, feeding, dressing, or bathing the young child*

1. Talk (and listen) to the child.
2. Pay full attention to the child with eye contact and touch.
3. Encourage the child to participate.
4. Teach the child something with each encounter (how to count, recognize colors, etc.).
5. Tell the child something that will build a healthy self-concept.
6. Play games (when appropriate).
7. Use this time to observe the child carefully.
8. Convey your enjoyment of the experience.

*Doctoring scratches and bruises*

1. Be helpful.
2. Sympathize: Say, "I know it hurts."
3. For younger children who want it, apply a bandage whether needed or not.
4. Give a hug, a kiss, or a love pat.
5. Be willing to hold them for a few minutes.
6. Accept appropriate crying. Ignore the inappropriate.
7. Do something. Apply ice, blow the hurt away, hold it under cold water, etc.
8. Tell them about a similar incident that happened to you.
9. Pray with the child.

*Practicing musical instruments*

---

1. Let him know you are always willing to help.
2. Show you are interested by saying, "When you are ready for an audience, I'd love to listen."
3. Sit down next to the child and listen for a few minutes even without an invitation.
4. Focus your full attention on the child while you listen.
5. Find something positive to say.
6. If you think you have some helpful criticism, cushion it by asking if the child wants advice.
7. Plan a performance time for the whole family.
8. Let the child overhear you telling another family member how well he is doing—but be honest.
9. When the child is discouraged, help him over a rough spot.
10. Attend the music lesson occasionally—if the child wants you to.
11. If you can, play something with the child.

*Housecleaning (cleaning one room)*

---

1. Work together in close proximity so you can communicate.
2. Sing as you work.
3. Tell a story or an experience that happened at work.
4. Make a game out of it.
5. Have a tea party when finished—just the two of you.
6. Compliment the child on something specific.
7. Plan a surprise for another member of the family together.
8. Make a cassette recording for the relatives by chatting back and forth while you work.
9. Offer advice judiciously.
10. Don't expect perfection.

*Preparing meals or washing dishes*

---

1. Let the child help with the planning.
2. Encourage the child to make one dish alone.
3. Make a point of telling the family about the dish your child prepared.
4. Don't rush. Plan a meal that is simple enough to prepare in the time allotted.
5. Don't expect perfection.

6. When mistakes are made, don't rub it in. Laugh, help clean up the mess, or tell the child about a similar incident when you made an even bigger mess.
7. Find a kitchen job that fits the interest and skills of the child.
8. While you are working, encourage the child to pull up a chair and read to you.
9. Have the children do their homework at the kitchen table while you are working, so you can be available to answer a question if they need you.
10. Work together on the dishes and clean-up.
11. Surprise the child occasionally by doing one of his routine kitchen jobs for him.

*Exercising and jogging*

---

1. Do it together.
2. Find something the whole family enjoys.
3. Talk as you exercise.
4. Exercise with one child alone. Make this your special time together.

*Shopping*

---

1. Take the kids along (sometimes one at a time for a special outing with Mom).
2. Give each child a list and have them find the right items.
3. Teach them how to compare prices.
4. Let them purchase something special that they want (within reason).

Prime-time parents who are trying to find value and meaning in the parenting experience, and especially in the time they thought they were wasting with their children, must realize that the very time they "waste" with their children will assure a growing, positive parent-child relationship. When it is time to launch your child, no amount of last-minute preparations can take the place of the "wasted" time you have freely given him throughout the growing years.

### Schedule Time Together

For many ambitious career-oriented parents, job obligations become so pressing that they take more and more time away from the family. Finally, time spent with the family can even be considered a waste of time, since parents don't see any connection between family time and career advancement.

In addition, when a man spends so little time with his young children that they hardly know him, the children will tend to seek out mother for help and attention and may actually reject their father's offers of help. Unless Dad is highly motivated to change the situation, he may leave more and more of the parenting responsibilities to Mom as he finds rewards and success in his career. When this happens, his wife and children see less and less of him and may begin to resent his career. They may even interpret the time he devotes to his career as an indication of his lack of love and concern for them. At the same time he may erroneously believe that he is showing his love to his family by succeeding in his career and making money to give them the things they need and want.

This situation can also occur with an ambitious working mother who leaves her children for long periods of time and consistently chooses to meet her job obligations rather than her family obligations. Eventually the children (and her husband) may grow to resent her job and question her love for them.

Harry Jones, a salesman, was asked to select the two things in his life that he considered most important. Without hesitation he answered, "God and my family." He was then asked to recall, hour by hour, how he spent his time for the last two days. Here's a sample of one of those days:

6:30   Got up before any of the family.
7:00   Hurried downtown to eat breakfast. (Justification: his wife likes to sleep later, and he

was able to make valuable business contacts while at the same time getting a wholesome, leisurely breakfast away from the mad scramble of getting the kids off to school.)

| | |
|---|---|
| 8:00–12:00 | Business. |
| 12:00–1:00 | Lunch with business associates. |
| 1:00–6:00 | Business. |
| 6:30 | Home at last, but he insisted on a half hour by himself to read the mail and wind down from a busy day. This also gave his wife time to feed the kids first so he could have a leisurely meal with his wife later. |
| 7:00 | Dinner with his wife while the kids were either watching TV or doing their homework. |
| 8:00 | Catch-up time with bills or reading the newspaper. |
| 9:00 | TV. |
| 10:30 | Bed, usually reading a religious book for a few minutes before getting too sleepy to continue. Wife usually stayed up longer since this was the quiet time in the house when she could really accomplish something. |

When contrasting this schedule with Harry's two highest values, God and his family, it appears that the way he was choosing to spend his daily time did not reflect his true values. Or could it be that his schedule reflected the things he really values, which have little in common with his stated values? Based upon his schedule, Harry's occupation seems to be of primary importance since he devotes 9 1/2 to 11 1/2 hours per day to his job, including both breakfast and lunch.

When Harry reevaluated his schedule, he felt that it was not essential to eat both breakfast and lunch away from his family. With some thought and planning, he decided that breakfast at home could become a real family affair. Some type of family worship could also be incorporated into this time, which would probably serve to bring the family closer together. His wife could join him for some of his luncheon appointments, or he could, with just a little more effort, drop home for lunch occasionally.

Harry was disappointed that he spent so little time with his children. After-dinner time was spent catching up with the bills, newspaper, and the TV. These activities were important to him, but this was also the only time during the day that he had an opportunity to interact with his children. The quality of his interaction with his children during this time was extremely low. It consisted of exchanges such as, "Joe, turn the stereo down, I can't even hear the TV." "Mary, finish your homework." "You've been on the phone long enough." "Larry, stop hitting your brother." "No, you can't have your allowance until Friday." All of these interactions took place while Harry was involved with projects of his own. He viewed them as distractions and annoyances rather than as ways of improving his relationships with his children and showing them the love he had for them. How could this situation be remedied without entirely eliminating the evening activities he enjoyed? Harry's solution was to schedule time with his children. One night a week was designated as family night when the family could choose a group activity. On another night he would do something special with just one child or his wife. This meant the children (and Mom) would have to take turns, but at least once every month each would have a special time with Dad.

Scheduling quality time together may be the only way busy families can ever find time for each other. But scheduling is just the first step. Keeping the appointment is equally important. A college classmate of mine often complained that her busy doctor father never came home when he promised. Once, when the family was packed and ready to depart for a vacation, there was a three-day delay as emergency after emergency came into the office and *had* to be handled. Certainly emergencies do occur and family appointments occasionally must be broken, but when this happens too often, children lose confidence in their parents' promises and are less likely to believe that their parents really enjoy their company. They begin to feel that everyone else is more important to their parents than they are.

Connie Gills had this problem. She had a demanding job as an executive for a large international firm. She kept all of her important appointments in her "little black book." Whenever her children wanted to do something special with her, she would take out her book to see if the time was free. In the majority of cases, she would have to shake her head and say, "No, kids, I'm sorry. I already have an important appointment."

One day her son asked, "Mommy, do you think I'm an important appointment?"

"Well, yes I do, Son," she stammered.

"Then why don't you write my name down in your book?"

Connie couldn't argue with that so she handed the appointment book to the children. "You kids decide what you want me to do with you and then find a time that is empty and write it down. Then it will become one of my very important appointments."

By planning time with her children weeks and months in advance she found it easier to schedule her business appointments around the children. She would just pull out her appointment book and if there was a conflict she would say, "I'm sorry, I have a previous commitment!" Those appointments to go backpacking, deep-sea fishing, rafting down the river, horseback riding, and stargazing are now among the family's most meaningful memories.

Every family should set aside a regularly scheduled family time with which nothing is allowed to interfere. I suggest a once-a-week STAFF meeting. (That is S.T.A.F.F., as in "Steps to Active Family Fun," if Mom and Dad plan to play games with their children. Or it could mean, "Steps to Airing Family Feelings" if a family council is needed.) You may find it difficult to turn down the chairman of the church nominating committee when he says, "We must meet Tuesday night," if you tell him that you had planned to pop popcorn and bob for apples with your children. But if you say, "Sorry, I have a STAFF meeting that night," he seldom will persist.

In addition to a weekly STAFF meeting, you may want to schedule some of the following daily, weekly, or monthly activities.

### Possible Activities for Family Scheduling

*Daily*

---

1. Meals that will be eaten together.
2. Exercise time.
3. Story time.
4. Family worship time.
5. Cooking, washing dishes, and clean-up together time.
6. Fifteen minutes or more of special time when you will do whatever a child wants you to do with him.

*Weekly*

---

1. STAFF meetings.
2. Shopping trips the children enjoy.
3. Sunday afternoon time with Dad (if the kids get all their work done before noon).
4. A special TV show the whole family enjoys.
5. Going to church or church activities together.
6. Inviting over a "family" guest.
7. Baking bread together.

*Monthly*

---

1. Observation at a child's special lesson (music, gymnastics, swimming, etc).
2. A special outing "field trip" such as the zoo, the beach, a camping trip, a picnic, etc.
3. A special "date" with Dad. Dinner at a restaurant, miniature golf, a concert, tennis, etc.
4. Catch-up day where everyone stays home and tackles a family project—like cleaning the garage, washing and polishing the cars, haircuts and permanents, refinishing a piece of furniture, etc.
5. A book the family would all like to read and discuss together.

When you begin to schedule quality time together, it is important that you and your child do those things that have the most meaning. List all of the family's favorite activities. Brainstorm. Then rank these items from the most important to the least important. Finally, schedule those items that have a high priority. If you schedule only the easiest activities, or those that take the least effort or time, you probably won't be able to do the most important ones.

Scheduling quality time together and meeting that schedule is an important step in finding and enjoying more quality time together.

# 2

# Sharing the Child-Care Responsibility

There is a basic amount of loving adult time that each child needs during his formative years if he is to grow up to be a competent, secure individual. There are no shortcuts. One individual alone doesn't have to fill this need, nor is the magic number two. It doesn't have to be just Mom and Dad and relatives. But *someone* has to provide consistent, stable, loving nurture.

After reading various case studies and interviewing a wide variety of parents who both work, I have come to the conclusion that families who are most successful at juggling parenting and outside job responsibilities fall into three categories. They can be characterized by the following formulas that add up to 1—the number that represents the total amount of time necessary to meet the children's needs.

1. $1/2 + 1/2 = 1$. Mom and Dad share parenting equally. Both have full-time jobs, both limit those jobs so they do not impose on the family any more than necessary, and both take active responsibility for child-care and house-keeping responsibilities. Additional help is hired when needed. Jan and I probably fall within this category.

2. $3/4 + 1/4 = 1$. In this category, one parent takes

primary responsibility for the children and the home and only works part-time, or at a fairly flexible job that is close to home. The other parent has an extremely demanding job that requires long or irregular hours away from home. Babysitting is used when necessary, and chores like weekly housecleaning are often hired out.

My friend Lenore and her husband have this type of relationship. She is the chief pediatrician in an intensive care nursery of a large hospital. The job is demanding, challenging, and time consuming. Her husband, an engineer, quit his demanding job with a large company to start his own "home-based" business so he could have flexible hours to get their four boys off to school, chauffeur them to their various lessons after school, and generally keep the family together during these critical child-rearing years. Now instead of having to consult two work schedules to plan vacations and free weekends, they only need to consult Mom's calendar and they are free to take off. And having Mom home is a privilege—the kids enjoy surprising her by occasionally serving her breakfast in bed. Everyone has benefited. Her husband is even completing the building of a home computer—something he has wanted to do for years but never had time for.

This somewhat unequal method of sharing child-care responsibilities works well as long as each parent is happy and respects the other.

3. $1/4 + 1/4 + 1/2 = 1$. In this category, Mom and Dad rely on someone else to meet the majority of their children's needs. Usually both parents work at extremely demanding jobs that require long and irregular hours. A live-in relative or maid handles all the housekeeping, and takes over the major responsibility for the children. When both parents have demanding jobs, however, it is impossible to have the same parental impact on the children. Successful child rearing can occur in these busy families if

someone is available to love and care for the children, *and* if Mom and Dad let their children know that despite the demands of their jobs, they love the children supremely and will spend quality time with them when they are all together. This usually means short surprise times during the week and on weekends, and fairly frequent vacations—at least more than two weeks in the summer. Some parents who fall into this category choose either not to work or to lighten their loads during the summer in order to spend more time with the children when they have summer vacation time. Scheduling time to be with the children is especially important for these families.

It is possible to be a successful parent and hold a demanding full-time job, but only if you can afford to pay for some of the services necessary to keep the family and home intact. Because single parents do not have the built-in support system of a spouse to help meet the time needs of their children, they usually opt for a less demanding job in order to provide the necessary flexibility to be home when they are really needed.

Actually, a single parent could fit into any one of these three categories, depending upon how much outside support is available or financially viable. Single parents in the 1/2 + 1/2 category generally share the child-rearing responsibility equally with another working parent who has a slightly different schedule, or with a babysitter. Their jobs are usually regular and do not require too many after-hour appointments, overtime, or travel.

The 3/4 + 1/4 category is the preferred arrangement of most single parents who only work part-time or seasonally. They take on the major child-care and home responsibilities and rely on others for only a small portion of the time.

Single parents who have highly demanding jobs must rely on someone else to take the major responsibility for child care—at least for preschool children. They may opt for a reversal of the 3/4 + 1/4 arrangement, utilizing one additional full-time or live-in person to meet most of the household's needs. Or they may choose the 1/2 + 1/4 + 1/4 arrangement, relying on several people to share some of the chores, but giving the major responsibility for the children to one full-time or live-in housekeeper.

Taking *sole* responsibility for parenting (child care) while holding down a full-time job is like trying to light a candle with just half of a match—it's a lot easier to get your fingers burned. And the chances of lighting the candle properly are just not as good. Sometimes it works—if it's a fairly easy candle to light or if the candle is older and has been lit before—but sometimes it does not. Some candles are just harder to light then others and require more time, and it's the same way with children. Some children are more difficult to rear and they simply require more time from one or a variety of caregivers.

The problem of finding someone to share the child-care responsibility must be faced and solved by each working parent. Sooner or later, you, as a prime-time parent, may find yourself in a situation similar to the following:

You just got a new job and your boss has made it clear that you are to be there on time. Aunt Sue was to arrive at your house thirty minutes ago to take care of the baby. There is no one else around to babysit. If you don't leave for work right now, you'll be late. What should you do?

Government officials are visiting your office today. You've just begun introducing them to the operation when you receive a message that your child is very ill and must be taken home from school immediately. What should you do?

You love your job. It's a dream come true, but your third babysitter has just quit and you can't find adequate care for your children. What should you do?

In order to keep your job, you must take a class two

nights a week. You've searched, but you can't find anyone to take care of the kids. What should you do?

You don't want to sacrifice your child's well-being for personal gain and satisfaction or even for financial stability. You want both. But the nitty-gritty reality is that *somebody has to take care of the children.* If you can't do it, how can you find someone who will give them the time, love, and discipline they need to become competent individuals?

Finding the type of child care that is right for you and for your child is a difficult, time-consuming task. But unless you are completely satisfied with the substitute care you find for your child, you will never eliminate those nagging guilt feelings.

### Type of Care

First, decide what type of child care you prefer for your child. Here are some of the possibilities, with some pros and cons for each.

1. *Live-in maid or relative.* Such a person can range from a full-time governess-housekeeper to a graduate student who will gladly exchange room and board to be a big sister or brother to your child. (Graduate students are particularly good for after-school and evening care but their class schedule must match your own needs.)

PRO: a. A live-in helper is always there and available. This is especially convenient for working parents with irregular and/or longs hours.

b. A live-in helper usually takes on more household responsibilities than a babysitter.

c. Stable and consistent care from one person is especially good for small children.

d. If child care is needed on a long-term basis, a live-in helper may become part of the family and parents' departures are not traumatic events.

CON: a. It is difficult to find someone who shares your

child-rearing philosophy and will get along with the children.

    b. If this person is handling housework too, the children may not, in the long run, receive as much attention as they would from a person hired only to care for them.

    c. This care is expensive and one must have an available room for living quarters.

    d. Because a live-in helper is always available, parents may be tempted to spend longer hours away from their children and take short vacations without the children, instead of giving the children as much parental time and attention as possible.

    2. *Babysitter coming to your house.*

PRO: a. Home care is excellent for younger children who find it difficult to adjust to new situations.

    b. Babysitters are usually paid to watch, play with, and care for the children. The children should receive their sitter's full attention.

    c. Parents can avoid the hassle of preparing diapers, bottles, toys, sweaters, changes of clothing, and everything else the child might need while he is away from home.

CON: a. Regular daytime care—when teenagers aren't available—is more expensive than taking the child to someone else's house.

    b. People enjoy being in their own homes, so it is not always easy to find a person who is willing to come to your home.

    c. A high turnover rate can be a problem since these individuals often find easier and more lucrative jobs elsewhere.

    3. *Family day-care "mothers."* These are individuals who are licensed to care for a certain number of children in their own homes.

PRO: a. Licensing insures that certain safety and health standards are met.

b. This type of care is easy to locate since a list of licensed homes is available through the licensing agency, which is usually the social welfare office in your area.

c. The children are in a home environment and usually have other children to interact with.

CON: a. Family day-care "mothers" sometimes have very little, if any, training for the job.

b. Such care is not always stable and dependable. When a family day-care "mother" becomes ill, wants a day off, or goes on vacation, there is no one else to care for your child. Also, in many states, if the "mother" becomes pregnant, regulations require a reduction in the number of children she can look after—and this could affect your child.

c. You have no control over the way a family day-care "mother" spends her day. She may do a beautiful job, or she may spend most of her time watching TV or reading magazines.

4. *Nonlicensed home.*

PRO: a. Taking your child to a friend's or relative's home can be an excellent solution if the caregiver loves and disciplines the child as her own, and provides appropriate learning opportunities.

b. Other children are often available for your child to interact with.

c. This type of care is usually flexible, which is important for parents who work irregular hours.

CON: a. You do not have the assurance that health and safety factors are met if the home is not licensed.

b. Care is not always available. Illness or other commitments may intervene, so you must have a back-up service.

c. Training is not required, so the quality of the care may not meet your standards.

5. *Exchanging child-care services.*

PRO:   a. If parents exchange services equally, no cost is involved.

b. Because you are caring for each other's children, it is easier to discuss your philosophy and techniques of child rearing and compare notes on the children's behavior.

c. Depending on the caregiver, this arrangement might offer more flexibility.

CON:   a. One parent could misuse the privilege.

b. It may be more difficult to make changes if you are not satisfied, because children other than your own are also involved.

c. It may be difficult for your child to share you with other children. This is especially true with young children.

d. Your child must spend twice as much time with other children than he would have to if you paid for child-care services.

e. After a busy day at work, you may not feel like taking care of someone else's children.

f. A back-up service is needed in case the caregiver is ill or has a conflicting appointment.

6. *Group care for children.* Group care can be lumped into three broad categories: nursery schools (which are usually partial-day programs); preschools (partial-day programs which are usually connected to a school program and may be more academically oriented than a nursery school); and child-care or day-care centers (full-day care and sometimes night care and after-school care).

PRO:   a. Care is always available on a regular schedule —which is great if the hours coincide with your work hours.

b. Teachers have training and/or experience.

c. Teachers have no other responsibilities than to watch and teach the children.

d. A wide variety of toys, play equipment, and learning activities are usually available.

e. There is a planned curriculum and a regular schedule of activities.

f. Centers must be licensed, so they should meet safety and health requirements.

g. Government funded programs usually have a graduated fee scale to make such care available for everyone. If you are a single parent with a low salary, or returning to school, this care might be very reasonable for you.

h. Many centers have additional services, such as counseling, extended day care for older children, or bus service.

CON: a. Group care may be more expensive than babysitting care.

b. The center may not be open when you need its service.

c. The center may not take children on a flexible schedule if your job is irregular.

d. Most centers are licensed to take children in a particular age group—usually two through six years of age. They may require the child to be toilet trained. Infant and toddler programs are available in some communities, but without government funding they are very expensive.

e. The program is only as good as the director and teachers.

f. Some children (usually the younger ones) find it difficult to adjust to a group experience and may be happier in a home situation with fewer children.

g. The larger the child-care center, the more institutionalized the program. It's difficult to find a "homey" atmosphere in a large center.

For parents who are students or who are working part-time and only need child care for a small portion of the day, or during odd and irregular hours, the following types of arrangements might be beneficial.

7. *Babysitting pool.* A large group of parents sign up to take care of other children in exchange for irregular or part-time child care of their own. This is similar to exchanging child-care services, but it is handled on a larger scale.

PRO:   a. There is no cost involved if you exchange child care evenly.

b. A large number of caregivers are available.

c. This type of care can function as emergency back-up when you need extra services or your regular sitter is not available.

CON:   a. You must be willing to babysit other children.

b. Since there are a large number of caregivers, your child may not have the consistency of one caregiver.

c. Such care can be used only in limited ways, and it is not very practical for parents who are working more than part-time.

d. Someone has to keep the records. The bigger the babysitting pool, the more complicated the record keeping becomes.

8. *Home play group.* Usually four or five mothers with similar-aged children organize a morning or afternoon program where all the children rotate to a different home each day or each week. The mother in charge becomes the teacher and plans learning activities for the children while the other mothers can enjoy a few hours of "free" time. Even though the children may rotate to different homes, the schedule of activities is usually similar. There is no extra charge involved in this type of care because each mother contributes the necessary supplies and time.

PRO:   a. The children are in a home setting with familiar caregivers.

b. The children receive a nursery school-type program without cost to you.

c. Parents are involved in the child care, planning together what type of program they want for their children.

d. The parents establish a group with friends who have similar interests and child-care problems.

CON: a. A parent's working hours must coincide with the hours when care is available.

b. Your child is at a different house each day or each week depending on the schedule.

c. It may be difficult to find a group of parents who want to establish this type of care system and who hold similar child-rearing philosophies.

d. The system breaks down when someone is sick, unless others are willing to substitute.

9. *Parent cooperative nursery schools and day-care programs.* These programs are owned and operated by the parents who participate. Most programs are partial-day programs, or full-day programs that cater to student families on college campuses. Participating parents must be involved a designated number of days in the teaching program or they must volunteer to fulfill other needed services. A minimum fee is usually set to hire one teacher-director to keep the program running smoothly.

PRO: a. The child has a nursery school-type experience that is fairly inexpensive.

b. The child has a consistent environment.

c. The parents, fathers as well as mothers, are involved in the child's program.

d. The teacher is trained and will usually have in-service training sessions for the parents.

e. Most parents find that a close community spirit develops in programs where parents are working together for the same goal—quality care for their children. They make good and lasting friendships.

CON: a. You must have time to donate to the program.

b. Irresponsible parents can be very detrimental to the program.

c. The program is only as good as the hired teacher-director.

d. The requirements for in-service training and the attendance of various organizational meetings may be too time consuming.

### Qualifications of the Caregiver

After choosing the type of child-care service that best meets your needs, you must decide what type of person you want to influence and teach your child when you are away. The type of care you select is only as good as the person who will actually be caring for your child, whether it be your mother-in-law, a maid, a family day-care mother, a babysitter, or a teacher. For example, live-in help may be ideal for your schedule, but if the only person you are able to find is not the kind of person you want your child to grow up to be, then you should look at alternative types of care.

Prime-time parents continue to have the major influence on a child's life, but this influence may not be strong enough to combat the negative influence of a caregiver. The more time a child spends with another adult, the more he learns from that adult, the more he models that adult, and the more his life is influenced by that adult. This is especially true during the early years, but must be carefully considered even during the teenage years.

The effect on the child's self-concept must also be considered. Feelings of self-worth are influenced by the attitudes of those around us. Therefore, if a caregiver doesn't like your child (or doesn't like children in general), this attitude will be reflected in your child's feelings about himself. If the caregiver disciplines a child in a way that generates feelings of guilt or shame, this diminishes a child's self-concept. If the caregiver doesn't meet the child's need for love and attention, a young child often feels that he or she is at fault. This feeling can spread and the child may even erroneously reason that he is to blame for his parents' absence. He may believe that they leave him because they don't like him or enjoy being with him. Thus, his self-concept is further diminished.

Your success as a prime-time parent is partially determined by your ability to find the "right" person to care for your child. As you make your selection, consider these essential qualifications of the ideal caregiver.

1. *The caregiver should be supportive of the parents.* Leslie, the mother of three small boys, was going through a very difficult period in her life. She was forced to keep a demanding full-time job because her husband did not have a regular job and was very irresponsible about his family obligations. Leslie had searched for the right type of care for her children and finally found another mother of three who was willing to watch her boys for a reasonable rate. Leslie promised to pick up her children before suppertime each evening. But she was not able to keep her promise on certain evenings when her husband took their only car and did not return on time. This, of course, infringed on the caregiver's family because they wanted to have supper alone. The caregiver would put the three little boys in another room and feed her own children. When the boys would cry, "We're hungry," the caregiver would say, "I'm sorry. Your mother promised to be here to pick you up before supper and if she really cared about you and loved you she would be here."

Such a seemingly innocent remark. But in reality this was much more painful to these little boys than a spanking would have been. When this was said every time Leslie was unable to pick up her children on time, it slowly destroyed the children's belief that their mother really loved and cared about them. And in their confusion of feelings they began to reason that if their mother, their very *own* mother, did not love and care for them, then they must not be very worthwhile little people.

Do not let this happen to your children. Be very careful to communicate with the caregiver so she can support you and help your children understand how much you love them even though you must be away from them part of the day. Your child's identity, his personhood, is all wrapped up in you, his parents. He is part of you and any words that demean you, demean that child too.

When interviewing a prospective teacher or a long-term babysitter for your children, you might ask some of these revealing questions. "If I come home later than I promised, what would you tell my children?" "If you don't agree with the things I do and the way I spend my time, what would you say?" "If you don't like what I've told you to do or what I've asked you to see that the children do, what attitude would you exhibit in front of the children?" Of course, there is no guarantee that a person will follow through on his answers, but it is important to discuss your differences and the attitude that you would like the caregiver to display when he is with your children.

The undercurrent of a negative attitude can affect the caregiver's behavior toward your children in subtle ways. Therefore, let the caregiver know that you expect her to discuss any disagreements or conflicts with you immediately. You want to have a chance to explain the reasons for your behavior and clear the air. If your child is aware of a gulf between you and the caregiver, that can be very damaging. It's similar to a child's reaction when Mommy and Daddy disagree. Because the child loves both, he does not know which side to take. You want your children to know that you and the caregiver are in complete harmony. You may choose to act differently, but the principles behind your actions should be the same.

Establishing a harmonious rapport with someone takes

time. If you want to have an understanding like this with your child's caregiver, it is essential to spend time with this person. Some mothers schedule a half hour a day to discuss the day's routine, the activities the child enjoyed, any behavior problems that occurred, and the interesting things the child said.

Thirty minutes a day is not necessarily the magic amount of time it takes to establish rapport. A five-minute talk when you collect the children, a telephone call during the day, or an occasional invitation for dinner might be sufficient. The important thing is to establish a regular channel for communication and evaluation.

When children are in a nursery school or day-care center, it is essential to exchange a friendly greeting with the teacher at the door each morning and evening. Linger for a moment, looking at your child's creative work or a new toy in the room, to give the teacher an opportunity to comment about the day. Closing time may be a busy time for the teacher, so if you have a question that requires more than a "yes" or "no" answer, you might want to jot it down and ask the teacher to call you in the evening (after the kids are in bed), or set up an appointment to talk more leisurely.

Teachers, for the most part, want to share their day with you. Working parents, however, are so busy that they often can't afford to linger too long. Teachers sometimes feel that the parents really don't care what is going on in school. Therefore, don't wait for a teacher to tackle you; take the offensive and actively encourage good communication. He or she will be much more understanding and supportive of you.

2. *The caregiver should be a master at combining love and discipline.* Too often, babysitters allow the children to get away with murder. On the other extreme, they may dictate and punish the child into submission.

The prime-time parent should not leave his child in someone else's care unless he is convinced that this person understands the age characteristics of children. A caregiver should also know how to require obedience in a firm but loving way, without resorting to harsh physical or psychological punishment.

When interviewing a prospective caregiver, don't be afraid to ask, "What would you do if Johnny stole a dollar from your purse or told you a lie or called you names?" Think of the worst situation possible. If you are satisfied that the answer is acceptable, you can probably assume that milder offenses will receive appropriate action.

Don't strip the caregiver of all authority. Disciplinary problems should be handled as they arise. A prime-time parent wants to be greeted with open arms, enthusiasm, and a recital of good things that the children have done— especially when the children can overhear. Negative tidings dampen the homecoming. If a problem arose during the day that needs your attention, ask the caregiver to phone you. Then you will have time to brainstorm together on a combined strategy to cope with the problem. Don't allow the caregiver to criticize the child or discuss the problem in front of the family. No child (or adult) likes to have his faults talked about. But don't be indifferent to your children's problems. Problem behavior is a sign that all is not well in the child's life. The sooner this is analyzed and solved, the happier the child will be.

3. *The caregiver should be open and willing to learn.* It is difficult to work with anyone who thinks that she knows all the answers. A caregiver should be open to new suggestions, and should not feel threatened when you disagree. She should be capable of making good decisions without having to ask you for detailed instructions. On the other hand, don't abdicate your responsibility as the parent and take a back seat when it comes to child rearing. The parent-caregiver relationship is most satisfying when there is mutual respect and an ability to talk things over on equal terms. If the parent seems to know it all, this often brings

out the defensive nature of the caregiver. If the parent takes the position that the caregiver knows best, this may create a superiority attitude. When both are willing to consider the position of the other and learn from one another, the relationship will be a good one and the children will benefit.

To find out how your caregiver feels about certain child-rearing philosophies and disciplinary techniques, choose one or two good books that you have found helpful and ask the caregiver to read them. Then discuss the books when you have time for a lengthy chat. By taking time to talk with each other in this manner you should both learn a great deal from the other.

4. *The caregiver should be the kind of person you want your children to grow up to be.* Because children are master imitators, you want them to spend time with someone who has personality traits that you will enjoy seeing exhibited in your children's behavior. Look for a happy, enthusiastic, optimistic person who loves children. Next, look for evidence of orderliness, honesty, integrity, firmness to principle, and patience.

Because children have a way of bringing out the worst in some people, you will want to know how the caregiver deals with frustration and anger. Does she take it out on the children? Does she pout? Does she scream? Is she willing to explain her feelings to the children before they become so intense that they cannot be contained, controlled, or diverted into constructive activity? Is her speech a good model for your child to follow?

Don't be afraid to level with a prospective caregiver about the kind of example you want her to set for your children. Then ask her if she thinks she can live up to these expectations.

5. *The caregiver should be willing to teach your child.* A good caregiver should be willing to teach whenever the teachable moment occurs. If everyone is sunbathing outside and your child is busy watching a line of ants and asks,

"Where are the ants going?" you don't want the caregiver to say, "I'm reading a book, don't bother me." Rather, you want her to put down the book, get up and say, "That's a good question. Let's follow them as far as we can." Your children should have every learning opportunity that they would have if you were home with them full time.

The teaching of values should not occur only when you are home. It is important that children know what other people consider right and wrong, valuable and good. Because this is such a sensitive area, you will probably want to choose a caregiver who shares your values and religious beliefs. If she doesn't, you will want her to understand your family values, and uphold those beliefs and principles when she is with your child.

To help you choose the best caregiver for your child, you may want to ask some of the following questions.

### Sample Questions to Ask When Interviewing a Caregiver

1. Tell me about yourself. Do you have family or relatives here?
2. What is your educational background? Do you have any special training?
3. What do you consider your best qualifications for the job?
4. Why did you decide to apply for this position? (What made you decide to become a teacher?) If you could do or be anything in this world, what would you choose?
5. Have you ever done this type of work before? What was the reason you left?
6. Do you have a driver's license? Transportation?
7. What are your long-term goals? Do you forsee any reason why you might not want to stay a full year?
8. For what reasons would you consider asking for extra time off?
9. How do you feel about working overtime if an emergency comes up and I can't get home?
10. Do you have trouble getting places on time?
11. What are your major interests outside of taking care of children?

12. What do you find most depressing? Does this happen often?
13. What activities do you think you might plan for my child?
14. What child behaviors irritate you most? What do you do in these situations?
15. Do you like to cook? Take children on field trips? Garden? (List other activities that might be included as projects the caregiver might do with your child.) How do you feel about children being included in these activities?
16. What would you do if my child got a nosebleed? Tummy ache? Burn? (Choose minor medical problems that do not need special medical attention.)
17. What would you do in case of a medical emergency?
18. How would you settle a problem if Mary and Johnny were fighting over a toy?
19. If Johnny says he doesn't want to eat what would you do?
20. What would you do if you disagreed with the way I wanted something done?

During the interview, clearly state the guidelines you want the caregiver to follow when working with your child. To avoid misunderstandings these should be given to the caregiver in written form. A sample set of guidelines follows.

## Sample of Child-Care Guidelines
*Guiding principles*

1. Place my child and his needs above everything else.
2. Treat my child as you would your own—with unconditional acceptance, reasonable firmness, and respect.
3. Use your common sense.

*Child-related activities*

4. Teach my child what is appropriate.
5. Read to him daily.
6. He should have at least one outdoor play experience (even if it means taking a walk in the rain). Be sure he is dressed appropriately.
7. No TV (except "Mr. Rogers" on occasion).

## Discipline

8. Discipline my child when necessary but never when you are angry. Use logical consequences as much as possible. Avoid conflict by catching problems early. Only spank when the child is belligerently defying your authority and then only two to three swats on his buttocks. Be sure you follow this with a positive affirming experience.

## Meals and routines

9. Meals should be served on a regular schedule with *only* juice between meals.
10. Encourage my child to eat one bite, but don't force.
11. Teeth should be brushed after every meal.
12. Naptime should be for approximately one hour between 2 and 3 P.M.

## Housekeeping

13. The house should be kept orderly, dishes washed, floor swept. Encourage my child to put one toy away before playing with another.

## Friends

14. Neighborhood friends of my child can come to visit for short periods if this is convenient with you.

## Emergency

15. In an emergency, call me immediately. If you feel medical attention is needed and I'm not available, call the ambulance or take the child to the hospital emergency room. (Be sure you as the parent leave signed permission for medical care to be administered to your child in your absence. This can be left with the caregiver, or kept on file at the emergency room.)
16. Call me if you have important questions that can't wait.

### Environment

The third step toward finding quality care for your child is to determine the kind of environment that will suit your child's needs if he is not in your home. For young children, this is what you should look for.

1. *The environment should be as homelike as possible.* Home is usually a place where children are free to go inside or outside whenever they want. They can play in little private corners without someone looking over their shoulders. Usually there is not a rigidly prescribed schedule of crayoning for ten minutes, stories for fifteen minutes, and puzzles for another ten minutes. People come and go; you get to watch the garbage man, greet the mailman, and answer the doorbell. There are usually curtains on the windows, pictures on the walls, a comfortable rocking chair, and carpets on the floors. Even if the facility does not look like a home, you want to make sure that the program scheduling and the atmosphere feels more like a home than like an institution.

It is naturally easier for a small center to be more homelike than a large center. In fact, centers that serve over sixty children find it more difficult to maintain a homelike quality of care. The more children there are, the more regimented the program tends to become.

2. *The environment should be healthy and safe.* Licensing does not insure that safety and health conditions will be completely met for your child, but it is a step in that direction. The room and yard should be clean, neat, and free of broken equipment, and there should be adequate and convenient toilet facilities for the children. Drinking water should be available both inside and out, and a nutritious hot meal should be served. For naptime each child should have a cot and blanket of his own.

There should be a fenced yard with both sunlight and shady places to play. Grass, plants, and trees add to the aesthetic aspects of a facility. Because of the danger of environmental pollution, the home or center should not be too close to a busy street or freeway, nor should it be downwind from factory smoke.

Be sure to ask if emergency procedures have been carefully worked out in advance. Find out what the caregiver would do if your child was involved in an accident and needed medical attention. Ask if there is an isolation room for sick children so others are not infected.

3. *The environment should be conducive for learning.* Make sure there are adequate toys and games, trucks and tricycles, and outside play equipment. Are there books, records, and musical instruments that the children can handle?

The children should be introduced to a variety of learning and creative activities throughout the day. They should be free to choose what they would like to work with. When children are regimented into a nonflexible program that is not responsive to their needs, learning is stifled.

### Evaluate

After you have chosen the type of program, the caregiver, and the environment, continue to evaluate the quality of the care and your child's reaction to that care.

If you have established certain guidelines for your caregiver (see previous section), periodically check to see that these are maintained. This can be done in the following ways.

1. Observe your child with the caregiver.

2. Ask the caregiver how she handled certain problems. Be specific. Listen to more than the words. Your impressions are important. If you feel a caregiver is not really leveling with you, say, "I have a feeling there may be more to the story. Can you think of anything else that may have contributed to the problem?"

3. Question your child. "How are things going? What do you really like or dislike about your caregiver? What activities does she plan for you? What special things do you do together?" Your child may be your most accurate source of information. On the other hand, such information may be biased because of anger, retaliation, or self-justification. Avoid tattling behavior. If your child gives you a negative report, simply say, "I'll check it out." Don't say anything in front of the child that will lower his respect for the caregiver.

4. If you have real questions about the caregiver and her relationship with your children, drop in unexpectedly. Have your neighbor observe or ask a friend to drop by and watch the situation for a while.

5. If you see a potential problem, solve it at that level. Don't let it grow out of proportion.

Some children have a difficult time adjusting to new situations. Even though the situation seems ideal to you, your child may not be happy with the care that you have arranged. To ease your child's adjustment, let him get to know the caregiver in your presence. Act confident and matter-of-fact about the decision that you have made. If your child preceives that you are hesitant about the child-care arrangements and feel guilty about leaving him, he is more likely to put on a good crying show for you and give you plenty of reasons for staying. If you feel confident, that attitude will help your child to adjust to the new experience.

If you have chosen a group child-care program or a home that is unfamiliar to your child, then it is important that you allow your child the time to develop trust in the new adult. Make sure he feels comfortable in the new environment before leaving him alone. During this time, do not make any attempt to push the child away from you. If a child feels pushed, the tendency is to hold on all the tighter. After an hour or so most children tire of sitting on Mommy's lap and will begin to look around the room. The teacher or caregiver should be friendly—but not over-whelmingly helpful. That may frighten the child. During this get-acquainted period, don't suddenly disappear when your child seems involved in another activity. If possible, let your child make the decision about when you can leave. If he knows you won't leave until he thinks he can handle it, he is free to become acquainted with the other children and the environment without having to worry that you will disappear when his back is turned.

If your child is too young to make such a decision, then tell him frankly that you are leaving for a specific amount of time and will return. Then go without any hesitation; no looking back or peeking around the corner. Stay away long enough to give the teacher a chance to comfort your child and establish some rapport. When you return, that should be a sign that it is time to leave the center and go home.

Don't be surprised if your child breaks down in a flood of tears when you return, even though he may have been happy and contentedly playing while you were away. This is natural. He has experienced many emotions during your absence and the sight of a familiar person will release all these emotions at once.

Continue with the care you have selected long enough to give it a fair chance of working. But if your child is still unhappy after a month, reevaluate your choice and con-sider other alternatives that may more readily meet your child's needs.

Continue to evaluate. Remember that your child's needs will change as he grows, and the quality of care may also change over time. A situation that is ideal now may be less than satisfactory a year later. Don't be afraid, at this time, to reevaluate and determine whether better child-care arrangements can be made. Here are a few questions to help you evaluate and continue evaluating the child-care choice that you have made.

## Child-Care Evaluation Checklist

*Type of care*

___

1. Does this care meet the current needs of my child?
2. Is it appropriate for his age?
3. How long might I expect this care to be appropriate?
4. Is this care the best for my own personal needs?

*Caregiver*

___

1. Am I convinced the caregiver is the best I can find for my child?
2. Is the person specifically interested in my child?
3. Has she established a rapport with my child?
4. Is she able to discipline my child in a firm but loving manner?
5. Does she support me?
6. Is she willing to talk to me about my child's progress as well as the problems?
7. Is she encouraging to my child—as well as to me?
8. Am I convinced she can act wisely in case of an emergency?

*Activities*

___

1. Are the activities my child is participating in appropriate for his age?
2. Is there adequate freedom within the environment so he can make appropriate choices to work or play with materials on his own time schedule?
3. Is he able to work at his own level of ability without any pressure to perform just like other children?
4. Are there a variety of activities and materials available to encourage learning?

*Environment*

___

1. Is the environment wholesome, healthy, and safe?
2. Is good food served regularly?
3. Is there an adequate resting period that is encouraged but not forced upon the child?
4. Are there adequate emergency procedures?

*Miscellaneous*

---

1. Is my child happy and satisfied?
2. Does my child talk positively about child care?
3. Is he eager to go or accepting of the situation?
4. Are there any signs in my child's behavior that would indicate unhappiness: sleeplessness, excessive crying, regression to immature behavior, excessive aggressiveness, destructiveness, listlessness, a tendency to withdraw, nervous habits—nail biting, twisting hair, etc.?
5. Are the children he is with the type of children I would want my child to have as friends?

Even if your child-care arrangements pass the test and seem ideal, almost all preschoolers go through periods of not wanting to go—or of not wanting Mommy or Daddy to leave. You must accept your child's feelings, but you don't necessarily have to give in to his wishes. Try to find out what the reason might be. Often, tensions in the home might trigger such a reaction, or you may be so busy that you have not spent enough time with your child. Sometimes a slight change in a routine, such as having Daddy drop him off at the babysitter's, or the promise of a special activity with Mommy after work, will be enough to satisfy your child. If his reluctant behavior becomes habitual, reevaluate the child-care situation. There may be a problem that can be solved by talking to the teacher, or you may want to change your arrangements for a while, or permanently. It is important to feel you have options available if you need them.

As you consider all the alternatives, don't be afraid to consider the advantages and disadvantages of quitting work or taking a leave of absence for a while until you can find the right child-care situation. We begin to feel uncomfortable and dissatisfied with our lives when we don't feel free to make decisions that affect our lives and those of our children.

**Questions about Child Care**

Here are some of the questions that I am frequently asked about child care.

1. How do you handle your own jealousy when your child seems to like the babysitter more than you?

*Answer:* Spend more time with your child. This is a sign that you have not spent enough quality time together with your child so your relationship has not continued to grow. Be thankful you have found a person your child enjoys so much. If the caregiver is supportive of you, you have nothing to worry about.

2. When hiring a regular babysitter to come to my home, how businesslike does this arrangement have to be?

*Answer:* You should have a written job description that includes specific housekeeping duties you might require. You should pay at least the minimum wage. Pay periods should be regular. Check with the local Social Security office about reporting earnings, making payments for Social Security insurance, and filing quarterly statements with the IRS. Benefits are usually given. Allow at least one day of sick leave a year for every day of the week worked. Vacations should include holidays and a yearly two-week vacation for a full-time worker. You can pay on an hourly basis or a salaried basis. This agreement should be signed by you and the employee. You should agree to an evaluation in one month as well as a quarterly review. Let the sitter know that the arrangement will be terminated before a specified trial period is over if you do not feel things are going well. Ask for two or three weeks notice if the caregiver wishes to quit.

3. When are children old enough to stay by themselves?

*Answer:* This does not depend entirely on age. It depends on the maturity of the child, the length of time the child is left alone, and the proximity of help should he need it. Certainly, a child should not be left without any type of supervision before seven years of age. An eight- or nine-year-old may be able to handle an hour or two occasionally. By ages ten to twelve a child usually has developed enough maturity to stay alone during the after-school hours until his parents arrive. Even during the teenage years most children need and desire some type of occasional supervision. Lonely children are prime targets for unwholesome experimentation and rebellion. Teenage pregnancy, drugs, alcohol, smoking, delinquency, and accidents are often the result of lack of adequate adult supervision.

4. What guidelines should I give my school age children when I leave them alone?

*Answer:* Children should not be frightened about being home alone, but it is important to give them the following common-sense instructions:

a. Keep the doors locked, even if you only leave the house for a short time. Keep an extra key holder outside the house in case you lose your keys.

b. If someone comes to the door, don't open it unless you recognize both the name and the voice. Don't tell anyone that you are home alone. Politely ask them to come back later, or ask them to go next door if they need help.

c. Don't give your name when answering the phone. Don't tell a caller that you are alone. Take a message and tell the caller that your parents will return the call.

d. If you receive a crank call, hang up immediately.

e. Don't entertain friends without first getting parental permission.

f. If in doubt about the safety or sensibleness of an activity, ask your parents' approval first.

g. Be predictable. Be where your parents expect you to be at the time they expect.

h. Keep emergency phone numbers handy.

i. Write down the procedure to follow in case of an emergency, such as fire, accident, or illness.

j. Keep the house neat and do what you can to prepare for your parents' arrival. For example: finish your chores and your homework; start dinner if you have your parents' approval; and think of something you can do to pleasantly surprise your parents.

At times, every working parent must rely on others to fill some of his child's needs. If you plan thoughtfully and choose the right person to share the child-care responsibility, your life as a prime-time parent will be more satisfactory.

# 3

## Working Parents and Their Problems

The combination of working and parenting is not a problem-free relationship. To discover the kinds of problems that working parents face, I conducted a small informal survey at Loma Linda University and Medical Center. I was not surprised by the results, since I have had personal experience with each! In addition to inadequate child care, three major problems that parents cited were: 1) not enough time; 2) too much guilt; and 3) illness and fatigue. And every one of these problems was compounded for the single parent. But for every problem, there is a solution. This chapter will focus on these solutions.

### The Problem of Not Enough Time

One parent expressed the problem in these words: "There is never enough time to get everything done at home that needs to be done. It is the same on the weekends. Just about the time I feel I have everything done in the home, and want to settle down with the kids or do something for myself, it's Monday morning again."

Another mother commented, "Monday after work there

are piano lessons; Tuesday, continuing education classes; Thursday, voice lessons; Friday, choir; Saturday night, extra shift for extra money. Only Sunday and Wednesday evenings are free. Sunday is housecleaning day, car cleaning day, yard day, basement cleaning day, wash day, shopping day, and if I work Saturday night, it is also sleeping day. What doesn't get done one week waits until the next. There is just never enough time."

Time is a relative concept. I've found that responsibilities and duties seem to accumulate to fill the time available. There's always something to do, whether you're a full-time working parent, a part-time working parent, or a non-working parent. The important thing is to realize that your children are the first priority. The rest of the time must be planned accordingly. Once a mother chooses to work, it is impossible for her to continue to do everything she did when she was a nonworking parent. You have to make choices and decide what is really important for you, and eliminate the rest or find other ways to accomplish the same things.

Regardless of the child-care arrangements you have chosen, lack of time will probably continue to be a problem. Here are some solutions that may help you find more time to be with your children.

1. *Take turns.* In order to stretch time to meet all your commitments, it is vital to share responsibilities. Such sharing must be flexible, based on the individual's needs and the particular situation. If one parent tries to shoulder all the responsibilities in one particular area all the time, he or she is likely to feel overwhelmed, resentful, and exhausted.

Some families utilize this concept creatively by allowing each parent "free" evenings. Prime time with one parent is better than halfhearted time with two. Monday and Wednesday are Mom's evenings to go shopping, write letters, visit friends, or whatever. Dad knows that Tuesday and Thursday is his time off. Just an hour to do your own thing can give you a new lease on life and you will return to your children with renewed energy and enthusiasm for parenting.

In our family, Jan is a fairly regular 8 to 5:45 person. But I leave the office early each day to pick up the children from school, so I must do some of my work at home. Because of this arrangement, my work never seems to be done. Therefore, Sunday morning is Jan's time with the children so I can catch up with my work. The children each make a list and when their chores are completed, Jan does something special with them. One rainy Sunday they visited the nearby electrical plant; in winter they enjoy sledding in the mountains. Summer may find them swimming in the swimming hole up the canyon. That's his prime time with the children—and they love it. I do too, for I can accomplish twice as much with no distractions.

Jan and I share household tasks as well. If Kevin's room is a mess and I have my nose in the typewriter trying to meet a deadline, Jan helps Kevin with his room. If I have a late class and students linger to talk, I know Jan will feed the children. When Jan has extra commitments, I'm happy to teach the children how to play baseball, build a tree house, or trim the hedges.

A more formal arrangement is to actually contract who will fulfill certain responsibilities. In this way each partner knows exactly what he or she is expected to do. Hopefully, misunderstandings and omissions can be alleviated. Avoid inflexible schedules. Parenting is filled with many unanticipated problems and responsibilities. Either build flexibility into the scheduling or be willing to fill in when your spouse finds it impossible to meet his or her obligations. The contract should be evaluated regularly.

2. *Establish a routine.* It can save precious time, since everyone knows what to do next and what his or her responsibilities are. It is also true that when children know what to expect, they can be more helpful.

Children, especially young children, need the consistency that routines assure. As a nursery school teacher I often observed the difficulties that a child had when a mother worked irregular hours. The child would be brought to the center at various times—in the middle of a story, during art time, or even halfway through naptime. These children usually had severe adjustment problems—unless they were highly adaptable children. Farewell time was especially difficult since they never knew when Mom would show up again. If the parent brought the child to nursery school on a regular schedule, the child could adapt more easily to the idea of separation. In a nursery school program it is not only the number of hours that a child is away from his parents, but also the consistency of those hours that is important for the child's adjustment. This may not be quite so important when a babysitter is used, since the child is not expected to fit into a regularly scheduled program. Of course, if you are able to limit your number of working hours, I would recommend working the shortest number of hours possible—especially if you have young children.

Flexi-time, which allows you to choose the hours you want to work, is especially helpful for working parents with school-age children. Mom can go to work when the children leave for school and be home when they return. Companies that have put this plan into action have found an increase in employee satisfaction.

Sharing a job, including the benefits, is an option many mothers have chosen. This allows working mothers to take a "full-time" job even though they only work half-time. Some husbands and wives have chosen to share a job so each can have the opportunity to be with the children as much as possible.

Many institutions and businesses are now realizing the value of a long-term, part-time employee, and have begun to offer these individuals the benefits previously available only for the full-time employee. This makes part-time work much more attractive.

The four-day work week can allow more time with the family, *if* the children are not in school and the "day off" is used for family activities. But once the children are in school, this working arrangement reduces parent-child time because four days of extended work hours make it more difficult to establish a routine time together.

All children need a regular time each day at home with their parents. Children's problems and concerns must be handled as they occur. If parents are not there to interact with their children and smooth the path of living, these problems and concerns may grow out of proportion and require professional help. Both children and parents are growing and changing daily, and if you habitually miss daily time together, you soon realize that you don't know each other very well. In addition, there is a warm sense of security that pervades children when they know their parents are consistently there when they need them.

Some jobs require hours that do not allow parents to be home when their children are usually awake. For example, when my brother was on the police force, he worked afternoons and evenings, arriving home about 10 P.M.—past the regular bedtime for most children. But his wife and preschool children adjusted their schedules so the children would not be deprived of their special time with Daddy. Supper was served at 10 P.M., next came the routine playtime with Daddy, and then the whole family slept until ten or so the next morning.

What about traveling jobs—truckers who are away for days at a time, sales personnel who are gone for weeks, or consultants who may be out of town for months working on a special project? Surely it is all the more important that the "stay-at-home" parent fill in at these times and be supportive of the parent who must be absent. But traveling parents can still keep in touch daily by telephone calls at a specific time each day or each week, by a letter, or even by establishing a special time when the family knows Mom or Dad is thinking particularly about them.

3. *First things first.* For prime-time parents this means that relationships with self, spouse, and children come first. Avoid the tyranny of doing what always seems important by doing something you really want to do, whether or not it is really essential. One evening when I was in the middle of updating my address book, Jan questioned my priorities. "I thought you had a deadline coming up on that book you are writing."

"I do," I answered, "but this is prime time for me." The address book wasn't an essential, but I felt better when it was finished, so I'm glad I finally elevated that task to top priority!

Jan and I gave an adult dinner party the other night and took our children over to a friend's house for the night. That was prime time just for us. Children benefit when they observe their parents placing a high priority on the time they spend together.

A physician I know is on call at the hospital from 8 A.M. Tuesday morning to 8 A.M. Wednesday morning, and then continues to teach classes on Wednesday morning and see clinic patients in the afternoon. No time for his kids for over forty-eight hours? No, he makes time. During that forty-eight hours he is in contact by phone as often as his schedule will allow. The children know they come first even though Dad cannot keep his regular playtime with them.

In order to have time to spend with each other, every family has to make certain choices and sacrifices. As you set your priorities and select the things that come first in your life, think about the following possibilities.

Limit newspaper reading and watch thirty minutes of daily news on TV instead or listen to the radio while you are involved in another activity. Limit TV viewing. When you do watch, combine it with another project. TV is not conducive to quality interactions among the family. If your time is limited, don't waste it on activities that don't contribute to the prime-time parenting goal.

Let the nonessentials wait. As you plan your day or evening, list everything you'd like to do, then rank these items in terms of their importance and level of interest for you. Start the day—or evening—with the most essential, highest-interest activity and proceed from there. Prime time is too short to get bogged down with nonessentials.

Evaluate the time spent on various activities. Hire out activities that someone else can do more inexpensively than you, *unless* you love doing it! Although I like to sew, I no longer do because it's just not worth my time. Keeping my house and yard spotless is too time consuming. My motto is "orderly, but not immaculate." To help save time I encourage the children to, "Never put it down—put it up." However, I still find it extremely helpful to hire a teenager for a couple of hours a week.

4. *Think convenience.* When you decorate your home think about convenience. Semigloss paint is easier to wash than flat. Wallpaper should be vinyl coated for easy cleaning. Solid dark or light carpets show more dirt than medium-toned multicolored carpets. Waxing floors is a hassle; choose nonwax vinyls. Cleaning up spills is much easier on a tiled or vinyl floor surface than a carpeted surface. Dust and fingerprints are twice as visible on glass coffee tables. Scotchgard upholstered furniture helps safeguard against spills and staining.

Never buy a knickknack unless you really want to invest time in dusting it. If possible, display collections behind glass. Put as many things as possible behind closed doors. They don't have to be opened for company!

Fresh flowers may boost your spirits. If so, fine. If not, decorate your home with dry flower arrangements or fabric flowers. A few easy-to-care-for plants add freshness to your home, but remember that they must be watered.

Appliances may add hours to your week—if you don't have a storage problem. But use them wisely. It may take more time to clean an appliance than it would take to grate the carrots by hand!

When organizing the kitchen, place everyday tableware at a level easily accessible to the children. They can more readily set the table and unload the dishwasher this way. Convenience foods can add a quick zest to a meal, but they can also just as quickly deplete the food budget.

5. *Limit nonfamily outside social activities.* Instead, plan social activities that include the family. Don't be afraid to ask, "Mind if we bring the kids along?" When entertaining business associates why not invite them home for a simple meal and an evening with your family, rather than subjecting them to another restaurant. They probably will never forget the occasion. Plan weeknight social events that begin after the kids are in bed so they aren't denied daily contact with Mom and Dad. Or choose a weekend evening after the children have been "parented" all day.

Every adult needs adult social experiences, but don't let these take significant time away from your family. A forty-hour-a-week career schedule leaves precious little time for the family. When Mom and Dad spend a significant amount of this leftover time seeking their own social experiences, children can easily resent their parents' careers. Instead, make the job a source of social activities for the whole family. For example, "The office has tickets to the ballet. Do you kids want to go?" Or "I just heard at work that there is a trail up Mt. Jasper. What about trying it with some people from the office next Sunday?" If the office parties have been restricted to adults, why not suggest a picnic in the park, a potluck supper at your home, or some other activity that includes children?

6. *Wait until the kids are in bed.* The evening hours—from the moment you walk through the door after work until the children's bedtime—should be prime time for the children. For most kids, these hours are the best part of their day. And if you aren't careful, this prime time will be eaten up by various projects that, with a little planning, could be scheduled after the kids' bedtime.

7. *Get organized.* Work efficiency is diminished in the midst of chaos. Searching for lost objects can waste valuable minutes. Effective organization does take time, but it takes less time to handle things consistently than to wait until a situation has grown out of proportion.

A good principle to follow is to eliminate the unnecessary. When your family accumulates too many things—toys, clothes, whatever—you'll have to spend a greater proportion of your time dusting and putting away.

If the children are encouraged to keep their rooms neat, cleaning is relatively simple. But when clothes, books, and toys are left scattered all over the floor, both children and parents panic at the sight. The job looks almost impossible and it takes a good deal of parental guidance, encouragement, and assistance to get the job done. How much better to stay on top of clutter!

8. *Don't go it alone.* The most successful prime-time parent does *not* do all of the housework, cooking, laundering, and yard care alone. We all need help and support, even if it's just emotional support. We all need people who care. When we feel we are solely responsible for the awesome task of child rearing, we may begin to feel very lonely and frightened, and become extremely sensitive to any type of helpful criticism. Open yourself up to others who want to help you. Accept their advice and assistance happily and thankfully. Don't hesitate to ask for help when you need it. There is no need to feel guilty.

If you do not already have a support system, start by offering help and support to friends. Involve your children in these activities. Reaching out to help and encourage others can bring added benefits to your own family.

9. *Plan special ways to spend time together.* Every family has to find its own special ways and times to get together. Some families enjoy eating out together, even if it is at the corner drive-in. Others enjoy concerts or church programs on a regular basis. Some families have invested in a Ping-Pong or pool table or even a swimming pool to provide family recreation right at home. Others invest in a motor home or boat to encourage more family excursions and vacations. Whatever your family chooses, carefully consider your favorite group activities and plan specific ways your family can participate in these activities more often.

10. *Pretend Mommy's in Africa.* Every prime-time parent occasionally must spend extra time on a project in order to meet a deadline. When children's emotional needs are adequately filled on a regular basis, they can usually cope with short periods of less parental attention. When this happens in our family we play the "Pretend Mommy's in Africa" game. I'm always pleasantly surprised by the self-sufficiency my children exhibit during these times. They even pride themselves on helping me with my normal housework and meal preparation activities.

During an "African trip" to finish this book, a note was pushed under my study door. "Dear Mom, Do you have time to fly home and give us a backrub before bed? Yes?_____No?_____ Love, Kim, Kari, and Kevin." I marked "yes," and delivered the answer in person. After all, I'm a prime-time parent!

### The Problem of Guilt

Guilt is another major problem of working parents, especially mothers. They feel guilty about working while their children are small; guilty about leaving them with babysitters and in day-care centers; guilty about their absence when baby says his first word or takes her first step; guilty about their older children coming home to an empty house; guilty about being unable to participate in the children's daytime school activities; guilty about feeling too tired to enjoy the children in the evening; guilty about getting angry and yelling and spending precious time together in conflict; guilty about not having time to make fancy birthday cakes and Halloween costumes; guilty that the house never seems spic-and-span. The list is endless.

Guilt is debilitating, discouraging, and defeating if no effort is made to eradicate the feelings. Yet the advice, "Don't feel guilty," is difficult to accept. However unrealistic these feelings may be in a broader context, if you share them, they are both genuine and painful for you. The only solution is to recognize guilt and reduce it by taking positive action.

If you repress too many negative feelings, you won't be able to fully experience the more positive emotions of happiness and joy. But, if you recognize your negative feelings, you can work with those feelings rather than letting them mount until the frustration level becomes unbearable.

What happens when you bottle up negative guilt feelings? Let's consider a typical, imaginary situation. You have had a particularly hard week. The boss demanded that you work overtime, and you didn't get home until after the children's bedtime. You feel guilty that you haven't spent more time with the children. On Monday, you realize you're beginning to feel depressed. You can hardly get up in the morning and get the children off to school. You arrive at work full of resentment toward the job and toward your boss who makes so many demands. Because you feel guilty, depressed, and resentful, you can't seem to get organized and your efficiency is significantly reduced. By 5 P.M. you still have a stack of work on your desk and you're feeling guilty about your work load. You come home frustrated and yell at the children for innocently giggling and goofing around. They stop immediately and put their arms around you, saying, "We're sorry, Mom." You push them away. "I just need to be alone," you tell them. Later, when the house is quiet, you begin to feel guilty about screaming at the children. Is there no way out of this endless cycle of guilt?

Now, replay the scene with a few modifications. When you wake up on Monday, face those feelings of depression and guilt. After thinking about some possible solutions, you make up your mind: *no more overtime*. It just cuts too deeply into your time with the family. Making that decision is a relief, although you're somewhat scared to tell the boss. You kiss the kids good-bye with a cheery, "See you at five." When you get to work, you confront your boss immediately. "I felt guilty all last week because I couldn't spend more time with my children so I can't work overtime anymore. I'm willing to work lunch hours, but my children need me after school. They are disappointed when I'm late. I hope you can understand my decision."

What was the difference between the two scenarios? In the first, you felt guilty, but you didn't do anything about the feelings and they continued to build up. In the second, you recognized the feelings and took constructive action. As a result, the feelings disappeared.

Often, parents with the most training in developmental psychology and human behavior feel the most guilty. They know what effective parenting entails, and can easily see the disparity between their behavior and that elusive goal. Research findings or information from a best-selling parenting book can generate guilt about past behavior toward the children—which at this point cannot be changed. For example, one book may advise you to forget about toilet training because the child will train himself when he is really ready. A second book notes that two-year-olds can and should be toilet trained. The third book says you can toilet train your child (when he's ready) in twenty-four hours. The first book may generate guilt about being too hard on your child. The second book makes you feel guilty if you were too soft. The third book encourages guilt if you weren't able to do it in twenty-four hours.

The only possible benefit of considering your past mistakes is to help you make better decisions in the future. Parents need to realize that they are going to make mistakes in their job of child rearing. They may get angry and impatient; they may demand too much of their children; they may not always be there when their children need them. Learn to say, "I'm sorry," and sincerely try to do better the next time. It is not the occasional mistake that shapes children's lives. It is the prevailing attitude of the parents and the atmosphere of the home.

Working parents often blame themselves (or the fact that they are working) for their children's problems. Friends, neighbors, and relatives can increase such guilt feelings by wagging their tongues and fingers disapprovingly, "If only she'd stay home and be a mother, she wouldn't have problems with her children." Research does not support this idea. Nonworking mothers have as many problems with their children as working mothers. If a mother is happy, whether she is working or not, her children tend to be fairly well adjusted.

An outside job may actually be a necessary escape for a mother who can't cope with her child's problem behavior. Work may be an oasis for you if you have an extremely difficult child, such as a handicapped child. You can return to your child with renewed enthusiasm and energy. The responsibility of child rearing is sometimes overwhelming. You should not feel guilty when you must ask others to help.

If you continue to feel guilty about working, carefully consider the reasons. Does it contradict your childhood values? Values *can* change. If work is not an economic necessity, consider part-time employment or a less demanding job when the children are young and need you most. If you have to work, dwell on the positive aspects of the job rather than the negative.

Does your spouse disapprove of the fact that you're working when the children are small? If he does, and you still choose to work, make a pact to be honest, open-minded and respectful of one another. Then try this exercise. Make a list of the negative and positive aspects of your job. Be specific. Ask your spouse to do the same, then compare the two lists. Look at the positive side first, and try to agree on as many positive points as possible. Then compare the negative side of the list. Brainstorm possible solutions for each negative point. Quitting would be one answer. Continuing to work without any changes would be the opposite extreme. Be willing to compromise. Consider some of these ideas: part-time work; hiring a housekeeper; fixing meals ahead of time; arranging a more flexible work schedule; taking a less demanding job; working closer to home or moving closer to work; hiring a live-in babysitter; coming home promptly after work.

Do your relatives, friends, or fellow church members disapprove of working mothers? If so, you must evaluate the importance you place on their opinion, and decide to what degree their beliefs should influence your life. At times you must learn to say, "I am unique. My situation is unique. I will do the best I can for my immediate family." The opinions of the church, neighbors, and relatives are *less* important than your own feelings about what is best for your family's happiness and well-being.

Do you feel guilty because you don't like your job, and would prefer to stay home? If you are unhappy and have a choice, *quit*—if you are sure that nonworking status will bring happiness. In many cases, however, a new job will alleviate such feelings.

Is your guilt caused by exhaustion or your inability to

find the time to meet all your household obligations? You may be trying to do too much. Hire help, or ask your family to provide more help. Be specific in explaining your needs. Get to bed an hour earlier—whether or not your "homework" is done. Make sure that you are physically fit. Begin a regular program to improve your health habits.

Do you feel guilty because you sense that your children are receiving inadequate child care? If so, thoughtfully write down the specific incidents that justify your feeling. You may want to counsel with others to check if your perception is realistic. Then if the situation cannot be remedied, your only option may be to quit work until good care is found. If you continue to work when you feel your child is definitely receiving substandard care, it will be almost impossible to relieve your guilt feelings. You cannot continue to live happily with this conflict brewing inside you.

However you choose to deal with guilt, do *not* allow occasional guilt feelings to affect your parenting. The following list includes the most common child-rearing mistakes made by guilty parents.

1. *Overprotecting the child.* "I'm not home very often, so I want to compensate by being with my child whenever I'm home and carefully monitoring her time when I'm not home." Children thrive on age-related independence—not smothering.

2. *Giving unnecessary gifts.* Some parents believe that they can make up for their absence by giving gifts. Presents never take the place of parental presence.

3. *Giving in to demands.* Children often play on a parent's guilt feelings to get what they want. Parents fall into this trap by trying to meet every desire and whim of their child. In such situations, the child runs the home—and it's not a happy place for either parent or child.

4. *Feeling sorry for the child.* "Oh, you poor dear. I feel so sorry for you when I have to work. You don't have a mommy here when you get home from school." This atti-

tude only encourages the child to feel sorry for himself. Instead, help your child see the benefits that can be derived from your work.

5. *Allowing the child to escape home responsibilities.* "After all, this poor child has a mommy who works, so the least I can do is to make it up to him by doing his chores and picking up after him." Balderdash!

6. *Ignoring misbehavior.* "I don't want to cross my child since I'm home so little. I'll leave that to the baby-sitter. I want my child to like me, so I'll just ignore the bad things he does." This attitude is particularly dangerous because you are encouraging your child to exhibit more of this antisocial behavior.

Children need parents who are willing to parent—and that includes healthy doses of both love and discipline. Don't deny your child his valuable training because you feel guilty about working. Instead, do your best, keep happy, apologize when you fail, and plan ways to avoid repeating the mistake. Follow these four steps:

1. *Count your blessings.* Each day try to learn new ways to fill your life with enjoyment, fun, and contentment. Don't focus on the negative aspects of life, focus on the positive. Count the blessings that work brings into your life and the lives of your children: new contacts and friends, new challenges; a focus for your creativity; new ideas to share with your children; colleagues that your children enjoy; a whole new set of "uncles" and "aunts"; a broadening of interests, and extra income. Children benefit by seeing their parents take on different roles willingly—Dad doing the cooking and Mom attending a convention. As children get older they benefit by feeling needed. They can be an important contributing member to their family by carrying more and more of the home responsibilities.

2. *Realize you can't be perfect.* No parent is perfect—at least not for long. Work toward this goal, as expressed in a jingle adapted from the Danish poet, Piet Hein.

*The principle of perfect parenting is simple to express.*
*Err, and err, and err again, but less, and less, and less.*

3. *Stay on the cutting edge.* Try to minimize pain, conflict, jealousy, and boredom by solving problems as soon as they develop. Look for the first signs of dissatisfaction. Talk to the person involved immediately. "You look as if what I did made you jealous (or whatever). What can I do to avoid such misunderstanding in the future?" Be willing to apologize first. The words, "Forgive me," are often met by a response like, "It really wasn't all your fault." Then you are in a good position to solve the problem at an early stage. If you are busy solving problems as they arise, there is little time left for guilt. When you allow problems to build, they seem insurmountable, and it's easy for a flood of guilt feelings to take over and destroy your family's chance for quality time together.

4. *Finally, play the "What would happen if" game.* This is a way to discover the best alternatives for your family. For example, what would happen if you quit work? What would happen if you only worked part-time, or said, "no overtime"? What would happen if you went back to school? What would happen if you decided to change jobs? To play the game fairly, you must remain open to a wide range of possible answers to each question you might pose. Don't kill this game in its prime and say, "What would happen if I quit work? Well, we would all starve!" Speculate on possible changes you could make in your life. You may find a whole new exciting life waiting for you.

Bruce Bogan and his wife did just this. Bruce was an aeronautics engineer; his wife was an artist. They felt guilty about raising their children in the rat race of a large city. They began to ask the question, "What would happen if we gave up our city jobs and moved to the country?" The move might be more conducive to an artist's career, but what would an aeronautics engineer do? They decided to make the move and Bruce applied his engineering expertise to sculpturing. His success exceeded his wildest expectations. But the real benefit was more quality time together with the family and no more guilt.

Playing the "What would happen if" game makes you realize you do have a choice about how you are going to live your life. When you feel that you have no options or choices, then you are ripe for a heavy load of guilt, and you will find yourself relentlessly pushed down the path of least resistance.

### The Problem of Illness and Fatigue

Most parents don't consider the possibility of fatigue and illness, whether their own or their child's, when they plan their life with children. Stark reality is expressed vividly by Jayme Curley, a working mother who wrote in her diary, "Shana has caught the cold I have just recovered from. David and I were up six times with her last night, she was sweaty and coughing. Of the 203 days of her life, she has been sick fifty days with colds, two with stomachaches. I've been sick seventy-four days with colds and the breast infections. David, fifteen days with colds. What a mess we've been."*

How do prime-time parents cope with illness and fatigue? Prevention is the best answer. As one mother told me, "I don't have time to be sick, so I put all my effort into prevention." It is also important to be realistic about our body needs and the effect that pregnancy, the postpartum period, and aging will have on our fatigue level and our general state of well-being. We must also plan realistically to deal with our children's illnesses.

* Jayme Curley *et al.*, *The Balancing Act* (Chicago: Chicago Review Press/Swallow Press, 1976).

## Prevention

There are three general principles to follow to prevent illness and fatigue.

1. Keep your family in good physical condition by getting regular checkups at least once a year. If you have a minor problem, have it taken care of immediately. Don't allow it to develop into a difficulty.

2. Maintain good eating habits, drink plenty of water, and don't indulge in harmful practices such as drinking alcohol, taking drugs, or smoking.

3. Use your body carefully. Get plenty of rest and regular exercise (the kind that strengthens the heart muscle and lowers the heart rate). Do not abuse yourself with inactivity or drive yourself too hard.

Health habits are established early in life, so by the time you need to present a good example to your children, your own poor health habits may be deeply ingrained. But change is possible. And change may be necessary if you want to solve the problem of illness and fatigue. Belloc and Breslow* found that the people who observed all of the following health practices were healthier and lived longer than those only observing a portion of these habits.

1. Usually sleep seven or eight hours.
2. Eat breakfast almost every day.
3. Eat between meals once in a while, rarely, or never.
4. Weight
    a. For men, between 5 percent under and 19.9 percent over desirable weight for height.
    b. For women, not more than 9.9 percent over desirable weight for height.
5. Engage in active sports, swim, or do physical exercises, or take long walks or garden.

* Nedra B. Belloc and Lester Breslow, "Relationship of Physical Health Status and Health Practices," *Preventive Medicine*, Vol. 1, No. 3 (August 1972): 409–421.

6. Have no more than four drinks at a time.
7. Never smoke cigarettes.

In addition to following these specific health habits, here are some further tips for the prime-time parent.

### Coping with fatigue

If fatigue is your problem, be sure to get enough sleep each night and take a few catnaps during the day. Find a place where you can nap during your break time. When you return home, take a fifteen minute nap before settling into the evening routine. Perhaps the babysitter can stay a little longer to give you this necessary rest period, or ask your spouse to take over for a while.

Exercise is a good way to get rid of fatigue. Get up for five minutes every hour and move around briskly enough to feel your heart pump a little harder. Try a number of exercises to stretch and move each part of your body. If your office building has stairs, use them. If the lounge has space to jump rope—jump. If there is a recreational facility at your place of employment or nearby, use the swimming pool, racketball or volleyball courts, or the gym.

Donna Kenmore, a reporter for a local newspaper, solved her fatigue problem when she discovered running. Now up at 6 A.M., her goal is to put in five miles before breakfast. Running has not only brought her increased energy, but also social experiences. She runs and socializes at the same time with her neighbor. Often, her eight-year-old daughter joins her. Meeting the challenge of a competitive race has become an ego-building experience for both mother and daughter and has brought them closer together.

Diet not only affects your general health, it can also affect your level of fatigue. Diets that are high in sugars, starches, and fats have a way of slowing down the system. Eat a balanced diet with plenty of energy foods, such as vegetables and good protein. Avoid fad diets and concentrate on eating a good variety of simple, natural foods. The amount of water you drink may affect your fatigue level because wastes that accumulate in your body create fatigue.

The way you feel relates directly to how you act. When your body is run down, when you are tired, when your head aches, it doesn't take very much pressure to push your emotional temperature to the breaking point, and coping with the children and the job becomes an unbearable task.

### Special situations

Pregnancy, postpartum adjustment, breastfeeding, and early infant development are sometimes difficult periods for the prime-time parent. Some women continue working without difficulty. Others find the combination almost impossible. The stories of Jean, Sally, and Joyce illustrate some of the problems that can arise during this time.

Jean had never been sick a day in her life. She was a perfect specimen of physical fitness—and then she got pregnant. During the first three months she was so sick that she couldn't even hold down water and had to spend a couple of weeks in the hospital. She existed through the fourth and fifth month, but by the sixth month she was hospitalized again, and fluctuated between her bed and the hospital doors until she delivered.

Sally sailed through her pregnancy with flying colors. Her first child was born after only five hours of labor, so she was looking forward to another easy delivery—since everybody told her the second one would be even easier! It turned out that after hours of labor, the baby was breech and she was rushed to surgery for a Caesarian section. Then a slight bladder infection turned into a major kidney infection and her temperature zoomed. A simple birth turned into a life-and-death struggle. Finally, after fourteen days in the hospital, Sally went home to the demands of two little girls—a two-year-old who couldn't understand why the family needed another little girl when she was still in good condition, and a tiny baby. Returning to work in the near future was not possible until Sally regained her strength and dealt with the demands of her family.

Joyce had a different experience. She worked right up until the day Timmy was born, and was back on her own feet within a day or two. "I'll be back to my old routine in two weeks," she told her friends at work. But little Timmy changed all that. Within four days he developed jaundice and went back to the hospital. Joyce caught a cold, and had to give up breastfeeding temporarily. After three weeks she tried breastfeeding again, but little Timmy continued to have difficulties, and it was a continuous round of doctor's appointments, medications, and hospital visits for the next eight months. How could she, during this critical time, give her tender child over to some other caregiver? Her two week vacation-leave to have the baby was extended for a year until life began to smooth out and Timmy seemed stronger.

Many women are surprised by the exhaustion they feel during their pregnancy and the first few years of child rearing. The changes that occur in a woman's body during the first three months of pregnancy cause her to feel especially tired. Then, because the body is pushed out of shape and it is more difficult to get around with the extra load, a woman tires more easily as she nears the final months—the last stretch. Labor is tremendously hard work, as its name implies, and most women need a week or two (or more) before they regain their strength.

Breastfeeding can be a real joy and an extra benefit to the baby, but it does cause fatigue,* and it can have some

---

* Someone once told me that breastfeeding a child was as tiring as working eight hours a day. Can you imagine how tired a woman will feel if she tries to do both without getting an adequate amount of rest?

handicaps for the working mother. If it is necessary to be away from the baby eight to ten hours a day, then breast-feeding is impossible. But many mothers work part-time or come home for lunch and continue breastfeeding their infant. The baby receives formula supplements or bottled breast milk when Mother is not around. This system has its drawbacks when Mother comes rushing home from work to find the baby full of formula and sound asleep. She is then faced with the problem of painfully full breasts which will probably need pumping.

The second handicap for mothers who breastfeed is that when Mother is home no one else can do the feeding. For the first six months or so, Mother will be awakened two or sometimes three times per night to feed her little one. Jan helped me through this time by awakening at the first sound of a cry, changing the messy diaper, and bringing our baby to bed for me to nurse. When the baby had finished, Jan dutifully got up again and carried him back to his own bed. But not every father is a light sleeper! As long as your infant continues to wake you during the night you are going to need extra rest during the day to make up for these interruptions.

Breastfeeding is ideal, but you need to be realistic about the difficulties that might occur, especially during the first month. Keep the local La Leche League number close at hand and don't be afraid to call for help if you need it. If job demands or other problems make breastfeeding impossible, consider the blessing of being able to share the feeding responsibility with your husband, or your babysitter. Remember, they too can benefit from the closeness of the feeding relationship.

### When your child becomes ill

A child's illness presents a special problem to the prime-time parent who does not have a full-time caregiver at home. Here are the options that are usually available when illness strikes.

1. *Stay home.* If possible, try to stay home with a sick child. If a child is too sick or contagious to go to school or to a babysitter's house, then the child usually enjoys the comfort of his own bed and the warm security of his own parents meeting his needs. This can be a prime time to enjoy your child alone, without the interference of the rest of the family. Both you and your child can benefit by this closeness.

Ask your employer about the possibility of using sick-leave benefits when your child is ill. It may be possible for you to stay home part of the day and let your spouse take over for the other half. You could also hire someone to come into your home and babysit your sick child.

If the child is not contagious or seriously ill, then one of the following plans might be suitable.

2. *Take the sick child to work with you.* This is only possible in certain work situations. You must consider the age of the child and the nature of the illness. When it is possible it can have advantages. You can still do your job (although your efficiency may be somewhat diminished) and you and your child are together. One day when Kim was four and did not feel like going to nursery school, I took her to my university class with me. It turned out to be a real education for her. After my lecture to students sitting in nice neat rows, she said, "Mommy, I didn't know that is how you taught. I thought you sat on a little chair and all the students sat on the floor." Her concept of a teacher was obviously colored by her nursery school experience.

3. *Ask a friend to babysit.* Sometimes, a friend who has young children or children in school might be willing to come to your home for the day and watch your sick child. If the illness isn't contagious, the sick child can be taken to your friend's home. This solution is fine if your friend is available when you need her. Think ahead about

who you might call in case of an emergency.

4. *Send the child to school.* If the illness isn't contagious and the child just has an early morning slump that may be remedied as soon as he sees his friends, send him off to school. If the illness is contagious or the child is too ill to get anything out of school, then you must make other arrangements. If staying home alone with Mom becomes too special, children can retreat from normal pressures of school and act sick in order to get their parent's full attention. This situation should be avoided.

Some day-care centers have a special isolation room for children who are sick. But even without this convenience most children can return to a child-care facility even if they are still plagued by a runny nose and an occasional cough because the contagious part of a cold is usually during the first three or four days. Most centers require a doctor's permit if there is a question about contagion.

5. *Staying home alone.* Some older children enjoy the independence and responsibility of staying home alone for part or even a whole day. Parents should be available by phone, and should call to check on the child throughout the day. If possible, a neighbor should be alerted to the situation and asked to check on the sick child occasionally. Be sure a list of emergency numbers is available. Choose this option only if your child feels good about it and you feel he can be trusted. The seriousness of the illness must be assessed before this decision is made. The length of your absence is also important. Four hours may not be too long, but ten hours may.

These suggestions may help you to plan realistically for future illness. Planning ahead will help a prime-time parent cope more effectively with a child's unexpected illness.

Prime-time parenting is not problem free. But your attitude toward your working and parenting roles can make the difference. If you are optimistic and willing to turn prime time with your children into quality time, and you have established good substitute child care, then your children can accept your busy schedule. They can see the rewards of having parents who work rather than dwelling on the disadvantages.

# 4

## The Prime-Time Parenting Personality— Fulfillment for All

If working parents want fulfillment, satisfaction, and pleasure from their parenting career, they must develop a prime-time parenting personality; their attitudes, behavior, and habit patterns must be conducive to fostering fulfillment in each family member. Personal fulfillment comes in the process of helping others. The only way to develop a prime-time parenting personality is to immerse yourself optimistically in family relationships and work to make these relationships as meaningful and harmonious as possible. Book learning, theorizing, and philosophizing cannot substitute for practical experience. However, immersing yourself in family relationships that will lead to fulfillment in others does not mean that you must deny your own needs.

Every grown-up has a "child" hidden within his adult frame. This part of you is made up of feelings that must be expressed, needs that must be met, and dreams that must be fulfilled. Working parents sometimes have a tendency to repress important needs under the guise of altruistic service to others. They rationalize that the children and their job must come first; that self must be sacrificed. Other parents err by selfishly pursuing their own desires to the neglect of their family's needs. Successful parenting is not possible when you concentrate on meeting your family's needs to the exclusion of your own. Nor is the opposite extreme any better.

At times, it is necessary to sacrifice for the family; to put the family's needs ahead of your own; to give time to the children when you would rather be doing your own thing. To do so, a parent must keep his own container of personal happiness, satisfaction, and fulfillment filled to the brim so he has something to give at these times.

That is why it is important sometimes to put yourself first. Don't deny your need for intellectual pursuits, challenging work, time away from the family, or travel. Never say it is impossible unless you have made a valiant attempt. Carefully consider your options—the advantages and disadvantages of fulfilling your personal dreams. Children can adjust. In fact, your children may thrive when you put yourself first occasionally—*if* their basic needs are being met and they are assured of your unchanging love. Children benefit by living with parents who feel personally fulfilled.

Regardless of your personality, you can contribute to your own fulfillment by following these six steps.

1. Concentrate on the positive.
2. Realize your true value.
3. Get to know yourself and accept what you can't change.
4. Choose to be the kind of person you want to be.
5. Meet your own needs without sacrificing the family.
6. Live a balanced life relationally.

**Step 1:  Concentrate on the Positive**

Attitude shapes behavior. Repeated behavior forms habit patterns. And your repeated behavior patterns have the greatest effect on your children. An occasional mistake, an occasional release of pent-up emotions will not scar a resiliently healthy child. But repeated neglect, hostility, anger, and depression make an indelible impact.

Therefore, your attitude toward life, toward your job, and toward your family is vitally important. It can affect the entire atmosphere of your home. A positive attitude is conducive to a child's growth. A negative attitude can have a deleterious effect. For example, a negative attitude that results in a lack of maternal warmth is the primary cause of the failure-to-thrive syndrome observed in some infants.

Attitudes have predictive power. Children who approach an exam with confidence tend to do better than those who anticipate failure. Postoperative complications are rarer among patients who are optimistic before an operation. It has been demonstrated that you can even think yourself thin. Positive thinking generates a mental image, a belief in your ability to surmount obstacles. It is an attitude that increases your chances of success.

Even the health status of family members can be affected by attitudes. For example, when Norman Cousins, editor of the *Saturday Review,* was stricken by an illness his doctors considered fatal, he prescribed for himself heavy doses of laughter, love, faith, hope, and a will to live, along with massive amounts of vitamin C. He believes that his change in attitude contributed significantly to his recovery.

Attitudes are contagious. One downcast family member can discourage everyone else. The opposite is also true. When things look hopeless, take advantage of the contagious quality of attitudes. Call up or visit the most optimistic person you know and get a dose of positive thinking. A number of weeks ago the children and I were sure our Shetland pony was going to die. In the depth of our discouragement, Jan came home smiling and optimistic. "Oh," he said, "I think the colt looks a lot better. See how he is holding up his head. Here, let me try to give him some water." He proceeded to give the colt a vigorous rubdown, telling him how good he looked and predicting that he would be well in the morning. The children and I felt better almost immediately. We all laughed and optimistically called the pony our little miracle pony. The pony was still sick, but our attitude, and the quality of our family interactions, changed significantly. And sure enough, Jan's prediction came true—the pony recovered.

Attitudes have a magnetic quality. Positive attitudes tend to attract others; negative attitudes repel. Prime-time parents must realize the devastating effect that negative attitudes can have on family morale. The following personality traits can lead to such a negative, devitalized attitude. I call them the deadly D's. Don't let them crowd out your chances for personal happiness, satisfaction, and fulfillment.

*Dependency:* A dependent parent has difficulty making decisions. He tends to live his life through others—even through his children, forcing them to meet his needs for companionship, support, and decision-making. He takes little or no responsibility for mistakes and tends to blame those who made the decision. Dependent parents face major difficulties when their children become teenagers and struggle to break free of parental ties. The children either leave home—probably feeling guilty and bitter—or stay home and cater to their parents and jeopardize their own personal happiness. Single parents must be particularly careful to avoid the tendency to become overly dependent and expect their children to fulfill all their needs.

*Denial:* Parents who cannot admit their own mistakes or faults seriously jeopardize their relationship with their children. This kind of denial is equally deadly when parents refuse to face family problems or difficulties, and continue on a collision course without seeking needed help. Parents who blindly defend a family member without a realistic appraisal of the situation create problems for the family as well. And the parent who denies himself to such an extent that he feels trampled on and used is ultimately going to rebel. Denial of self is not always negative, and it is often required of parents. But martyrdom in any form must be avoided at all costs.

The martyred parent gives to others at great personal expense, and if all does not go well he often plays on the ingratitude of the unappreciative child. "Remember all those nights I stayed up late just to iron your dresses? Don't you think your poor old mom deserves a child who treats her with more respect?" "I gave up the football game just to stay home with you kids, and all you do is quarrel. See if I ever do that again!"

*Defensiveness:* A defensive parent takes everything personally and interprets casual remarks, and even compliments, as attacks or insults. This attitude is often the result of a poor self-image and fosters a rigid, narrow outlook. Any attempt to make changes is interpreted as a personal attack. Rather than being open and willing to change, the defensive parent defends the old ways until death, divorce, or desertion. This type of parent is a master at driving children away.

*Defiance:* The defiant parent boldly resists the authority or opposition of others. He is openly hostile and challenges those who do not share his views. He often appears to have a superiority complex and tramples those around him in order to get what he wants. As children grow older they naturally develop their own ideals. If their emerging values are ignored or ridiculed by a parent with a superior attitude, the children are not likely to spend much time with that parent.

*Demeaning:* This type of parent constantly puts other people down with comments that degrade them or cause them to think less of themselves. The underlying attitude is "I'm okay but you're not." Demeaning is a method of psychological pressure used to force children to act in appropriate ways. But when children hear words like, "Can't you ever do anything right?" they are not likely to improve their behavior or actions. In fact, such words usually have the opposite effect. Children's behavior mirrors their parents' expectations. They will continue to repeat negative behavior patterns to punish their parents, or because their confidence has been shattered by their parent's attitude.

*Depreciating self:* This parent exhibits an inferiority complex. He feels he can never do anything right. It is depressing to be around a self-depreciating person. You try to help him realistically consider his strengths and good points, but to no avail. As fast as you can dish out the compliments, they are shredded into pieces. A self-depreciator plays the game, "Build-me-up-after-I-tear-myself-down." A child will play along for a while, but soon the game becomes stale and the child wants out.

*Depression:* A depressed parent feels so woeful about his world and himself that he tends to withdraw from others and the responsibilities of the household. He is consumed by feelings of gloom, discouragement, and inadequacy.

Many working parents suffer from depression after hard days of work at unfulfilling jobs, only to come home to a new set of problems—poor housing, financial difficulties, and delinquent children. When parents lose hope in the possibility of a better life, they cease any efforts to make changes. This attitude affects every member of the family, and children grow up with one goal in mind—to escape the situation as soon as possible. Often, they marry early and find themselves in similar circumstances, and the cycle is repeated. If you want a better life for your children, never give up your dreams, never cease to work toward your goals, and never let discouragement encompass your family.

*Detachment:* Detachment is the net result of uncontrolled depression. Instead of seeking to communicate and share with others, the deeply depressed parent wraps his thoughts about himself and withdraws. An attitude of detachment may be fueled by worries about the job, finances, or an impending crisis that a parent doesn't want to share with his family. Rather than talking it out, the characteristic method of handling problems is to retreat. This is devastating to family life. Parents might also become detached because they really don't understand their children, aren't very effective in relating to them, and try to deny these inadequacies and problems by withdrawing. Whatever the reason, the family suffers.

Life is not always easy for the working parent, but your attitude toward problems will determine whether or not you find personal fulfillment. The negative components of your life must *not* be denied. Place them in the proper perspective. Don't allow them to outweigh the positive. When you are discouraged and depressed, prime the attitudinal pump and take advantage of the placebo effect. Do this by finding something positive, then express thanks and joy. Once you experience the exhilarating effect of these positive emotions, they will act as a catalyst and raise your spirits in general.

But can you find something positive in problems, pressures, conflicts, illnesses, crises, failures, disappointments, and less than ideal situations? Consider some of the following possibilities:

1. Children can learn how to deal with problems by watching their parents cope.

2. Experiencing negative situations fosters a greater appreciation of the positive.

3. Solving problems together can bring the family closer together.

4. A special sense of satisfaction develops when problems are solved.

5. Learning to develop coping procedures to deal with small problems will give you confidence to deal with bigger problems.

List the negative aspects of your life on one side of a page and then write at least one positive aspect of each on the opposite side. When you are tempted to feel discouraged or depressed about the negatives, think about each positive point and be thankful.

Concentrate on becoming a dynamic, positive person who has control over his life; who is dedicated to his family; who is optimistic and energetic; and who is willing to change when change is necessary.

Remember, your attitude toward problems will determine whether or not they will stand in your way of attaining personal fulfillment.

### Step 2: Realize Your True Value

You are a special person. Nobody else feels exactly as you feel, values exactly what you value, behaves exactly the way you behave, has the same needs as you have, or can accomplish exactly what you can. Because of your uniqueness, nobody can tell you exactly what you must do to realize your value and find self-fulfillment.

Every person is of equal value. This is a part of your birthright. You should feel a healthy sense of self-worth because you exist and because of your potential to create something. Realistically, however, society, classes, and individuals have demeaned others to such an extent that it becomes extremely difficult for some individuals to accept their unique value. Life's circumstances may make it more difficult for you to reach your ideal, but your worth remains the same. However, the fact that you are as valuable as other individuals will *not* have a positive effect on your life *if you do not believe it*.

A low sense of self-worth usually develops through years of interactions. People learn that they can't do things as well as others, that they are poor decision-makers, or that they make too many mistakes. To rise above these feelings is by far the hardest task of the prime-time parent. But it is vitally important if one is to grow.

Each person must come to the realization of his innate value *in his own way.* Individuals who believe in God can find self-worth in the knowledge that God created them, that God has a plan for them and accepts them. Self-worth can develop in a special relationship that offers unconditional acceptance. It can develop in a stimulating job where colleagues respect you and seek your advice. It can be found in a satisfying parent-child relationship. It can be found by being true to yourself and consistently doing what you believe to be right. It can be fostered by realizing your own creative potential. It can develop by realistically accepting your strengths and making progress in diminishing your weaknesses.

### Step 3:  Get to Know Yourself and Accept What You Can't Change

Only when you know yourself well enough to visualize your potential, accept what you are, and to initiate plans to reach your ideal, can you ever hope to find personal fulfillment. Start by asking yourself these revealing questions:

What are you like? Describe your physical self; your emotional self; your spiritual self. What do you like about yourself? What do you dislike? What are your major interests? How do you enjoy spending your time? What really makes you feel like a valuable person? What makes you feel on top of the world? What contribution would you like to make to society? What would you like to do if you had no family commitments? What do you value most highly? What are your priorities in life? Would you like to get a better education? Would you like to be a better parent? Would you like to be a better lover? What would you like to be ten years from now? What kind of a person would you really like to be?

Although you can choose to change your attitudes, your behavior, and your habits, there are aspects of your life that are difficult to change—your physical looks, for example, a physical handicap, the family situation, your job, your previous mistakes. If a positive, dynamic attitude is to prevail, these aspects of life must be accepted. Don't waste valuable energy by worrying, fretting, and complaining about the things you can't control. Accept them, and channel this energy toward improving those aspects of life that can be changed.

Accepting yourself is the major prerequisite for accepting others and for giving yourself to others. If you haven't mastered the art of getting in tune with yourself and accepting what you find, it is difficult to enjoy helping someone else. If you feel inferior, unattractive, and incapable of achieving your goals, it is almost impossible to free your mind from these overwhelming concerns and concentrate on the needs of others. Little children's cries for help become an imposition on your time; your spouse's request for attention appears selfish; and your aging parent's need for closeness seems like meddling. However, if you know yourself well enough to take little daily steps toward fulfilling your own needs and goals, you can concentrate on others and give of yourself more freely.

Part of self-acceptance is the ability to accept those to whom you are committed. If you are married you have a certain commitment to love, to respect, and to be loyal. Fulfilling that commitment brings contentment. If you have children, you must provide for their physical and emotional needs. Fulfilling this commitment to the best of your ability will bring a measure of satisfaction. Ignoring your commitments will create conflict in your life, and personal fulfillment is impossible to achieve when this tension is present. The answer is to accept your responsibilities with a positive attitude.

**Step 4: Choose to Be the Kind of Person
You Want to Be**

Personal fulfillment is possible when your ideal self is similar to your real self, and when you are systematically setting and reaching goals that bring you closer to your ideal.

Personal happiness, satisfaction, and fulfillment are impossible to achieve if you feel you have no control over your life. Abandon such thoughts immediately. You may not be able to change the world or your family situation, but you can change yourself. So focus on what you consider to be the ideal you. List as many characteristics as you can and plan ways, starting today, to systematically reach your goal.

For example, consider happiness. Everyone wants to be happy. But happiness is not a goal that one can pursue. It is an attitude that must be cultivated as one pursues other goals. It's a by-product of living a satisfying life. Here are some suggestions that will help create the right climate for happiness.

1. *Think interesting thoughts.* Conversations about gas bills, leaky faucets, and dirty dishes won't make you a very interesting person to be around. Do some creative thinking. Read a challenging article. Tackle some new vocabulary words or learn a phrase or two of German. Plan an exotic vacation. Read a joke book or learn some riddles. Then surprise the family by sharing your thoughts with them.

2. *Do something interesting.* Get out of your easy chair, break free of stagnant routine, and play basketball with the kids. Give them a piggyback ride. Teach them a new tumbling trick. Hunt shark's teeth, pan for gold, climb a mountain, build a sailboat, design a solar heating unit, buy a French cookbook and treat your family to some gourmet cooking, take the dog to obedience school, paint a picture, organize the photo album, or sign up for karate lessons. Forget your age and, within reason, forget the cost. Do

something you always wanted to do but never had the time or the courage to try. You will become a much more interesting parent, and life will take on more meaning.

3. *Be satisfied, but keep dreaming.* The expectation, the planning, the wishing, and the saving for some desired pleasure is an indispensable part of happiness. Too many parents think that happiness is bound up with the number of possessions they have. In reality, happiness has nothing to do with what you own. It is a by-product of your ability to enjoy what you do have, accept what you don't have, and hope for something better.

4. *Surprise others with kindness.* Immerse yourself in doing good for others and happiness will find you. A few months ago our family decided to surprise some friends by showing up unexpectedly for supper. We packed a basket of food and headed out, eagerly anticipating the fun we were going to have yelling, "Surprise!" Halfway there Jan abruptly stopped the car and made a U-turn. The children protested because they thought Jan had changed his mind. But the reason for the hasty U-turn became evident when he pulled up in front of a donut shop. *"Donuts! Daddy buying donuts?"* The unexpected treat of donuts added to the excitement of surprising our friends and resulted in increased happiness for all concerned.

### Step 5: Meet Your Own Needs Without Sacrificing the Family

The logical consequence of realizing your value as a person is to accept the fact that you have certain needs that must *not* be denied or repressed. Your responsibility then is to develop a plan to meet your needs without sacrificing family needs.

Almost all parents need: 1) private time of their own; 2) supportive adult friends; 3) time to pursue their hobbies and interests; and 4) someone to take over the household tasks occasionally. Prime-time parents can meet these needs in various ways.

*Need #1: Finding a private time of your own.*

1. Regularly schedule quality private time. Some people need daily private time, others opt for one complete day a month, or a week's vacation each year. The amount of time is less important than the quality of that time. If private time is not regularly scheduled, busy parents usually neglect this aspect of their lives in the hustle and bustle of family interactions. Giving up private time is analogous to forgetting to eat a meal. Missing an occasional meal will not noticeably affect your weight, but allowing this to happen on a daily basis will soon have a significant impact. Missing a private time occasionally will probably have no noticeable effect on your own sense of satisfaction. But continual neglect of this need will reduce your sense of personal satisfaction and harm the quality of family relationships.

2. Use travel time as your personal time. Read your favorite book or work on your needlepoint (if someone else is driving). Listen to cassette tapes of stimulating books and lectures. Enjoy the pleasure of quiet, creative thinking.

3. Get up an hour before the family and do something you really *want* to do. Wait until the family is up before getting out your "Things-to-do" list.

4. Combine your private time with an activity that is uplifting or beneficial. Many prime-time parents combine exercise time with their private think time. Others climb mountains by themselves, fly airplanes, or take long walks.

5. Plan your work schedule to allow a half hour at home alone after everyone else leaves for work or school. Enjoy the refreshing quiet of an empty house. Resist all temptation to turn on the TV or radio.

6. Many women find that a weekly two-hour appointment at the hairdresser is a satisfying oasis in their busy schedules.

7. Combine private time with lessons or courses that will contribute to self-improvement. Consider art lessons, ceramics, creative writing, upholstering, photography, or hundreds of other courses.

8. Find a hideout close to home where the family can't find you. Try sitting on the roof, locking the bathroom door, sitting in the car, or holing up in the children's playhouse.

9. Reserve the first fifteen minutes after you get home from work as your private uninterrupted time. If the family knows how important this time is for you, they will be happy to allow you these few minutes alone.

10. Buy a headset or earphones and put on your favorite record.

11. Set the policy, "From nine until ten o'clock is Mommy's time—don't bother her!" Let the phone ring. Calls have a way of eating up valuable personal time.

12. Reserve lunch hours for yourself. Find a comfortable, private place and kick off your shoes. Put your feet up and indulge in a good book, newspaper, or crossword puzzle.

*Need #2: Supportive adult friends.*

1. Be friendly. Don't hesitate to be the first one to speak. Show a genuine interest in others. Discuss the other person's interests.

2. Seek friends who have families with children of a similar age. When you plan activities together, the children can enjoy themselves and you can enjoy adult friendship.

3. Invite friends home. Don't isolate yourself by using the family as an excuse. Don't apologize for less than ideal surroundings—breakfast dishes that are still in the sink.

When appropriate, ask the family to join the conversation. Children benefit from encounters with other adults. Don't complain when your spouse brings home an occasional friend. Enjoy the experience.

4. Take a special trip occasionally—without the children. Children should realize that their parents need a life of their own.

5. Take a honeymoon at least once a year. This is a time when you and your spouse can enjoy each other without interruptions from the children.

6. Offer to help another working parent when help is needed. When you see the need, fill it without waiting to be asked.

7. If possible, combine socializing with something you have always wanted to do. Attend adult education classes. Go back to college. Take a refresher course. Join a Bible study group. Join the YMCA or YWCA. Join the tennis club.

8. Visit places where other adults are likely to congregate.

9. Volunteer your time to help in some worthwhile cause.

10. Make friends with the people you interact with on a fairly regular basis. Get to know, on a first name basis, the librarian, the clerk at the grocery store, the gas station attendant, the mailman, your child's teacher, the barber, or the bank teller. When you see them you can enjoy a more meaningful relationship.

11. Enroll in a seminar, such as marriage encounter, stop smoking, financial planning, or weight control, and make friends with people whose interests are similar to your own.

12. Cultivate friendships. Don't give up a good friendship just because you moved across town. Write letters, telephone, and plan special times to get together.

*Need # 3: Finding time to pursue your own hobbies and interests.*

1. Include the family. Encourage them to participate with you. Help them get started on a similar project that you can work on together. Share your interests with the family.

2. Set up a regular time each week to pursue your hobby or interest.

3. Work together with other adults who have similar interests.

4. Go through your complete schedule and eliminate unimportant activities wherever possible. Or use some time-saving devices and techniques and try to carve out at least fifteen minutes a day for your special project.

*Need #4: Finding someone to take over the household tasks occasionally.*

1. When the children are young, hire someone. Budget for the expense.

2. Share the tasks with your spouse and/or your children.

3. Hire a babysitter who is also willing to do housework.

4. Contract with a family member to do one of his chores if he'll handle one of yours.

5. Pay your children to do tasks that you would normally pay someone else to do.

6. Don't feel you are indispensable. Let others help with the housework even though their work does not meet your standard of excellence.

7. Make a bargain with the children. Purchase something they want if they will consistently help you with certain tasks.

Using these ideas to stimulate your own thinking, complete the following project to determine what your real needs are and how you plan to fill them.

Task 1: Define what personal fulfillment means to you. Be specific. Brainstorm. Don't reject any idea because it sounds silly or frivolous. Consider the following: Does it mean time alone? A better job? Pursuing your hobby? Reading a book? Being a better parent? Having satisfying adult relationships? Being a better spouse? Upgrading your business skills? Making enough money to live comfortably? Getting an education? Losing twenty pounds? Keeping your house spotless? Going out to eat? Managing your budget?

Task 2: Rate each entry according to its importance in your life. Write the number 1 next to top priority items— those that you consider essential. Write the number 2 next to those items that you could live without but would add a great deal of pleasure if they could be realized. Write the number 3 next to those items that are not really essential.

Task 3: Now list the top priority items in their order of importance.

Task 4: Take each top priority entry (starting at the top of the list) and write down all the ways you can make this item become a reality. Be as specific as possible. Repeat the process for the items in the number-2 category.

Task 5: Develop a daily or weekly plan to fill each of these needs. Remember that your life needs balance. Personal fulfillment cannot be found if the family's needs are neglected in the process. Wherever possible, think of methods that combine family needs with your own.

Task 6: Don't overlook the items in the number-3 category. Although you can live happily without them, they may add a special sense of satisfaction to your life.

Until you begin meeting your own needs, without sacrificing the needs of the family, you will never find personal fulfillment and experience the exhilarating feeling of self-worth.

**Step 6:  Live a Balanced Life Relationally**

Prime-time parents must establish balanced family relationships if they hope to find personal fulfillment for themselves and for each person in the family. There are three essential relational qualities that must be kept in constant balance among family members to insure healthy interactions. These are love, freedom, and responsibility. Each person in the family can be happy only if he receives unconditional love, if he feels free to make the decisions he is capable of making, and if he is willing to take the responsibility for these decisions. If any of these components is missing, or if any component reaches harmful extremes, the result is family disharmony and conflict.

*Love: Relational component #1*

Love is the first and most crucial ingredient for a balanced, harmonious family life. If love is freely given and freely accepted with no strings attached, individual freedom and responsibility can develop. Unconditional love (acceptance) means that each person is loved because he exists and not because he gets good grades, keeps his room clean, brings home a decent paycheck, or has dinner ready on time. If you feel that others love you only because of your looks, behavior, or accomplishments, you will feel used and exploited. When conditional love is expressed in the family, relationships are thrown out of balance because the person who feels loved conditionally tries to mold himself to fit the desires of the others. You can never be comfortable with yourself or with others if you feel loved in this manner. The absence of love—rejection—also causes relational imbalance. When needs are neglected, feelings are scoffed at, and closeness is spurned, family relationships die.

Love is the strongest power that we all have at our disposal. Experiencing it, and helping others to experience it, will change the most hopeless and discouraging circumstances. Love can even bring major family upheaval and disorder into balance.

### Freedom: Relational component #2

Freedom, especially the freedom to make choices, is a vital factor in everyone's life. Although family commitments carry certain limitations, these very limits can be advantages, and can open up new possibilities. Your power to make choices can actually be expanded because you are committed to the good of others.

The freedom to make choices is enhanced in love relationships because each person is assured that if he makes a poor choice and fails, he will still be loved. It is also easier to accept the responsibility for your decisions if you know you are loved. You don't have to blame other people to bolster your self-esteem. You can enjoy the people you live with. You can treat them as individuals by allowing them to make their own choices, rather than using them to support your demands. Love that encourages freedom creates a climate of mutual respect in the family.

### Responsibility: Relational component #3

Responsibility is the third vital relational quality. Taking responsibility can mean two things: 1) fulfilling the duties that are clearly yours; and 2) taking responsibility for the decisions that you make. When each family member accepts the responsibilities that are rightfully his, he controls his own destiny and his self-worth is enhanced.

However, there are extremes to be avoided. The first extreme is to shirk the responsibilities that are yours and to blame others for your own mistakes. The second extreme is to take on too many responsibilities. To avoid this problem follow these two rules: 1) never consistently do anything for your children that they can profit from doing themselves; and 2) never take on an outside responsibility that will harm your family's relationships.

If any family member leans to an extreme in any of these three areas, his life will be thrown out of balance. If a parent's life is out of balance it affects the lives of those he is living with. It's similar to the building of a tower. If the foundation stones are not properly balanced, anything placed on top of those stones will lean. As the tower grows, the lean becomes more accentuated, and the lack of balance threatens to destroy the whole structure. In the family, parents are the foundation stones. If their lives are not balanced, the rest of the family is pushed out of balance, and it becomes almost impossible for them to experience personal fulfillment. Other family members are forced to adjust to the tilt or compensate for the imbalance.

Do you feel your family life is in perfect relational balance? Does the rest of the family agree? Are their lives in balance too? Remember, true balance can only be achieved when each life is in balance. Get to know yourself through the eyes of your family by asking each member the following questions. The revelation may be painful. But it can be a growth experience for you, *if* you can accept the constructive criticism without casting blame or seeking to justify yourself and *if* you are willing to change.

1. Is the LOVE factor balanced? When do you feel you are loved conditionally? When do you feel rejected?

2. Is the FREEDOM factor balanced? When do you feel I am making poor decisions? When do you feel I am making too many or too few decisions? What decisions would *you* like to be making? Why?

3. Is the RESPONSIBILITY factor balanced? When do you feel I am taking too little responsibility? When do you feel I am taking too much responsibility? In what areas would you like to have more responsibility? In what areas would you like to have less responsibility?

True personal fulfillment for a prime-time parent does not mean meeting your own needs at the expense of others. It means finding ways to meet your needs within the family context. It means getting to know yourself better and seeing yourself as a valuable person. It means making the changes in your life that will help you realize your goals. It means relating to family members in such a way that personal fulfillment can be a reality for all. This is what it means to have a prime-time parenting personality.

# 5

## Becoming a Child Development Expert

It is impossible to be an effective prime-time parent without a knowledge of children. First, it is important to understand normal child development and learn how to spot a potential behavior problem. Then, you must get to know and understand how to work with the characteristics of your own child. Finally, in order for your child to develop according to your highest expectations, you must seek to become the type of person you want your child to be. Achieving these goals is not easy. It takes study, as well as practical experience, to become proficient in the prime-time parenting career.

Children develop best when parents act on knowledge and educated common sense and not instinct or guesswork alone. Most new parents are frightfully inexperienced and know very little about child development. Prime-time parents must be willing to learn and to continue learning through a child's growing years. Do away with rigid ideas that can't be molded by new information. Eagerly seek advice from recommended books or from professionals who have devoted their lives to studying children's development and behavior. The study of children must become an absorbing interest in your life. You must become an "expert" in the field of child development.

You can never learn too much about children. But remember, there are exceptions to every rule. Your child probably will not conform to all of the norms that have been established for children of various ages. Norms should be considered guidelines. If you are uncertain if your child is developing normally, it is always best to check with a professional who can advise you. Children develop best when a developmental lag or a behavioral problem is caught and treated early.

Certain behavior can be expected in the various developmental stages of a child's life. By talking to experienced parents, you can learn how they dealt with problems similar to your child's problems.

A child's behavior can be frustrating to parents if they do not realize the behavior is normal. Consider, for example, the crying of a newborn. Few parents realize how often a baby will cry, or that crying will probably increase for the first two months! Then, when the baby is about three months old, the crying should decrease to about one hour a day. Becoming upset and frustrated will not help the crying—it only makes it worse. So, "Grin and bear it," is good advice. After you have made sure that there is nothing you can do, console yourself by thinking of crying as good exercise for the baby and shut the nursery door.

If parents have never studied or had much experience with babies and young children, their expectations may be unrealistic. Young teenage parents with little knowledge or experience often expect their children to do certain things before the child is developmentally ready. Vladimir de Lissovoy's study on child care by adolescent parents is a good example.* "In general," de Lissovoy states, "I found the

* "Child Care by Adolescent Parents," *Children Today* (July–August 1973): 22–25.

young parents in this study to be, with a few notable exceptions, an intolerant group—impatient, insensitive, irritable, and prone to use physical punishment with their children." I was shocked by this conclusion until I studied the following chart indicating the age at which these parents expected certain behaviors.

The expectations of these mothers and fathers differed considerably from expert opinion. In every instance, whether it was a social smile or a first word, these teenage parents expected this behavior weeks and sometimes months before the average child is actually capable. Imagine how much frustration and anguish these young parents would have been spared had they known what to expect.

At this point you may want to test yourself to see how well your expectations compare to expert opinion. At what age would you expect the following behaviors to occur. Your score may motivate you to learn more about children!

| Area of development and approximate norm in weeks (Opinions of experts are in the parentheses.) | | Parents' estimates in weeks | |
|---|---|---|---|
| | | Mothers | Fathers |
| Social smile | (6) | 3 | 3 |
| Sit alone | (28) | 12 | 6 |
| Pull-up to standing | (44) | 24 | 20 |
| First step alone | (60) | 40 | 40 |
| Toilet training (wetting) | (not given)* | 24 | 24 |
| Toilet training (bowel) | (not given)* | 26 | 24 |
| First word | (52) | 32 | 24 |
| Obedience training | (not given) | 36 | 26 |
| Recognition of wrong doing | (not given) | 52 | 40 |

\* Most experts would suggest sometime between 1 1/2 and 4 years of age, yet some children continue to have enuresis (bedwetting) problems into their early teenage years! Six months of age (24–26 weeks) is totally unrealistic.

1. Sitting up.
2. Purposefully reaching for and grasping objects.
3. Understanding when someone is talking about him.
4. Crawling (on stomach).
5. Creeping (on hands and knees).
6. Seeking for a hidden object.
7. Walking alone.
8. Understanding the command "no."
9. Speaking in simple sentences.
10. Sleeping through the night.
11. Peddling a tricycle.
12. Girls begin menstruation.
13. Able to draw a diamond.

(Answers: 1. 6 mo; 2. 3 mo; 3. 9 mo; 4. 7–8 mo; 5. 8–9 mo; 6. 5 mo; 7. 12 mo; 8. 9 mo; 9. 2 yr; 10. 6 mo; 11. 3 yr; 12. 11–14 yr; 13. 7 yr.)

In addition to understanding developmental characteristics, parents must learn how family circumstances can affect children. Parental illness, divorce, grandparents in the home, race and culture, social class, family size, and other family characteristics over which children have no control, all have an effect. Understanding this can help parents alleviate potential problems.

For example, the order of a child's birth can affect the child's behavior. First-born children have the advantage of being an only child for a time. They often receive more verbal interaction and attention from adults. They are more likely to fulfill their parents' expectation to behave properly and perform well in school. Middle children may get lost between the first born and the last born. Their achievements are often overshadowed by those of the first born. Nor do middle children receive the attention, assistance, and the lengthened period of dependency that last children enjoy. If parents understand the importance of birth order, they can guard against showing favoritism to the first, forgetting to praise the middle, and being overly protective of the last.

At the same time they can remember to encourage flexibility and playfulness in the first; to talk a great deal to the middle child; and to expect the last child to show self-reliance at an early age.

## A Child Development Guide for the Working Parent

Whether or not a parent is working does not make a great deal of difference in the basic development of a child. However, there are certain developmental concepts that are extremely important for prime-time parents to know. These concepts relate to the developing child's needs and behavior, and can cause family conflicts if working parents are not aware of them.

### *Infancy—the first year*

The first month of life is an adjustment period for the entire family. Baby is adjusting to life outside of his mother's warm "incubator." Mom is adjusting to breastfeeding and/ or getting her body back in shape. Dad is adjusting to a new mouth to feed. Dad and Mom are both adjusting to sleepless nights. Everybody is more tired, more irritable, and probably needs more attention than ever before. Mom needs Dad. Dad needs Mom. The older children need to be convinced that their place and importance in the family has not been usurped by the newcomer. And the baby seems to need everything!

The most important parental need at this time is usually someone who is willing to take over the housecleaning, meal preparation, and the other necessary tasks while Mom, Dad, and the children get reacquainted. This is the time for a family to establish a good foundation for growing together through the years to come.

Because this is an important adjustment period, many women find it difficult to return to work immediately. If you do decide to return to work, keep your life as uncomplicated as possible. Only take on responsibilities that are absolutely necessary. You might ease the transition period by working part-time for a while. Find someone that you can completely trust to provide for the baby's needs so you won't have to worry and spend extra time coaching an inexperienced babysitter. Budget for extra household help.

The first three months are very demanding in terms of physical child care, because the baby can't do anything for himself and older children need extra parental attention to be assured of your unchanging love. This period is also emotionally draining as you begin to realize the vast commitment and responsibility that is now yours. Before returning to work, be sure you are in good physical and emotional condition. Guard your strength by taking a lunch hour or afternoon nap, and get to bed earlier than usual to make up for the sleep you will lose during nighttime feedings.

Do yourself and your family a favor by taking time to strengthen the relationship between you and your newborn. Spend as much time together as possible. Psychologists consider this period prime time to establish the bonding process. Some people have the mistaken idea that once the bonding process occurs—when an attachment is formed with the newborn—you and your child are bonded or emotionally cemented together for life. Although this process does occur in some animal species, it is *not* true for humans. For example, during a critical period after baby ducks break out of their shells they become forever imprinted (attached) to the object that moves around them, normally the mother duck. Experiments have proven that ducklings will even become imprinted to a human or a moving box—if that is what scientists provide for them during this critical time. And once imprinted, the attachment lasts for life.

In our modern world of short order meals, crash courses, and instant solutions, many parents attempt to emulate the animal world and insure the bonding process in the first moments of life. Dad joins Mom in the delivery room and both parents take advantage of live-in arrangements with their newborn in the hospital. This is a positive step, of course. There is evidence that mothers who are allowed to touch, cuddle, and fondle their babies in the delivery room immediately after birth and during their hospital stay have a higher quality of interaction six months later than those mothers who do not have this experience.* But such early interaction will *not* insure permanent bondng. After enjoying this birth time together, far too many couples return to business as usual as soon as Mother brings her infant home. Father goes back to work, Mother-in-law takes over the care of the baby (after all, she is experienced), and Mother rests or tackles the housework and projects she left unfinished until she, too, disappears into the outside work world. And the bonding process which began so promisingly at birth is not allowed to grow. I call this phenomenon the "absent father syndrome." Obviously, this can occur just as easily with an absent mother, but our society makes it harder for a mother to be the absent parent. The following chart portrays the sequence of events.

The absent father (or mother) syndrome begins when Dad or Mom spend very little time with the infant. Time together is the one essential element necessary for bonding to occur. It is impossible to form attachments unless time is invested in a relationship. When the father fails to spend time with the infant during the first four or five months, the child doesn't recognize him as a familiar person; between five and eight months of age, he may even cry when the father picks him up. If the child doesn't know his father, he doesn't develop trust in him, so when the father tries to help the child, the child won't respond. He cries harder, pushes his father away, and if he has mastered his first word, he now uses it and yells, "Mamamamama." This situation is

* Marshall H. Klaus and John H. Kennell, *Maternal-infant Bonding* (St. Louis: The C. V. Mosby Company, 1976).

## The Absent Father Syndrome

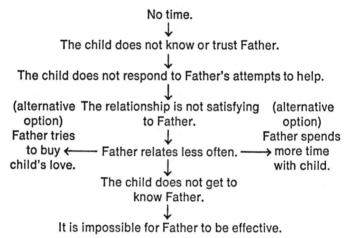

No time.
↓
The child does not know or trust Father.
↓
The child does not respond to Father's attempts to help.
↓
(alternative   The relationship is not satisfying   (alternative
option)                 to Father.                     option)
Father tries                ↓                        Father spends
to buy ←——— Father relates less often. ——→ more time
child's love.               ↓                        with child.
The child does not get to
know Father.
↓
It is impossible for Father to be effective.

obviously frustrating to the father who thought he and his child were bonded for life. He may silently vow, "Okay. I'll just wait until he can kick a football, and then I'll play with him." Because of the father's lack of satisfaction in the relationship, he usually will not respond as readily to the infant's future cries for help. Instead, he will call for his wife to take care of the infant's needs. The result, of course, is that the father spends less and less time with the infant. The child never really gets to know and establish a relationship with his father. Thus, it becomes almost impossible for the father to be effective in the care and training of his child.

In too many cases, the father continues to absent himself from the care and nurturing of his growing child. Instead of spending time with his child, he tries to buy the child's love and attention by offering him little gifts—until he willingly hands his sixteen-year-old son keys to a new Porsche because he feels guilty that he didn't have time to watch his son pitch a high school baseball game.

Surprisingly, during the preschool years this syndrome

has an inverse effect on the child's obedience. The child generally obeys the absent parent better because he does not have a wide variety of experiences that convince him of that parent's unconditional love and acceptance. In fact, he may believe that his father will only love him if he obeys. So when the father speaks, especially in a strong, commanding voice, the child quickly responds. Because he is convinced that the person who cares for him most loves him no matter what he does, he is freer to exhibit the normal autonomy and willfulness of two- and three-year-olds. But he obeys the absent father because he fears rejection. This syndrome can only be stopped by spending more quality time together with the child.

The more intense the initial bonding relationship is and the earlier it begins, the stronger it is likely to remain. This indicates the importance of establishing satisfying relationships during the first few months of your child's life.

Between the ages of five to eight months, the child begins to recognize familiar objects in his environment. Therefore, he develops a fear of the unfamiliar. He wakes screaming in the middle of the night because his room does not look familiar in the darkness. This is the reason he may even cry when Dad comes home, if Dad has been an absent father. If a working mother plans to use a babysitter during the first year of the baby's life, it is important to introduce the baby to the sitter early, so the sitter will be a familiar person when "stranger anxiety" occurs. Otherwise, it may be very difficult to leave the child with another person because he will feel insecure and cry for his parents. In order to avoid this scene, many parents seldom go out together without the baby. They figure it is just not worth the hassle of trying to make the unfamiliar familiar.

Try to avoid switching the child from babysitter to babysitter and from home to home during this time. It is best if the sitter can care for a child in his own familiar home territory. If not, select a place that will meet the child's needs for as long as possible, at least until the child is two years old.

During the first year, a child develops so rapidly that one must always be aware of new skills and capabilities in order to prevent accidents. I often hear parents lament:

"Yesterday he couldn't roll over. Today I left the baby on the bed for a moment and he rolled off."

"Yesterday she couldn't stand up in the crib. I left the guardrail down and today she tumbled out."

"Yesterday he couldn't grasp objects. I failed to pick up Junior's marbles and today he swallowed one."

"Yesterday he couldn't crawl. Today he scooted to the stairs and fell down the whole flight."

"Yesterday she couldn't walk. Today she toddled out into the street."

"Yesterday he couldn't grasp the door knob. Today he opened the door and I'm still trying to catch up with him."

This is a normal pattern during the first year, so it's vital to know what developmental changes to expect next. Then you can safety-proof your home and avoid needless worry about possible accidents. Put breakables or harmful substances away. Medicines and poisons should be kept in locked containers far out of reach. Caustic cleaning solutions should be stored in childproof locked closets. Discard broken equipment and frayed electrical cords. Place safety plugs in electrical sockets. Turn the temperature on the water heater down so a child can't get scalded with hot tap water. Remove poisonous plants from the house and yard. Fence dangerous equipment or swimming pools. Remove sharp-cornered furniture. Keep the doors of the older children's rooms shut. It is usually impossible to keep every potentially dangerous object out of reach. A one-year-old can cause major destruction in a very short time. When a baby has just destroyed some prized possession, it's not always easy to feel very loving.

When you know the developmental characteristics of your baby, you can prevent these problems and look ahead to the next stage of development with more confidence.

### Toddlers—from 1 to 2 1/2 years of age

This is the time when the child takes his first steps toward independence. He starts talking, so he can ask for what he wants. He perfects his walking, so he can go wherever he wants. He starts feeding himself, so he can eat what he wants. This all culminates in what people call the "terrible twos." But this child who is growing so independent continues to need people who will give him attention, affection, and affirmation of his worth. The toddler also needs firm, gentle, consistent discipline as he begins testing out parent-imposed limitations in his life. He must learn to distinguish right from wrong. This is the foundation period of intellectual development, language acquisition, and socialization. The toddler must be carefully taught.

Home care by a patient, understanding person is ideal for the active toddler. If you have access to a good family day-care situation or a quality infant-toddler program you might also consider these options.

### Preschoolers—from 2 1/2 to 5 years of age

This is the age when children become more interested in other children, and parents begin checking out the local nursery schools. Some parents have the mistaken idea that college achievement is tied to attendance at the prestigious nursery school. This is not true. Children, however, do need a consistent environment and an intellectually stimulating caregiver. They need a variety of toys and play equipment, and a place to play. They need stories, songs, finger plays, and language development experiences. They need someone to answer their questions about how cows make milk and why birds have beaks. They need to be introduced to their community—to have a chance to go shopping at a local market, take a trip to the barbershop, visit the fire station and the zoo.

Children of this age continue to thrive in groups with a small adult-child ratio. Obviously, the one-to-one relationship that a mother or babysitter can establish is ideal. But if a day-care center is selected, then be sure there are plenty of caring adults to meet your child's personal needs; people who will occasionally hold him on their lap, will read a story just to him, and will rub his back during naptime. One adult to five children is the ratio that most quality programs like to maintain. As the preschool child gets older, he will need less individual attention from the teacher. Make sure that the teacher is not overworked, loves her job, and shows an individual interest in each one of her little charges. (For more information on child care, see Chapter 2.)

Children need afternoon naps during this time. A nap is always a good idea for children of working parents, since it allows the child and parent more time together in the evening.

Preschool children may still seem hesitant to step into new situations. Therefore, it is important to evaluate child-care programs on the basis of their long-term possibilities for meeting the needs of the child. If possible, select a child-care situation where the primary caregiver is likely to continue working for at least a year.

Time is an abstract concept and means very little to the preschooler. Parents who are away for long periods of time seem to be gone for an eternity to a lonesome, hungry preschooler who has spent all day at a babysitter's house or a day-care center. Pick up your child promptly. Better yet, arrive before the child expects you so he won't have a chance to worry. If you must spend more than six hours at a time away from your preschooler, especially one under four years of age, try to break this time into two shorter periods. If possible, spend your lunch hour with your child. If this is only an occasional occurrence, some children may find the second good-bye even more difficult. But if you make it a routine, children can greatly benefit from a midday parental visit.

### The school-age child

Between six and twelve years of age, a child usually experiences steady, developmental progress. The first years in school are an especially important time for a child to learn to step out on his own and make new friends. Inviting a friend over to play or attending a birthday party becomes very important to a child. Working parents must plan ways for their children to enjoy socialization experiences after school.

These are the years of music lessons, Little League, Brownies, horseback riding lessons, and gymnastics, among others. Working parents may find it particularly difficult to make these special after-school activities available to their child. A broad base of friends who aren't working and who have children participating in these activities is essential. Another possibility is a babysitter or teenager who is willing to transport your child. In the early stages of lessons, especially music lessons, it is almost essential for a child to have someone supervise his practicing. One mother I know hired a teenager to babysit after school—her main job qualification was her ability to play the piano!

School-age children are interested in sharing school experiences with parents. No child wants to be hounded each night with the question, "What did you do in school?" But he does want Mom and Dad to see his classroom, meet his friends, and participate in some class activities if at all possible. The working parent should schedule at least one day a year to visit the child's classroom. This is just as important as bringing your child to your office for a visit.

School-age children are sensitive to slights. They want to be accepted. They need to discuss their conflicts with an understanding parent who will not belittle them. Relational problems aren't just blurted out at the dinner table. Children need time to find the right words to ask for help. A typical problem might be, "Mary was calling Julie names and made her cry. I still want Mary to be my friend, but I felt sorry for Julie. What should I do?" This is the time to establish the fact that you are interested in listening to your child's problems and will offer good practical advice. School-age children are much more interested in asking for and taking parental advice than teenagers. If you take the time to establish good communication with your school-age children, they will be more willing to accept parental counsel when they are teenagers.

At times most school-age children feel that they won't be able to meet their teacher's expectations. They don't want to fail. Parents can ease these feelings and increase a child's sense of competence by taking the time to listen to him read and help him with math problems. An enrichment program that a parent and child can enjoy together, such as visiting museums, art galleries, or attending concerts, may also increase a child's feeling of competence. If a child can begin his school career feeling competent and successful, this will set a good pattern for his future school years.

Schoolchildren don't want to be with their parents all the time, but they do enjoy knowing that their parents are around. They like their growing independence and may enjoy an hour home alone before Mom arrives. But few school-age children enjoy coming home to an empty house on a regular basis, especially if it gets dark before their parents come home.

This is the age when children need training in taking responsibility. They enjoy completing and checking off a list of chores that have been left for them. They also enjoy learning new skills and playing games. If you can't be home when your child comes home from school, hire a mature high school student who would love to play big brother or sister to your child and help him with his homework, toss a football back and forth, or let him win a game of chess. To insure adequate supervision, make regular telephone checks, or hire the teenager next door so his parents will be available if needed. Another possibility is to have your child go directly to the teenager's home if an adult is available there. Remember, there is a big difference between a six- and a twelve-year-old. It may not be appropriate to leave a six-year-old home alone, but a twelve-year-old may enjoy it. Consider your child's maturity, level of responsibility, and individual characteristics, and use educated common sense when making this decision.

### Teenagers

Working parents often think they're in the home stretch when their child reaches his teens. He is not as dependent upon his parents, and he is fully capable of taking care of himself. Therefore, when parents are away from the home they tend to leave teenagers with little or no supervision.

Some working parents, however, feel that it is even more important to spend time with their children during the critical teenage years. This is the age when children can reap bitter consequences if parents don't provide proper guidance and supervision. One parent stated, "To encourage and influence my teenagers, instead of threatening and forcing them, requires every ounce of my intelligence, judgment, and wit. I could not possibly leave the job of supervising my thirteen- and fourteen-year-old to another person. I enjoy working during the time when they are in school, but unless I have an emergency, I am home with them during the afternoon and evening hours."

Teenagers need attention. They need someone to talk to. They need someone who thinks they are special. If they don't receive this attention from their parents, and sometimes even if they do, they will establish this type of relationship with someone else. Members of their own peer group often fill this need, and without parental guidance they may be led into drug experimentation or questionable habits that make them feel important. Teenage pregnancies, one of the worst problems in our society, very often result from a lack of parental supervision. The lonesome teenager, left without proper parental guidance, invites a friend home to share the empty house.

Parents with full-time jobs won't be available to supervise afternoon activities. So it's especially important to plan ahead. Know exactly what your teenager is doing after school. Encourage him to participate in extracurricular activities. An afternoon job may help fill these hours constructively. If your teenager is self-motivated, encourage him to tackle homework, household tasks, or special projects and hobbies during this time. Teenagers need to be needed. They want to do worthwhile work. If your child is too young for an outside job, create one at home. Hire him to do various chores and pay him whatever you would pay someone else.

Your teenager should be in your thoughts and your plans as much as younger children. Your home must be as responsive to your teenager's needs as it was to your preschooler's needs. If it's not, teenagers will choose to spend their time elsewhere. One family I know spent their last nickel to put a swimming pool in their backyard and a pool table in their rec room so their home could become an attractive gathering place for their teenager's friends. In this way the parents were able to "unofficially" supervise.

One newly married college student was asked (with her mother standing nearby) if she had had a chaperone when she dated as a teenager. Without hesitation, she replied, "No."

"What do you mean, you never had a chaperone?" her mother said, looking up in surprise. "What do you think your dad and I were doing all those times we took you and your friends to the beach, to the concerts, and to the amusement parks?"

This time it was the daughter's turn to look shocked. "Mom, I had no idea you were chaperoning us. I just naturally thought that you enjoyed having our company as much as we enjoyed your company."

Teenagers need parents like that. What a challenge for the prime-time parent to find time to be that kind of parent to his *almost* emancipated child!

Now focus on your child and ask yourself these questions:

1. What do you think your child's basic needs are at this time?

2. How are you as a working parent meeting those needs? Is there anything else you feel you should be doing?

3. As you look ahead to your child's next stage of development, what changes do you feel you may have to make in order to better meet his developmental needs?

### Recognizing Problem Behavior

Every parent hopes that his child will glide through childhood and adolescence with nothing more serious than a few scraped knees and an occasional "blah" day. But many children do develop emotional problems, so it is important for prime-time parents to spot problem behavior in its first stages. In this way, necessary changes can be made before deep-seated emotional problems envelop a child's life.

Every child will go through good periods as well as bad periods when his life seems particularly confusing and he doesn't like himself. When things are going well for your child, it's time to rejoice in his happiness and well-being. But when things are beginning to slide downhill, it's your job to stop the fall as soon as possible. Don't wait to pick up the pieces after the crash has occurred.

In order to prevent emotional problems you need to be aware of the possible signs that may occur when a child does not feel good about himself and when he is experiencing an emotional problem.

### Signs of lack of self-worth

Low self-worth does not develop suddenly. It's a slow process that occurs when a child perceives that the significant people in his life don't think very much of him. In reality, they may love and care for him very much, but his perception is the important factor. If a child feels that his own parents don't love him or think that he isn't as good as other children, his belief in himself will be seriously damaged. Even if parents shower their children with love and support, there may be periods when he feels that other people don't like him, or that his friends are rejecting him. When this occurs, his self-esteem may suffer.

The signs of lack of self-worth are age-related. For example, excessive thumb sucking might be considered a sign of low self-worth for a seven- or eight-year-old, but could be very normal for a one- or two-year old. These signs are also situation related. For example, a certain behavior may occur when the child is with strangers or when he is very tired. This might indicate that he feels insecure only in certain situations or under certain circumstances.

The behaviors listed below might be considered signs of low self-worth for the preschool and school-age child. If your child exhibits some of these signs, *don't* assume that he has an emotional problem. Consider such behavior an indication that your child could use a little more quality time with you to convince him that he is a worthwhile person. After each sign, you will find some suggestions for bolstering your child's ego and helping him realize his true value.

*Signs of low self-worth\**
1. Child is unrealistically fearful.
    a. *Is afraid to play games because he might not win.*
       Play noncompetitive games. Give a prize for playing the game, not for winning. Teach the child strategies or skills that will help him be successful.
    b. *Does not ask questions or is afraid to answer questions.*
       Make it easy for the child to ask questions. Say, "It looks as if you have a good question for me." Encourage questions when you are alone with the child or in a safe family setting. Reward the child for asking questions by saying, "That's a good question," or "I can tell you were really thinking." In turn, ask the child questions. At first, make sure your questions have simple or obvious answers. Accept all answers by saying something like, "That's an interesting idea."
    c. *When asked to do something, immediately says, "I don't know how."*
       Reassure the child that it is okay not to know how. Say, "When I was your age I didn't know how either." Offer to do it and "hire" him as

\* Adapted from: Kay Kuzma, *Understanding Children* (Mt. View, Ca.: Pacific Press, 1978), pp. 133–134; used by permission.

your special assistant. Let him do every small part of the task that he is obviously capable of.

d. *Afraid to try things for the first time, even when a teacher or parent offers help.*

Reassure him that it is acceptable to watch. Let him decide when he will try something new. One way to do this is to ask him, "How long do you think you'll want to watch before trying?" After he indicates the amount of time he needs, tell him to let you know when he's ready so you can help him.

e. *Is afraid to be left in a new situation or with a new person.*

Stay with the child until he feels comfortable. Ask him to tell you when it is okay for you to leave. Don't appear anxious to go. If you have allowed a reasonable time, you might warn the child, "I will have to leave in one hour." When the hour is up, go to the child and say, "Good-bye," tell him when you will return, and leave. Keep your promise by returning on time.

f. *Does not ask for things he needs.*

Make it easy for a child to ask. Never belittle a child. Reward requests by saying, "I'm glad you asked," and fulfill the request immediately.

2. Child exhibits unusual or negative behavior.

a. *Cries, pouts, or exhibits other negative behavior when he doesn't win or get his own way.*

Ignore the behavior, but acknowledge his feelings. "It makes you sad when you lose or don't get what you want. I sometimes feel that way." Then give the child something positive to do. "This is what I do when I feel that way. . . . What are some other things you could do to chase away the sad feelings?"

b. *Carries a blanket or pacifier, or has thumb in mouth wherever he goes.*

Give the child an extra amount of attention, but don't let him know that this behavior bothers you. Keep the child busy. After three years of age the child can make the decision to give up a blanket or pacifier. Let him buy something he really wants in exchange for it. Let him actually give it away to the store clerk. But be sure it's the child's decision!

c. *Exhibits excessive, undesirable behavior, such as biting, kicking, hitting, or spitting.*

Use the behavior modification technique of "ignoring" negative behavior and rewarding positive behavior. (See Chapter 7.) Realize that these behaviors are indications of a discouraged, unhappy child. Encourage him. Find the little things he does well and capitalize on those. Stop the negative behavior by saying, "I can't let you hurt someone else," but don't belittle the child with criticism.

d. *Seeks attention by doing something prohibited, by acting silly, or by disturbing others.*

Ignore the behavior, but say, "I bet you'd like me to play with you. Let's go. . . ." Later, tell the child that he can use a magic word to get your attention. Invent a word so you'll both know what it means and the child won't have to resort to inappropriate behavior to get your attention.

e. *Exhibits such behavior as lying, stealing, or otherwise being deceptive.*

This behavior is often a cry for attention. Spend more quality time with the child. Don't be critical. Let him know that you can't be deceived. Say simply, "I know you took the knife. The consequence is that you must return it or pay for it." Don't get in an argument about the truth of a statement. If a child tries to argue that his lie is really true, give him the reason it could not be true and show you understand why he feels the way he does. Say, "I saw what happened but I can tell you really feel strongly about your point of view. That's exactly how you would like it to be, isn't it? How can I help you feel better about it?"

f. *Deliberately hurts others or himself.*
Simply say, "You may not hurt others or yourself." Stop the child. Hold him. Comfort him, Talk about the situation. "You were really angry. What happened? What else could you do when that happens again?" Make sure he knows that he is special and you won't allow him to hurt himself.

3. Child is overly concerned about being liked and accepted.
   a. *Constantly gives things to people to buy their attention and friendship.*
   Discourage the constant giving of gifts. Concentrate on showing the child how much you like him because he exists, not because of his gifts. Compliment him on things he can't change; for example, his blue eyes or black curly hair. Spend time with the child when it's not related to the receiving of a gift. Explain to a child that the most important gift is friendship because that can't be broken or lost. Encourage your child to invite a friend home to play. Help him to make friends without giving gifts.
   b. *Brings things from home to get teachers' and children's attention and approval.*

Make it a policy that the children can only take things to school for "show and tell" sessions. Invite the teacher or special friends to visit your home. Let the teacher know why you think your child is doing this and work together to meet the child's need for attention and approval.

c. *Often asks parent, "Do you love me?" Asks teacher and children, "Do you like me?"*
Read the picture book *The Way Mothers Are,* by Mariam Schlein (Chicago: Albert Whitman Co., 1963), to your child daily for a month and let your behavior give the child the same "I love you" message. Help the child to develop skills and interests that other people admire.

4. Child exaggerates or is unrealistic about certain situations.

a. *Complains, "They don't like me," or "They won't play with me."*
Don't disagree by saying, "That's not true." Use active listening techniques to draw the child out. Say, "You must really feel hurt. Tell me more," etc. Finally, encourage the child to think of ways to change this situation.

b. *Brags or boasts by saying such things as, "I'm better than you are."*
Shock the child by agreeing. "You are an important person and can do a lot of things better than _____. Let's list the things you can do better." (Think of the obvious. If a child is smaller, he can crawl through a smaller hole, etc.) Then talk about how everybody can do something better than somebody. But there is always somebody that can do something better than you.

    c. *Is jealous when a child, parent, or teacher shows attention to others.*

    Spend time with the child. Reassure him that he is important and that your love for him will never change. When a child's need for love and attention is met, he will not feel jealous.

    d. *Blames others for his own mistakes or finds excuses for his behavior.*

    Don't accept this behavior. Defuse it by showing the child that you understand how he feels. "It makes you feel terrible when you make a mistake, doesn't it? It's hard for anyone to admit they were wrong. It's okay to make mistakes. That's the way we learn."

5. Child has difficulty with social relationships.

    a. *Is extremely competitive with other children.*

    Deemphasize competition. Be sure that both your words and behavior give the message that the child is valuable whether or not he wins.

    b. *Does not defend self with words or actions.*

    Encourage the child to stand up for his rights by saying, "You are an important person. Don't allow others to hurt you needlessly." Then give the child words to use in future situations, for example, "You may not say those things to me." Role play the situation so the child can practice the words and the tone of voice to use in a safe environment.

    c. *Does not initiate contacts with others.*

    Show the child how to initiate contacts. For example, show a toy to another child or select a child that looks lonely and walk up and say, "Hi, I'm Jim, do you want to play?"

    d. *Is critical and judgmental of others—tattles.*

    Don't accept tattling and don't reward it. Instead, change the topic of conversation and give the child attention when he is not tattling. Talk to the offender in private, not as a direct result of the tattling.

e. *Calls others names, such as "baby," "dummy," or "shrimp," in order to make himself look better.*

Stop this behavior. Make up a story that will show him name-calling can hurt a child's feelings. After telling the story, ask, "How would you feel if you were that child? Why do you think the child called his friend those terrible names? What else could he have done, rather than hurt the child by calling him names?" Make sure the child understands the concept that we feel better about ourselves when we help others feel better about themselves.

f. *Does not participate in group activities.*

Don't force him. Let him know it's okay to be a bystander. Give him something special to do. Invite two or three children over to the house. Help the child feel comfortable with a few friends first.

### Signs of possible emotional problems

The signs of possible emotional difficulties are similar to those discussed above. In fact, they may be an outgrowth of a long-standing problem of self-worth, or there may be other reasons.

In order to catch emotional problems at an early stage, it is important to be alert to sudden changes in your child's personality or behavior. For one child, the lack of a smile and laughter may be an important sign that all is not well. For another child this might just be a characteristic from birth. The behavior itself may not be the problem—it is the sudden change in a child's behavior that is the key.

The following behaviors might indicate that all is not well with your child. Please note that none of these may be significant alone. But when they occur in combinations, parents may have a key to a developing emotional problem.

## Signs of Possible Emotional Problems

1. Extreme nervousness or irritability.
2. Inability to relax or rest.
3. Listlessness and/or excessive daydreaming.
4. Excessive inattention and tendency toward distraction.
5. Frequent unprovoked crying spells.
6. Lack of interest in surroundings or other children.
7. Unusual shyness and quietness.
8. Lack of laughter and smiles.
9. Overanxiousness about doing what is expected or "right."
10. Frequent hiding or attempting to run away.
11. Repeated aggression (both in words and in actions such as hitting or biting).
12. Destructiveness.
13. Frequent temper tantrums.
14. Frequent complaints of physical problems such as stomachaches or headaches.
15. Bed-wetting (after age four, five, or six).
16. Unusual or unreasonable fears.
17. Marked personality and/or behavior change.
18. Marked drop in grades (for child in school).

From: Kay Kuzma, *Understanding Children* (Mt. View, Ca.: Pacific Press, 1978), pp. 91–92; used by permission.

Emotional problems are often triggered by events and situations in a child's life that are particularly stressful. The following list indicates some of these potentially difficult periods.

## Potentially Difficult Times for a Child

1. Parental divorce.
2. Parental conflict in the home (family conflict as well).

3. Parental tension over work or personal problems.
4. Disruption of the home routine, such as too much company staying for too long a time.
5. New situations, like starting school or a new babysitter.
6. Dissatisfaction with one's own behavior, such as not being able to stay dry during the night.
7. Too much criticism of the child.
8. Unrealistic expectations of the child.
9. Lack of sufficient quality time together with the family.
10. Problems with making friends at school.
11. Scholastic pressures or difficulties (such as learning to read, meeting a deadline for an essay, etc.).
12. Illness, fatigue, or the death of a family member.

It is impossible to provide one exhaustive list of all the potential situations that might trigger an emotional problem in a child. Some events are obviously stressful while others are more difficult to discern. Situations that might seem ordinary to an adult, such as the disruption of a home routine, may be very disturbing to a child. You cannot assume that your child's feelings will mirror your own. But knowledge of your child's behavior and feelings will help you recognize those times when ordinary difficulties may cause potential problems.

When Kim was three, her grandparents stayed with us for a month. It did not seem like a stressful time. But Kim developed a stuttering problem. A week after the grandparents were settled in their own home, her stuttering vanished. The changes and disorganization that occurred in our home had a greater effect on Kim than we had anticipated.

Our friends had an almost continuous round of overnight company from Christmas until March. They didn't get stuttering, but their two-year-old would not let his mother out of his sight without erupting into a fit of terror.

Once in a while my work piles up and several deadlines come due at once. When pressures hit Jan at the same time, we often notice emotional and behavioral changes in our children. During one such period Kevin's behavior became atrocious. He refused to get dressed in the morning, he wouldn't brush his teeth, he wouldn't get into the bathtub, and once he was in, he wouldn't get out. He couldn't find anything to do at home, even though his room was filled with toys, so he would pounce upon me like a little lion cub. I shortened my working hours, said "no" to a couple of commitments, Jan submitted his grant proposals, and before long Kevin was back to being the spice of our lives instead of the fly that spoiled the ointment!

Some children seem to cope with these problems with relative ease. They are the "indestructible" children who are able to meet the challenge of any situation, sense that they have inner resources, and determine to make the best of a bad deal. Problems, pressures, and difficulties seem to bring out the best in these children. But the vast majority of children need support, encouragement, and perceptive parents who will be alert to the first signs of difficulty. Once you have observed potential danger signals in your child's behavior, what should you do?

First, look for the reason. Reconstruct the events of the last month or two. Did anything unusual or stressful happen during this time? Try to pinpoint the onset of this behavior to give you a clue to the changes that need to be made to prevent further problems.

Second, establish a closer relationship with your child. If your child is very young, spend more time together. Give him more attention and touch him frequently—rub his back or hold him on your lap. If the child is older, do something special together. Show that you are supportive and interested in the child in unique ways. Talk together. Be as open as possible about your feelings. When you say, "I feel sad when I see you unhappy," your child will be more open with you. Your child may not know why he is feeling as he is. Open communication which is supportive and noncritical will help bring out possible reasons for the problem.

Third, determine if the problem is a person-problem, a situation-problem, or both, and establish a plan of attack. A person-problem can only be solved by the person with the problem. A person-problem might be a child who bullies other children or a six-year-old who still sucks her thumb. When these behaviors become habitual, they are almost impossible to change unless the children themselves are willing to make a change. Person-problems can be solved by helping the child gain enough courage, determination, and self-confidence to do something about it himself. The vital ingredient necessary is self-worth. Unless a child feels that he is a capable person who can change, change is not likely to occur.

Situation-problems can only be solved by changing the situation. These can often be solved by parents, especially if a young child is involved. For example, a number of years ago Jan and I began noticing that the sunshine and laughter had disappeared from our little Kari. Her negative attitude was difficult to live with. She always seemed to be doing things that forced us to correct her. After realizing that our interactions with Kari were constantly critical, Jan decided to become her ally. I would continue to correct her when necessary, Jan would play the role of her advocate and support her, while we both would make a point of noticing and rewarding her positive behavior. Kari never knew anything about our plan, but within two days she was dancing circles around her daddy. "Oh, Daddy, I love you so much." "Daddy, can we go out and get the wood together?" "Daddy, I want you to sit beside me." Our little grouch had disappeared, and we were once more blessed with the warmth of her laughter.

In our analysis of the problem, we felt it was not Kari's problem per se, but a situational-problem brought on by our critical treatment. Our plan of attack, therefore, was to change the situation, and the problem was quickly resolved. If we had misdiagnosed the problem as a person-problem, we would have probably doubled our efforts at correcting and criticizing Kari and would have unknowingly contributed to the problem.

Not all problems are as simple to solve. Sometimes, you must change your plan of attack, or you must try a wide variety of solutions before you find one that really works. Often, situation-problems that could have been easily solved by a change in the environment become deep-seated person-problems that affect every aspect of a child's life. This is what you want to prevent.

Most problems are a combination of the two. A younger child is more likely to face situation-problems. Parents can be most effective in dealing with these problems since they are able to control many situations. The older the child is, the less control parents have over the child's environment and interactions. Therefore, unless the problem is directly related to the parents, the parents will have difficulty solving a situation-problem. In order to solve such a problem effectively, it is important to involve all of the significant people who are connected to the problem in the solution.

Not all emotional problems can be caught in their early stages. Children are sometimes masters of camouflage. Nor is it always true that parents are the only ones, or even the best ones, to deal with these problems. If you think that a certain behavior may develop into a full-scale emotional problem, seek qualified professional help immediately. Early signs of emotional illness are like early signs of a cold. If they are not treated they get worse. When the early signs of emotional illness are ignored, they seldom go away!

Start today to observe your child more carefully. List any behavior that might be an indication of your child's lack of self-worth. Is there any behavior that might indicate an emotional problem? What do you think might be the reasons for this behavior? Do you feel this behavior is a person-problem or a situation-problem, or a combination of both? What do you feel your plan of attack should be?

### Getting to Know Your Child's Individual Characteristics

You are a special and unique person. That is your right and your privilege. What about your child? Does he have the same right? All children are different; babies are different; even identical twins are different. From *birth* each child is unique. Parents do make a significant impact upon a child, but each child is born with certain characteristics that parents cannot control or change. When these behaviors persist, parents should not feel guilty, nor should they force their children to change. Parents must accept and work with what they have—a unique, special individual. Some children are simply more difficult to rear. For example, a child who is moody, and has irregular bodily functions, intense emotions, and slow adaptability is not going to be as easy to raise as a more pleasant, easygoing, adaptable child.

Parents who constantly monitor their own child's behavior and development by looking at other children are going to discover that their child is different in a number of ways. It is gratifying when your child appears to be advanced, clever, and cute. But what if your child is the opposite? Can you accept him as lovingly? Each child has his own rate of development. A boy who develops early has a better chance to do well in high school athletics. If your boy is a late developer, no amount of fatherly pushing will make this child a football star. Special abilities also vary. If a child has no musical talent and no interest or motivation in this direction, parents should not dream that their child will conquer the concert stage someday. Children should not be considered extensions of their parent's unfulfilled dreams. Your responsibility is to show your child unconditional love and acceptance—regardless of his individual characteristics or traits. Parents must realistically help a child accept his own strengts and weaknesses and grow toward his own unique potential.

However, although your child is unique, he probably shares many of the same feelings you had as a child. To better understand your child's feelings, try to remember your childhood. You may not remember the thoughtless words, but you can remember the pain. You may not even remember the type of punishment, but you remember the injustice. You may not remember the reasons why, but you remember the indifference. You may not remember the circumstances, but you remember when others were insensitive to your needs. Remember how you felt when someone called you a name, or spanked you in front of your friends? Remember that awful, sick feeling inside when your world was being torn apart and you had no one to turn to? Remember how you felt when you were small and made mistakes, had accidents, and said stupid things. How did the adults in your life treat you? Use these memories to guide your interactions with your own children. Here are some simple exercises to help you rediscover your childhood feelings:

1. Were you ever afraid when grown-ups said, "The Boogie Man will get you," "We'll just leave you here by yourself," "God won't love you if you do that," "I think Mommy and Daddy will just give you away"?

2. Did you ever feel stupid when grown-ups said, "That was a dumb thing to do," "Don't you know any better?" "It's obvious that's too hard for you," "I'm afraid you're not smart enough to catch on"?

3. Did you ever feel angry when grown-ups said, "Do this. Do this. Do this," "Stop whatever you're doing right now," "You'll get a spanking when you get home," "Eat everything on your plate or else"?

4. Now recall what your parents said or did to make

you feel: happy; loved; successful; attractive; ten feet tall; smart; timid; fearful; angry; resentful; unloved; embarrassed; dumb.

Remember, your child is likely to feel the very same way you felt as a child. Every interaction the prime-time parent has with his child should be tempered with this vital realization.

### Being the Person You Want Your Child to Be

Although you may not be able to change your child's innate characteristics, you can influence his development by being the person you want him to be. Children model adults—both the bad and the good.

Being the person you want your child to be is a difficult task. Even the realistic goals you have for your children's behavior may seem almost impossible to reproduce in your own life. You want happy children, but you often get discouraged. You want your children to be neat and orderly, but your own closet has needed a good spring cleaning for months. You want children who will control their tempers, yet you often scream at the kids for minor infractions.

There are two ways to cope with this dilemma. One is to ignore your deficiencies, kid yourself into believing that you are a perfect parent, and act as though you haven't a fault in the world—then hope that your children will grow up believing this is true.

The other is to recognize your deficiencies and be open about your struggles, mistakes, and bad habits, and let your children know how you are trying to overcome your own problems and undesirable traits.

In the first situation, you fool yourself into believing that you can hide your real self from your children while requiring perfection from them. This teaches the children a double standard: parents can do anything they wish, but children have to tow the line. Children who grow up in such an environment usually become more and more like their parents.

In the second situation, the parental example may be faulty at times, but a child benefits by observing how grown-ups deal with their bad habits and undesirable traits. Children learn methods of coping and ways of overcoming. They see their parents as real people who, like themselves, are striving to exhibit more appropriate behavior and wholesome character traits. A good parental model is not necessarily a perfect parent. Rather, it is a parent who is open enough to teach his children how people continue to develop their personalities and characters throughout their lifetime. It is important that children see that their parents never give up the hope that they, even as adults, can change.

What about all those bad habits you don't want your children to pick up? What about smoking, lying, cheating, showing anger, mouthing off, shirking duties, staying up late, or watching too much TV? You may not be perfect in all of those areas, but you *can* give your children these positive examples. Let them know that you want to and *can* change. Set short-term goals for your advancement, and meet those goals. Recognize your failures. Encourage the family to remind you when you start to fall, and accept your lapses with good humor. Don't be defensive and spout off hollow excuses. Finally, be willing to apologize when necessary. Don't blame someone else for your behavior.

Why do children always seem to model negative parental examples rather than positive ones? I'm not sure that they do. Actually, when they copy behavior that you don't like in yourself, it is easier for you to recognize it. Furthermore, negative examples are often highly charged emotionally; anger and aggression, for example. Such behavior is not only easy to notice, it is also very easy to model. The next time you raise your voice at the children and threaten them, listen. Before long you'll probably hear them threaten a younger sibling, curse the dog, or even yell at a toy.

Studies have shown that aggressive behavior will be modeled by children when they are put into identical situations. For example Albert Bandura and Richard Walters,* in their classic studies on modeling, found that if children see adults hitting a Bobo doll, they will treat the doll in the same way when they have an opportunity. And it doesn't matter if they see the adults in person or on television— or even if they see the whole situation cartooned. Aggressive behavior is still easily modeled by children when they are put into similar situations.

But if you take the time to notice, your children are also busy modeling your good behavior, as this personal example illustrates:

*"Girls, make your beds and pick up your clothing before we leave," I heard myself shout above the hustle and bustle of an early morning departure. I had thirty minutes of things to do in about half that time, so I was too rushed to supervise the clean-up operation I had requested.*

*Five minutes before departing time, I gave the last instruction, "Children, get into the car. We're leaving." They promptly obeyed as I grabbed my coat and purse from the bedroom and started down the hall. As I passed the girls' room I glanced in to make sure everything was organized for the day.*

*"Oh, no," I sighed. Their room was a mess. Nothing had been done. Impulsively, I started to yell, "Girls, get in here this minute and clean your room or else!" But I stopped myself. After all, it was partly my fault for not supervising them more closely—and they were already in the car. Rather than get everyone upset, why not do*

---

* Albert Bandura and Richard Walters, *Social Learning and Personality Development* (New York: Holt, Rinehart and Winston, 1963).

*it myself? Why not handle the situation with a little creativity?*

*I put down my purse and coat, picked up their clothing and hung it on the hooks in their closet and then quickly made their beds. The room looked presentable. Then I took a large piece of paper and wrote, "Dear Kim and Kari, I made your beds because I love you. Love, Mommy." I pinned the note to the top bunk bedspread, where it was sure to be seen and then got into the car without saying anything to the girls about what I had done.*

*When we returned home and Kim and Kari went into their room, I listened for their discovery. They seemed not to notice their room was in order, but immediately spied the note.*

*"What does it say?" asked Kari.*

*Kim went over to the note, unpinned it, and read it to Kari. "Dear Kim and Kari, I made your beds because I love you. Love, Mommy."*

*"Hey, she did!" exclaimed Kari as she glanced back at the beds.*

*"Ya," exclaimed Kim, "Mommy sure must love us."*

*About three weeks later I was again checking the girls' room. This time everything was in order. Then I noticed an interesting note pinned onto Kari's bedspread. I bent down and read it. "Dear Kari, I made your bed because I love you. I love you, Kim."*

*This time it was my turn to be surprised. It works! What if I had yelled at the girls and had dragged them back into the house by the scruff of their necks in order to make their beds? They probably would have turned around and kicked the cat—or little brother Kevin!\**

Are you the kind of person you want your child to be?

\* Kay and Jan Kuzma, *Building Character* (Mt. View, Ca.: Pacific Press, 1979); used by permission.

Remember your child's behavioral development will partially reflect the kind of person you are. You may not be able to change his rate of development, his basic inborn characteristics, or his feelings, but you can influence his behavior by being a good example.

# 6

## How to Tuck Love into Every Pocket of Time

One cold and dreary day last winter, I reached for an old comfortable coat—a favorite of mine. I thrust my arms into its ragged sleeves, buttoned the remaining buttons, turned up the collar, and shoved my hands down into its deep well-used pockets. Ah, it felt good. But what was that I felt? I pulled out the contents, and surprise! There was a twenty-dollar bill and a crumpled piece of paper. I unfolded it and discovered this note, "Dear Mommy, How are you. I am fine. I know how hard it is with us. I love you. I really do. Love, Kim (you know who)." What delightful treasures those pockets held!

Pockets are marvelous inventions. Pockets are meant to put things into. Pockets are meant to be filled. Pockets are meant to carry your treasures around in. Pockets are for surprises.

Time has pockets too; minutes or hours here and there that can be used creatively. When you think of filling your child's life with love, it seems like an enormous task. You hardly know where to begin. But you can start by viewing time in little pockets—five minutes here, ten minutes there —that can be filled to the brim right now—not tomorrow or next month or next year. Prime-time parents must cultivate the habit of immediately filling every empty pocket of time with love. Your constant thought should *not* be, "When will I ever find the time?" Rather, it should be, "I have a five-minute pocket of time; what can I do right now that will get the 'I love you' message across to my child?"

### How Do You Say, "I Love You"?

Most parents are willing to give everything they have to their children. They will sacrifice their own needs and work long hours to provide their children with the necessities, as well as the luxuries of life. However, possessions are only of secondary importance in the lives of children. Other people can give your children the things that you may not be able to give, and the child won't care who the giver was. But if a parent neglects to give a child love, no one else can substitute for that gap. The child will suffer. Parental love  is of primary importance.

Mr. Andrews was a successful businessman. He loved his wife and two children deeply, and wanted to give them the very best in life. In order to afford these luxuries he worked long hours at the office, brought his briefcase home in the evenings, worked weekends, and made frequent out-of-town business trips. The children had the best of everything throughout their lives. When his daughter, Marie, showed an interest in playing a harp, he purchased the best instrument available. But when she played at a recital, Mr. Andrews was unable to attend because of business commitments. Larry, his son, was interested in sports. His father made sure that he was on one of the best Little League teams and even purchased new uniforms for the entire team. But Larry's games took place during working hours and Mr. Andrews did not feel that he could justify time off to watch a child's baseball game.

The children went to the very best summer camps and

private boarding schools. The family was able to travel to Europe, Hawaii, and other interesting places. But Mrs. Andrews and the children often had to take sight-seeing tours by themselves because Mr. Andrews was tied up in conferences and meetings.

It was not until Marie and Larry finished high school that Mr. Andrews' dream for his children began to fall apart. Marie fell in love the first semester of her freshman year and announced that she wanted to get married at Christmas time. Larry refused to go to college. Mr. Andrews purchased a new Jaguar for Larry and extracted the promise that Larry would finish the first year of college. Larry went to college but he only passed two of the courses he took. When Mr. Andrews confronted both children with his anger and disappointment, they replied, "Why should you care what we do? You don't love us."

"What do you mean, I don't love you? I've given you everything you have," was Mr. Andrews' anguished reply.

What went wrong? Mr. Andrews meant well and thought he was working hard to show his family just how much he loved them. But his message wasn't heard because you can't say "I love you" with things. Love can be expressed by words and actions, but in order for either of these methods to be effective, a parent must spend time with a child. Love is communicated by the time spent individually with your child, and by the time spent in pleasant family activities. It is your "presence," not your "presents," that really expresses your love.

Filling each pocket of time with love is the only foolproof method of making sure that your child gets the "I love you" message that you want him to receive. This does not mean that you must spend every minute with your child. However, when your absence is necessary, you must continue to communicate love messages, and convince your child that your absence does not mean other people are more important to you than he is.

What if a child does not want to spend time with you? That's not a very pleasant thought, but it does happen. For example, a psychologist friend once told me about a family he was counseling. The teenage daughter was on drugs and had attempted suicide. Her father, a busy physician, was now willing to spend two to three hours each day with her —if she would allow him to do so. However, she really needed this kind of attention, love, and concern during her first ten years when her father was so busy establishing his practice that he felt he could spend time on nothing else.

Parents of teenagers have told me that they would gladly spend time with their children if the children wanted them to. Now they have the time. Their children are old enough to converse and enjoy some of the same activities their parents enjoy. But their teenagers often want nothing to do with them. "Dad never had time for me when I wanted him to take me hiking and fishing; why should I include him in my activities now?"

A parent's presence should not be forced on a reluctant child. The important thing is to make yourself and your love readily accessible. Be fun to be with. Create an atmosphere of warm acceptance and most children, including rebellious teens, will be drawn to you.

## Making Presence Qualitatively Meaningful

Since presence is the best way of tucking love into pockets of time, prime-time parents must understand how to make their presence qualitatively meaningful. Study the following model which outlines five meaningful levels of presence, then read the descriptions that follow.

The lowest meaningful level of presence is mental closeness: letting a person know that you are thinking about him even though you are away. You may not be physically close to your children all of the time but you can have them in

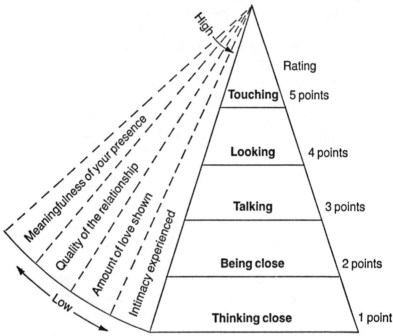

your thoughts. This is an important way of communicating the "I love you" message and it's worth 1 point.

The second level is physical proximity—when you are together, whether it is at home, in the car, shopping, or at the beach. You may not be talking, watching, or touching each other, but you are still enjoying each other's presence. This level is worth 2 points.

Talking (whether long distance or face-to-face) is the third level of meaningful presence. This level is worth 3 points.

The fourth level is looking. You can do a lot of talking and listening, even when you are close, without actually looking at each other. But when you really focus on the other person the level of meaningful presence increases. This level rates 4 points.

The fifth level is touching. When you care enough about a person to express yourself with a touch, this is the highest level of meaningful presence. This is worth 5 points.

As one moves up the levels, the value of your presence increases, and the quality of the relationship, the amount of love expressed, and the intimacy one experiences also increase.

Now comes the fun. Once you have mastered these levels and know their computational value, you can begin adding up the value of the time you spend with your children.

For example, let's take your homecoming—a five-minute pocket of time. The children are already home, and you are loaded with packages. "What a day," you announce to no one in particular. "Let me just sit down and get out of these shoes for a minute." The children are in the next room concentrating on their homework to the accompaniment of "The Brady Bunch." After a few minutes of rest you begin supper. You have earned only 2 points. You are physically close, but nothing else.

Let's try again. You come home loaded with books. (That's 2 points for being close.) "Hi, everybody, I'm home," you yell. "How did school go?" (That's 3 more points for talking.) You hand the children the books. "I knew you wanted these books from the library, so I thought I would surprise you and bring them home tonight. (That shows you were thinking of the children even though you were away. Give yourself 1 more point.) You watch the surprise on these faces (4 points) and reach over and kiss them each on the forehead (5 more points). Now add that up and you have a 15-point homecoming. That's a meaningful pocket of time!

Obviously, every moment of time your family spends together isn't going to be that rich, nor does every homecoming have to be worth 15 points. You may need that time completely to yourself so you can give a fifteen-point pocket of good quality time to your children later on in the evening. The important thing to remember is that sometime during the day, each one of your children needs those 15 points from you—a pocket of time that gives them the "I love you" message loudly and clearly. How you do it or when you do it is less important than the fact that they can depend on you to do it!

Now let's go through the day and see how you can get the most out of your time with your children.

1. Morning: Instead of just yelling, "Time to get up," walk to the children's bedroom, whisper in their ear that it's time to get up, and then rub their foreheads as they open their sleepy eyes.

2. Good-bye time: Instead of running out the door, say "Good-bye." Wink at the children as you turn to leave and then blow them a kiss from the car.

3. Midday: Instead of working straight through the day, take a break and think of a way you can communicate your love to your child. Call him at school, bring him something from the office, remember to tell him the joke you just heard.

4. Evening: Instead of letting everyone go about their different tasks, do a few things together. Talk, smile, laugh, and give your child a pat on the back when a task is finished.

If you are interested in getting as much as possible from your time together, remember to add one or two additional levels to the pockets of time you spend together and you'll find life with your children more meaningful.

## The Importance of an Unconditional Loving Relationship

The important key to helping our children develop desirable characteristics is love—unconditional love. No matter what mistakes a parent may make, if a child knows that he is loved, he can overlook many of these mistakes. And, with the sense of worth that love brings, he can grow into an emotionally healthy adult.

When parents begin tucking love into every pocket of a child's life, they must not base this shower of affection and acceptance on the child's behavior. The kind of love that must be tucked into pockets of time is the kind of love that is unconditionally given, no matter what the child does.

A study conducted at a church-related university* emphasizes the importance of making sure that children know they are loved unconditionally. In this study it was found that a large number of students were hostile toward authority figures such as the university and church administration. When the data were examined to uncover possible reasons for this attitude, it was found that those students who felt hostile toward the university and the church also believed that their parents loved them only under certain conditions.

If children feel that their parents won't love them when they misbehave, they will often go to great lengths to preserve the love relationship. If these children had negative feelings toward their parents, they had to repress these feelings and later transferred this hostility to other authority figures who were not as important to them. The normal little hostilities and grievances that children sometimes feel toward their parents were never brought into the open and were never solved at home. This affected the child's later

---

* Fred Osborne, "The Relationship Between the Disposition of Hostility and Non-self-confirming Experiences" (Ph.D. diss., The Claremont Colleges, School of Theology, 1972).

relationships with others. This study suggests that parental unconditional love and acceptance can have a tremendous influence on a child's life for years to come. The important thing is not just how a parent loves a child, but *how a child perceives this love.*

Therefore, let your love be completely independent of your child's behavior. Tuck love into every pocket of your child's life, not because you always feel like it, but because love is a principle of interaction that you choose to live by. You can decide today to act in a loving way. You can decide today not to let those little pockets of time slip by without any message at all, or worse yet, slip by filled with messages of disinterest and hostility. You can choose today to fill every pocket of your child's life with an "I love you" message. The rest of this chapter is devoted to ways that you can make this a reality in your busy life.

### Enjoy Your Child

It's always sad to hear parents say, "I can hardly wait for my child to get through the diaper stage," or "Thank goodness, he'll be in school next year," or "If I had it to do over, I would only have one child—or none at all."

Of course, most parents wouldn't say these things to their children, but if they don't really enjoy their children, this attitude will be reflected in subtle, indirect ways. And their children will get the message!

If you are really interested in filling every pocket of time with as much love as you can pack into it, you must enjoy being with your children. You have to enjoy them *just the way they are, at whatever stage they may be.* Here are some suggestions to help you create that sense of enjoyment.

*Be prepared.* Whenever you prepare for an event or an occasion, it becomes more meaningful because you added a precious commodity—your time. Husbands, how do you feel when your wife and children have truly prepared for your homecoming in the evening; when dinner is ready and the mail is lying in a place where you can find it? Wives, doesn't it feel good when your family anticipates your arrival and greets you with a clean kitchen and folded laundry? When someone has made an extra effort on your behalf, you know that person has been thinking about you. You feel loved. Children feel the same way. If you prepare for their birth and their various developmental stages, the time you spend with them will more likely be quality time. Becoming a child development expert (see Chapter 5) will help you enjoy your children to the fullest.

*Keep a diary, scrapbook, or picture album.* Collecting the children's cute sayings, anecdotes, photographs, drawings, and other interesting miscellany helps build memories for future enjoyment. Collecting and recording can add to your enjoyment right now, if you keep the task easy. Don't let things pile up. Be organized. Some useful ideas follow.

1. A memory box. Let every child have a memory box for his own things. Once a year—a birthday is a good time—sort through the box and add the little notes, letters, drawings, and cute anecdotes to the child's scrapbook.

2. A book of clever sayings and cute things the child does. You've got to keep such a book close at hand in order to write down the comments just as they were said. Be sure you put the child's name and date beside each entry.

3. A book of childhood prayers.

4. A scrapbook of memories. Keep the child's picture, notes, letters, and special cards. This type of book shows a child's development more graphically than dozens of journals and diaries, and it can offer a real picture of the child's personality and interests. Birthdays are even more enjoyable when the whole family gathers around to look at the birthday child's scrapbook of memories.

*Play games with your child.* Playing games with children means getting involved with them at their level; being responsive to their behavior. Start at birth. Play the "I'll-touch-your-nose, and tickle-your-tummy, and pedal-your-feet and stretch-your-arms-up-so-high" games. Watch for your baby's response to your touch. Infant games should mirror a child's growing skills. For example, the reach-for-the-toy game is a good one for a child learning to reach. When tiny infants begin imitating, play the stick-out-the-tongue games. Toddlers love the ride-'em-cowboy game, chase-me-but-don't-catch-me game, peek-a-boo and make-funny-faces game. Preschoolers enjoy finger plays, pretend games like let's-play-house or fireman, or going-to-the-restaurant. School-age children enjoy organized games like basketball, baseball, and Ping-Pong—if you are skillful enough to allow them to win without letting them know what you are doing. Although teenagers do enjoy simple table games, they also enjoy such high powered games as sit-down-Mom-and-Dad-and-help-me-build-this-computer!

When playing games with your children be responsive to their abilities and interests. If they can only grasp and pull, invent games that use these skills. For example, you can play the don't-pull-my-hair game as you lean over and allow the child to grab your hair. You pull back, shake your head in surprise and then lean over again, and again, and again. If they can only kick with their feet, play the don't-kick-me-in-the-tummy game as you are changing diapers. When they kick against you, jump back in surprise and then get close again. While these games are appropriate for the three-month-old they may no longer be appropriate for the twelve-month-old. The key to being a successful game player is to be responsive to your child's abilities and creative enough to make a game out of whatever you are doing together.

*Dovetail your interests.* There are two ways you can dovetail your interests with the child's interests: 1) become interested in your child's particular interests, and 2) make your own interests so exciting and geared to your child's level that he will naturally develop an interest in them.

The younger your child is, the more difficult it may be to interest him in your concerns, especially if your number-one interest is nuclear physics, or the socioeconomic interrelations of developing nations. Young children are interested in collecting earthworms and catching ladybugs, digging in the dirt pile or climbing the neighbor's tree. Forget yourself and enjoy your child's interests. Pull weeds while you're collecting earthworms, or finish your cross-word puzzle under the tree he is climbing. The important thing is that you are enjoying the activity that your child is interested in.

When you go on family excursions and vacations, think about your child's interests and try to gear your interests accordingly. For example, most toddlers couldn't care less about looking at a collection of old Indian relics when the "look-alive" mammals are in the next room of the museum. In fact, a toddler may be more interested in the drinking fountain than anything else! Don't get frustrated; gear your interests to his interests and enjoy things on his level. It won't be too long before your teenager will be leading you by the hand through the atomic energy museum, explaining the different exhibits to you.

*Do what you enjoy (or what you have to do) and take the children along.* Why not take the children along on a business trip if you think you might have a few pockets of time when you could enjoy each other? If your children are young, consider bringing a babysitter or hiring one at your destination. A colleague who works long hours and takes frequent business trips to Washington, D.C. takes each of his teenagers with him once a year. While Dad attends meetings, the teenager fills his mind with thousands of interesting facts and sights at the Smithsonian Institution. Each evening they do something special together. This prime time with Dad has been a memorable experience for each.

We have friends who love antiques. Although antique stores and little children are not generally compatible, this couple came up with a creative solution for the entire family. They started antique collections for each child. Now, when Mom and Dad go to an antique store or a garage sale, the children join them, looking for items to add to their collections. One boy collects antique marbles, another collects miniature German steins painted with mythology characters, and their daughter collects Victorian saltshakers. To make the activity more meaningful, each child has a book about his particular collection that gives historical facts and explains how to date various objects. This family activity has become so meaningful to the children that they have given presentations about their collections at school and are even thinking about writing an article or two! And all this came about because their parents chose to take the children along rather than leave them at home.

Antiques can be expensive but there are other possibilities for collections. What about rocks, grasses, wildflowers, or shells?

Do you go birding? Why not take your child along and teach him how to spot certain species? If photography is your thing, introduce your child to the darkroom. Choose an activity that you really enjoy and include your child, but remember his developmental capabilities. He may not be able to sit through a long meeting, hike ten miles a day, or fish on a quiet lake without rocking the boat, but with a little modification you may be able to take your child along and create a memorable occasion for both of you.

*Take time to enjoy each child individually.* Years ago I clipped a little story about a teacher who asked her group of children what happiness was. One of the children replied, "Happiness is when I go walk on the dunes with Dad.

Nobody else, just him and me." I've often heard my brother say that his most memorable childhood experience was when Dad took him fishing *all by himself.*

Ideally, each parent should try to spend some daily individual time with each child. Although family occasions foster close ties within the group, they do not substitute for individual time spent with a child. Finding this time is more difficult when families are large. With each new birth parents have less time to give the other children alone. This is especially true when children are born close together. Studies indicate that twins or siblings born closer than fifteen months apart have I.Q. scores that are slightly lower than other siblings. Many factors contribute to this finding, but parental time seems to be a major one. Studies have also indicated that children's I.Q. scores may drop as a family becomes larger (six children, or more). For example, as a child grows older his I.Q. score may actually drop as more children are born into the family. Intelligence is related to the amount of adult attention and verbal stimulation that parents give to their children.

One very busy traveling evangelist, who was also the father of six, solved this problem by making bedtime his time with the children. Every night when he was home, he scheduled their bedtime at half hour intervals. This gave him time to talk over the events of the day, read to the child, and listen to each child's prayers individually.

Never feel guilty about the time you are spending with your child. Remember that time spent with the child is never wasted time, unless it is NTT #1 (Negative Time Together) or NTT #2 (Nothing Time Together). Even if you are not accomplishing a specific end, the time you enjoy your child is the best investment you can make in your child's future happiness as well as your own. The quality of time you spend with each child will determine how effectively you get the "I love you" message across.

**Do the Unexpected**

I once read an unforgettable account about a father and his seven-year-old son. On an August night, the father bundled up the sleeping child and carried him out into the darkness. As the boy's sleep-filled eyes began to focus on his surroundings, the father shouted, "Look!" And there in the sky the little boy saw a star leap from its place and fall toward the ground. Then incredibly, another star fell, and another and another. That was all. But the boy never forgot that night when his father did the unexpected, and he determined that he would do the same some August evening when his boy was seven.

How often do we miss the beauty and richness of life because we are locked into routines and schedules, and we are afraid to take advantage of the unknown, the unplanned, and the unexpected? Don't miss an opportunity to fill a child's pocket with love when he is least expecting it. Keep a "Why-not" list. This is a list of way-out, interesting, crazy things to do with or for your children. When the opportunity is right and the children are least expecting it, surprise them with the announcement, "Why not . . . ?"

At the top of a Why-not list I suggest a love note. Why not write a love note when it is least expected? For years mothers have been tucking little notes into children's lunch pails, but have you thought about taping a note to his toothbrush, or on the ceiling of his bedroom so he will see it as soon as he wakes up, or putting it under his napkin at the dinner table? Imagine how astonished a child would be to find a love note in the classified section of the local paper, or to have a telegram delivered to him at school? Even a letter sent through the mail to your own home address (especially if you haven't gone anyplace) would probably be a loving surprise.

I'll never forget the love note that greeted me the first

Christmas vacation I arrived home from college in California. We lived in Boulder, Colorado, on one of the most traveled streets on the hill. Every Christmas we decorated the house with lights and a huge greeting card that Daddy painted. We had done it for so long that it had become a Humpal family tradition. So, as I drove up to the house, I expected the colored lights, but the love note on the greeting card filled my eyes with tears. It simply announced to the whole town, in letters a foot tall, "WELCOME HOME, KAY."

Another working mother told me, "I remember once when I went to parents' night at school, a working friend older than I suggested that I surprise my daughter the next morning by leaving a note in her desk praising what I saw of her work on the wall. I flipped! It was an enchanting idea. It worked. I may not have been a room mother, but it showed I cared."

This is what I call intensive reinforcement. Working parents may not always be available to give the "I love you" message, but with a little creativity, they can do it more inventively, thoughtfully, and meaningfully.

The secret of writing a meaningful love note is to be specific. A couple of years ago, Jan and I started the practice of writing our children love notes and serving them for breakfast. Soon our children were writing love notes too. Kim left this specific message on Jan's pillow early one morning after Jan and I had returned from a weekend trip. "Dear Dad, Thank you for carrying me to bed. So I don't have to walk to bed." I once received this charming note: "Dear Mom, Thank you for picking me up at 3:00. I like to be picked up at 2:20 or 3:00. But not later! I hope you got the house cleaned. It's about time I say good-bye. Love, Kim." (I've always been grateful there was not a period after "It's about time!")

So, if you are wondering how to tuck love into every

pocket of time, why not write a love note and tell your child something special that you appreciate about him.

The second item on a Why-not list might be a surprise visit to your child when he least expects it. Why not stop by his classroom for an informal visit? Why not drop by during gymnastic practice, or stay for a piano lesson? Of course, you don't want to embarrass your child, but most children whose pockets are consistently filled with love are mighty proud to introduce their parents to their friends.

Here are some other "Why-not" ideas. Why not take the child to some unexpected place or do something out of the ordinary? Why not milk a cow? Why not go up in a hot-air balloon or take a helicopter ride? Why not glean the sweet potato field? Why not visit the local radio station? Why not paddle down the river or float on inner tubes (if you've got a river close by)? Why not hunt for valuables at the city dump, junk yard—or even go after high-class junk and visit the flea market? Why not ride a bucking bronco, or try to rope a calf? Why not sit on the roof and watch the full moon come up? Why not search for four-leaf clovers? Why not catch butterflies, or fly a kite, or have a three-legged race? Why not go frog hunting and enter a frog leaping contest? Why not camp out in your backyard with sleeping bags and a campfire? Why not take your child out of school and play golf for the afternoon, or walk on the beach, or go fishing? Why not make reservations for two at the fanciest restaurant in town and ask your daughter (or son) for a date? Why not just stop in the middle of your ironing or dusting to read your child a story?

You just have to have a creative mind and be willing to say, "Why not?" when your children make simple requests. "Mommy, can we stop by to see the Cassidys?" "Daddy, can we feed the ducks at the park?" "Can we climb that tree?" "Can we watch the telephone repair man?" Why not tuck a little more love into those pockets of time and do the unexpected?

**Open Doors for Your Child**

One of a parent's greatest privileges is to open new and wonderful doors of possibility to a child. One day, after winning a tennis tournament, the young teenage winner was asked when she first became interested in tennis. She thought for a moment and replied, "It was the day my father gave it to me." The reporters, not understanding her reply, tried to clarify. "You mean, when your father bought you a racket and ball?"

"No," she replied, "it was the day Dad took off from work and played with me. That was the day he gave me tennis."

Opening doors for your child does not necessarily mean that he will become a tennis pro, a Globe Trotter, a Nobel prize winner, or a concert violinist. You are just showing him what is available, giving him more options in life, and increasing his understanding and appreciation of events and people.

When parents open doors for their children, they do not always have to go through those doors together. The child will sense your love for him when you share ideas and suggest activities that he can do on his own or with others.

You may have read a best-seller. Share it. Open the door of quality writing to your child. You don't have to read the book together. You may have just heard a new song on the radio. Pick up the music on the way home and leave it on the piano. Your child might find a new inspiration. Open the door to good cooking by sharing kitchen responsibilities with your child. Let her read your cookbook or take her out to eat at a gourmet restaurant and then encourage her to experiment on her own. Open the door to the artistic world by frequenting art museums and galleries. Find a local artist and let your child watch him or study at his side. If your child wants to whittle, see if you can find a wood carver who will give him a few pointers. If he wants to tie-dye, visit the little shops until you find someone who is willing to teach him the trade.

Your child may not want to take advantage of every opportunity or walk through every door. That's fine. Just keep opening them, and freely allow him to enter those he wishes. Plan to open a door for your child today.

## Be an Effective Communicator

The interest and concern you express when your child talks to you is an excellent way to tuck love (or disinterest) into little pockets of time. Studies on teenage runaways suggest that the most important way a parent can help a troubled adolescent is to listen. Running away is a desperate attempt to communicate what parents were not willing to listen to before. Being a good listener is a simple way to show you understand and care about another individual. Here are some guidelines to follow:

1. Show interest in your child's conversation. Look up. Make appropriate comments. Stop what you are doing. Interpret body language as well as verbal communication.

2. Don't correct his speech while he is talking to you.

3. Focus on the hidden message—if you think there might be one.

4. Don't contradict his story or the points he is making until he has finished and wants your opinions. Don't cut him off prematurely by arguing with his point of view.

5. Listen with a soft touch. Don't squelch a child when he voices offbeat values or comes to an impossible conclusion. Don't laugh, make fun of, belittle, tear down, or in any other way make it more difficult for a child to open up his heart and ideas to you in the future.

6. Be an active listener. Active listening means active involvement with the person who is communicating. To show that you are actively listening, make little expressions of understanding, such as, "Yes, ah ha, I see," etc. Make

clarifying comments when necessary. "You mean that . . . It seems as if you . . . Do you mean . . . I hear you saying . . . You must have felt. . . ." Share yourself with the person as well as allowing the other person to share with you. If you try to listen to something else (like the TV) while you are trying to listen to your children, by the time they reach their teens (and often before), they will cease to even try to compete. It takes time to listen actively. But this is the only kind of listening that will give the "I love you" message to your child.

7. Encourage your child to talk, to express himself, and to share his values and goals. One way to encourage the child to share his world with you is to have a talk-about-it bowl or basket that sits on the kitchen table. During the day, the children can put objects, notes, newspaper clippings, or articles into the bowl that they would like to talk about during dinner. Even the most reluctant child will probably speak up at a show-and-tell dinner.

Write a variety of questions on paper placemats. Cover them with clear contact paper so they will last. Choose questions that will stimulate a good conversation. When the dinner conversation seems to drag, read off a question, like, "What would you do if you just inherited a million dollars?" Or, "If you knew you were going to die in one month, how would you spend your time?"

Play the Ungame or Social Security or some of the other commercial games that encourage a person to give his ideas on certain subjects. Get a good book on values clarification* and try some of the suggested strategies. This is a surefire way to encourage conversation. As the children get older, read articles or books together and discuss your feelings about them and the meaning they have to each of you.

Have a weekly family council. Ask each family member to bring up problems or issues and discuss possible solu-

* Sidney B. Simon and Sally Wendkos Olds, *Helping Your Child Learn Right from Wrong* (N.Y.: Simon and Schuster, 1976).

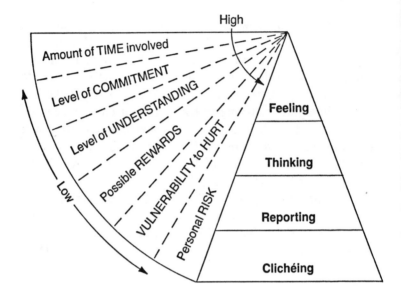

tions or changes that might be made. Establish ground rules that are conducive to open discussion. Use this opportunity to teach the children how to bring up points of contention in diplomatic ways.

When you encourage your children to communicate, you will be better able to assess whether or not you have been filling their pockets of time with love. Then you can make the necessary changes so every minute together can be quality time.

8. Children should be encouraged to communicate on the feeling level. There are four levels of communication: the lowest level is clichéing, the second is reporting, the third is thinking, and the fourth is feeling. See the diagram above.

When you use the higher levels of communication, you will have to spend more time and make more of a commitment to the other individual. But your conversations will be more meaningful and more rewarding. You will also become more vulnerable to hurt. Now let's look at the various levels.

The clichéing level of communication consists of such phrases as, "Hi, how are you? Fine. See you later." If families aren't careful, most of their communication can degenerate into this kind of uninvolved small talk. Clichéing is sometimes necessary, but it does not convey the "I love you" message. It takes very little time and requires no commitment to another individual. It results in very little understanding, and it is not rewarding. There is no risk involved because you're not expressing feelings or thoughts.

The second level consists of reporting facts, telling others what you've heard, seen, or read. No one can argue with a report, unless you have reported erroneously. There is very little risk, but it takes a little more time.

The thinking level involves communication of your thoughts. There is risk involved because someone can disagree with you. But this type of communication is also more rewarding. You can learn a lot more about an individual when they communicate with you on the thinking level.

The feeling level is the most difficult level of communication. It reaches far beyond thoughts and ideas and strikes at the heart of the matter—your internal reactions to various things—your gut feelings. Most people find it much easier to cliché, report, or merely think about things than to analyze their feelings and communicate those feelings to others. When you choose to do this, the rewards are great. But the risk of misunderstanding also increases and you become more vulnerable to hurt. Communicating on this level as you rush out the door is impossible. It takes time.

Communicating on the feeling level is only appropriate when you are committed to someone else. Baring one's soul to perfect strangers is not appropriate. Your home is the place to express yourself on the feeling level.

When you choose to communicate your feelings, other family members can fill *your* pockets with love. A woman I know had returned to college to finish a nursing degree. One morning she got up early, folded the wash neatly, and put it in the ironing basket. When she was ready to take the clothes to her ironing lady, she noticed that the basket was a jumble. She knew what had happened. Her seventeen-year-old son had been looking for his blue shirt. She was angry that her son would act so irresponsibly when she herself was so busy. She picked up the basket in a flurry and started toward the car. Then she realized that if she didn't say something to her son, she would remain angry all day and would not be able to concentrate on her studies. So back up the stairs she went, calling out to her son, "Bill, I am angry at the way you left the ironing basket."

"Oh, sorry Mom," he replied as he breezed into the room. "Let me help fold those things." He took the basket from her and began folding the garments. When they were finished, he bent over and gave her a kiss on the forehead and said, "Don't study too hard . . . and by the way, thanks for washing my shirt." Now she could enjoy her day because she had chosen to communicate her feelings and had allowed her son to tuck a little love into her day.

If, through your example and your encouragement, you can help your children to communicate their feelings as Bill was able to do, you just might find it easier to show them how much you love them.

9. You must allow children to communicate both positive and negative feelings. If children do not feel free to communicate their negative feelings, the feelings build up and are eventually acted out. If a child feels angry and can't express his anger in words, he will usually hit, kick things, blame others, or stomp around the room.

If children are going to learn to communicate their feelings, then you must encourage them to do so. When they say, "I hate you," you must be willing to acknowledge their feelings by saying something like, "You *are* angry," rather than punishing them for their verbal outburst. You must accept their feelings, including their negative ones, and help change the situation so positive feelings can dominate.

Does your child know that it is safe to say: "Mommy, I feel sad. Hold me a little bit." "Mom, I feel discouraged. Do you have a minute to talk?" "Dad, I got angry when you spoke to me like that. Can we discuss it?" "I'm afraid you don't really love me when you do things for others and don't have time for me."

When your children can be this truthful, when they can learn to recognize their negative feelings early and express them, problems can be handled in their early stages. Then parents can get on with the business of tucking love into the little pockets of time.

What kind of a communicator are you? For one hour while your whole family is together, tape-record your conversation. Then analyze your interactions by asking yourself these questions.

1. Did I show interest in what my child was saying?
2. Did I listen without correcting his speech?
3. Did I focus on the hidden message? What did I learn?
4. Did I listen without contradicting his story or interrupting him?
5. Did I listen respectfully (with a soft touch)?
6. Was I an active listener?
7. Did I encourage my child to talk? How?
8. Did I encourage my child to communicate his feelings?
9. Did I accept both positive *and* negative feelings?

If you answered "yes" to all of these questions, you were an effective communicator. Keep up the good work! If you slipped up in a few areas, pick another hour or mealtime and try again. Being an effective communicator does not come easily to busy parents.

### Preparation for Separation

Very young children often think that Mom and Dad don't love them very much if they have to go away. They may feel rejected and hurt and often find it difficult to understand the real reasons for a separation. School-age children may feel that other people or a job is more important to Mom and Dad if they are frequently absent and don't take the children with them when it is feasible to do so. Teenagers may even resent a parent's absence, especially when their friends' families spend a lot of time together.

Parents should be willing to take the necessary time to prepare a child for their absence. This means planning ways to fill a child's pockets of time with love during their absence, and making sure a child understands the reasons for the separation. Therefore, before leaving, the prime-time parent should consider the following questions:

1. Is it really necessary to go away?

2. Will my child receive good quality care from someone he enjoys?

3. Would my child be better off staying at home with someone else?

4. What modifications might be necessary in order to take my child along?

5. If I must go away, how can I prepare my child for the moment of departure?

6. How can my child's pockets be filled with love while I'm away?

When these questions are carefully considered, the final decision will be easier because you will be sure that it is the best possible decision that can be made under the circumstances. Children are able to adjust to separation better if they know their parents aren't torn and guilty and grieving for them while they are away. They want to be missed, but they don't want to be responsible for their parents' misery. When a separation must occur, it should be handled in a matter-of-fact way, and that is only possible when parents have made a carefully considered decision.

It is often easier for children to accept their parents' vacations or business trips if they know that they will be invited along some other time. Children suffer most when they don't know when or why their parents are leaving, and when they feel that they will never be able to join their parents. One couple decided, even before they had children, that they would never let their children interfere with anything they wanted to do. The two children are now four and six years of age, and it is true, the children have never interfered with their parents' pleasurable pursuits. But the children are miserable. They never know when Mom and Dad are going to leave them. It is not uncommon for them to be left at a babysitter's house, thinking they will be picked up in a few hours, only to discover later that their parents have flown off to some exotic vacation resort and won't return for weeks. Such separations can destroy love relationships and make a child feel rejected by his parents.

One summer our three little ones scrambled into Aunt Joanie's and Uncle Dick's van for a ride to Colorado to spend three weeks with Grandma and Grandpa. We could have simply hugged and kissed them, admonished them to be good, and waved "good-bye." But we felt that it was important to do more. First, we carefully considered the questions listed previously. We talked about the possibility of the trip. We let the children know that it really wasn't necessary for them to go. We did explain that I had to teach a summer school course and do some writing during this time, so I would have to leave them with a babysitter for a good part of the time if they stayed home. After considering all of the possibilities, they decided that they would prefer spending this time with Grandma and Grandpa and their cousins.

Once the decision was made, then we started talking and planning for the trip. We talked about certain hypothetical situations that might come up, such as getting lonesome, and how they should handle it. Maybe they could tell Grandma that they needed a little extra hugging. Maybe they could call us. Maybe they could work extra hard to make someone else happy, and in doing so would forget their own loneliness.

Then we sent certain things along with them so they would be better able to share their time away from us once we were together again. I loaned Kim my camera so she could record the memories she wanted to share. I gave them a scrapbook so they could collect leaves, flowers, ticket stubs, programs, or anything else they wanted to save to remind them of the trip. Jan gave them each five dollars that they could spend on special things they wanted to buy. Then I bought them little presents, which they were to open on the trip. With this preparation we sent them off with hugs and kisses, reminding them that we would be thinking about them at bedtime every night.

As soon as they were gone, I went to my typewriter and wrote to them so they would have a letter the day they arrived. And every few days while they were gone either Jan or I would write to them. We always addressed the letter to Kim, Kari, and Kevin Kuzma, and not to Grandma and Grandpa, so the children would feel it was really meant for them. We would tell them the little things that were happening around the home, such as getting medicine for Missy's (the dog's) eczema—things that no one else would be interested in! We always told them something that we appreciated about them, encouraged them to do their best, and would try to enclose something special for them. When I wrote, I would include a little limerick and draw a silly picture to accompany it. It always had something to do with the children and the situation they were in. For example, I drew a picture of a van full of quarreling children traveling to Colorado and penned this verse:

There once was an Auntie named Joan,
Who told all the kids to lie prone.
  But five was a lot.
  They talked and they fought.
And all she could do was to groan.

When young children are separated from their parents, the most difficult part of the day is often bedtime. One parent solved this problem by reading stories to her child over a cassette tape recorder. Her daughter was reminded of Mom's love at the end of every day when she heard her mother's words, "I love you and miss you. So snuggle up in your warm, cozy bed. I'm going to blow you a kiss. Did you catch it? Now there's a special story for my special little girl."

Separation time can be a good time to send a child the "I love you" message. But separation *without preparation* can be interpreted as indifference and rejection.

### Take Advantage of the Prime-Prime-Times

Every minute with your child should be considered prime time. But there are extra-special times when your presence or absence will have a tremendous impact on the child. I consider 1) arrival and departure times, 2) performance time, and 3) bedtime as prime-prime-times.

1. *Arrival and departure times*. Arrivals and departures should be family celebration times. No matter how insignificant these times may seem, make some preparations and take some time off from your busy schedule to affirm your love for the arriving or departing member of the family.

To prepare for arrival times, I try to finish whatever my children wanted me to do while they were gone. I also try to plan an occasional after-school excursion. Children eagerly await school dismissal time when they know that we might be stopping by the library or department store for a special purchase.

If it is impossible for you to be home when your child arrives, you can still make homecoming special. A tape-recorded message or a love note is a good welcome for a child. One mother I know even takes a few minutes one morning a week to lay out a treasure hunt for her child with a treat hidden at the end. The child never knows which day to expect this surprise, which adds to its suspense and effectiveness. You might also leave special exciting announcements for the child, such as "Sakala is coming over tonight! Be sure to get your practicing done." Then make sure that your own arrival is a happy one and that you have time for hugs and kisses and a word of appreciation for each child.

Departure times can be more meaningful if they are not rushed. In most homes, including ours, the average after-breakfast departure time is a disaster. "Grab your lunch pail." "Kevin, get your shoes." "You forgot to wash your face." "Remember to walk to Daddy's office after school." "No, I don't know where your note that I was supposed to sign is." Finally, when they are gone you collapse in the midst of dirty dishes, thankful that you have once again lived through the departure hurricane that has just swept through your house.

Again, preparation is the key. Our most pleasant mornings begin the night before: the children have prepared their box lunches, set the table, organized their clothes, and put everything they have to take to school by the back door. It also helps when they get up early enough to get themselves ready and still have time to help Jan and me with breakfast. Then we have time to enjoy each other. We even have time to read the children a character-building story at the breakfast table and thank the Lord in a proper manner for a good night's rest and the blessings of a new day.

2. *Performance time.* A child's performance time is a prime time for parents to show love and support. Children enjoy attention—but applause from strangers is not nearly as meaningful as the approval of Mom and Dad. It doesn't matter how small a part your child has in a performance, your presence is meaningful. At such times, parents should support their children because they are trying, and pat them on the back even if they strike out or fumble the ball. Children's baseball, football, and soccer games have been distorted by parents who urge their little ones on to super-kid performances while yelling curses at the opponents. This is not the kind of support your children need.

3. *Bedtime.* Bedtime is by far the nicest, coziest, and most enjoyable part of the day. If I could choose only fifteen minutes a day to spend with my children, it would be the fifteen minutes before bedtime.

Bedtime can be a hassle if it's not well planned—if the kids are dead tired, haven't done their homework, and are bickering about who should pick up the dirty clothes left in the bathroom. To set the stage properly, there has to be adequate preparation and planning. Bedtime is most enjoyable when the children are not exhausted or rushed.

This is the time when I listen to my children's prayers, tuck them in with a hug and a kiss, and then linger around after the lights are off to chat, rub backs, and snuggle—if they feel like a snuggle. Bedtime is a prime time to fill a pocket of time with a loving touch.

Never let your children go to sleep with criticism, angry words, or threats (such as, "If you get out of bed or call me one more time . . .") ringing in their ears. Make bedtime a time for loving rituals. I don't think my dad ever said "Good night" to us without adding, "Sleep tight and don't let the bed bugs bite." And if he wanted us to go to sleep quickly, he would always add, "Remember, the first one to sleep say, 'Potarimus.' " Of course, the magic word was never said, but it was a special way Daddy had of building sweet dreams and pleasant childhood memories.

A parent can never give too much love to a child. Love does not spoil a child; too little discipline spoils a child. An abundance of love does not mean indulging, overprotecting, allowing wrongdoing, fostering dependence, smothering a child's individuality, or showering gifts, bribes, and rewards on a child. Parents who truly love their children will provide a warm, pleasing, and happy environment for their children. Love—unconditional love—is the substance that builds a child's feelings of self-worth. Why not start today to fill every pocket of your child's time with a heaping amount of love?

# 7

## Prime-Time Discipline:
## The Preventive Approach

The goal of effective prime-time discipline is self-discipline. That's the preventive approach. Working parents can't oversee and police all their children's activities. Therefore, they must teach their children how to make good decisions about their own behavior. When children are self-controlled rather than parent-controlled, it frees time for more creative, enjoyable, and happy family interactions—more quality time together.

Prime-time discipline is based on principles and goals rather than on past experience or present feelings. Parents must resist the strong tendency to say *thoughtlessly*, "My parents' methods worked for me so why shouldn't they work for my children?" Or, "I resented the way my parents handled me; I'll never do that to my child." It is equally harmful to allow feelings to control your actions, and assume a laissez-faire attitude or become harsh and punitive in an attempt to win power struggles.

Unreasonable punishment can result in good behavior, but it can destroy a child's self-worth. A child can have many excellent qualities, but if he lacks a wholesome sense of self-worth, he will be handicapped throughout life. When

## A Model for Prime-Time Discipline

The guiding principle: "Will my actions enhance my child's sense of self-worth?"

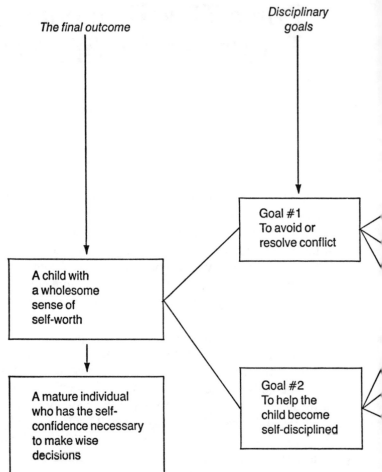

*The final outcome*

*Disciplinary goals*

Goal #1
To avoid or
resolve conflict

A child with
a wholesome
sense of
self-worth

A mature individual
who has the self-
confidence necessary
to make wise
decisions

Goal #2
To help the
child become
self-disciplined

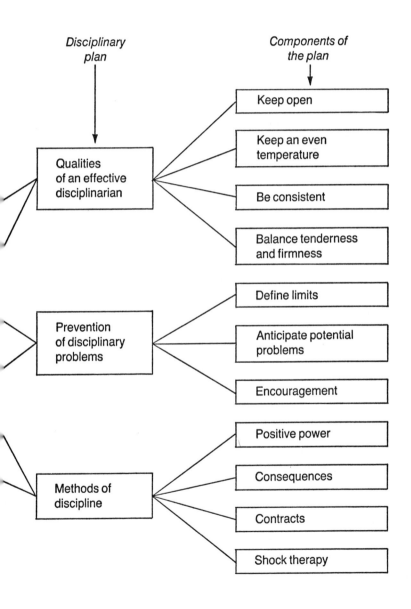

a child feels good about himself, he can choose to become the kind of person he would like to be. He can choose to avoid or resolve conflict. He can choose to be self-disciplined.

Parents are primarily responsible for helping a child to feel worthwhile. Ask yourself, "Will my actions enhance my child's self-worth?" This question should be the guiding principle that monitors all your interactions with your child —especially the disciplinary ones.

To avoid discipline that is irrational and haphazard, parents need a disciplinary model that is based on principles and goals. The following model will foster that important sense of self-worth, and will help you raise a child who has the self-confidence necessary to make wise decisions.

### The First Goal for Discipline: To Avoid or Resolve Conflict

Prime-time parents want to establish joyful, loving, high-quality relationships with all their children. Obviously, fighting, arguing, demeaning, yelling, ridiculing, swearing, hitting, and threatening are not conducive to such a goal. Such behavior only leads to conflict. After the battle you can kiss and make up, but the bumps and bruises—the physical as well as the psychological ones—are not easily forgotten. It is much better to prevent conflict if it is possible to do so.

Of course, family members should disagree, should stand up for their rights, and should voice their points of view. Family growth is possible only if individuality in thought, as well as behavior, is encouraged. But it is important to settle differences before battle lines are drawn, and before weapons destructive to a child's self-esteem are aimed and fired. Prime-time parents should not waste potential high-quality family time in conflict.

Children's inappropriate behavior ranges from childish

irresponsibility (such as forgetting to feed the dog and accidentally spilling the milk) to willful defiance of parental authority. In between these two extremes there is a wide range of "normal" misbehavior by children who persistently challenge the limitations imposed by adults. The task of prime-time discipline is to teach a child responsibility and to successfully meet each childhood challenge in a way that will prevent the development of a willfully defiant attitude. A child's willful defiance results in conflict that can destroy parent-child relationships. The following model shows the inappropriate behavior continuum.

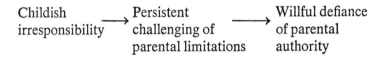

Childish ⟶ Persistent ⟶ Willful defiance
irresponsibility   challenging of        of parental
                   parental limitations  authority

The earlier that intervention (effective discipline) can occur in this inappropriate behavior continuum, the less conflict a family will experience.

In order to avoid unnecessary conflict, a parent must understand the difference between discipline and punishment. Punishment is a *penalty* imposed upon a child for a wrongdoing. Punishment involves the experience of pain, loss, or suffering for a mistake a child has made. Parents usually punish with the intent to hurt a child (physically or emotionally) so that he will learn that it is painful to do what is wrong and thus choose (or be forced to choose) to do what is right. Parents often punish their children to satisfy their own anger. At other times, parents punish because of a mistaken sense of justice that demands that a child must pay a penalty for his "crime." Too many people confuse punishment and discipline. They believe that a parent must use punishment to produce a well-disciplined child; a literal "spare the rod and spoil the child" attitude. Actually, when parents punish to eradicate childish irresponsibility and persistent challenging, they may be setting the stage for family conflict. Outward conflict can develop because a child may decide to fight against what he considers unjust treatment. Inner conflict may arise because arbitrary punishment can generate feelings of rejection and mistreatment, and a child may bottle up intense resentment toward his parents.

Discipline, on the other hand, is a *teaching* process. It leads to the prevention or the resolution of conflict. Discipline helps a child improve himself. It helps him learn lessons that will make him a better person. The primary aims of discipline are to resolve impending conflict and teach a child self-discipline.

Punishment is arbitrarily imposed; discipline relates directly to a child's inappropriate behavior. For example, Tim was late getting home from school and had not notified his mother. If she chose to *punish* him, she might take his bicycle away for two weeks and spank him for his irresponsibility. If, on the other hand, she chose a *disciplinary* action, she might not allow Tim to watch his favorite TV show that evening so that he could have the time to finish the homework and chores he'd neglected by arriving home late. She might also set up some careful limitations for future behavior. "Unless you call home and receive permission for a variance, you must be home thirty minutes after school each day or no TV that night." When discipline is effective it avoids needless conflict and enhances the possibilities for more quality family time.

### The Second Goal for Discipline: To Encourage Self-discipline

The second goal of discipline is to teach a child to make wise decisions on his own. Busy working parents aren't always available to discipline their children. Therefore, they must encourage their child to make wise decisions about his own behavior as soon as he is capable of doing so.

How can you determine when your child is capable of making his own decisions? A knowledge of child development is helpful. At birth, children are completely dependent upon the significant others in their lives to make decisions for them. But as soon as a child can get around on his own, he begins to seek independence. As his abilities and skills develop, he can make more of his own decisions.

Clearly, a child is not capable of making wise decisions in all of the areas he *wants* to. It is the parents' responsibility to teach him what is appropriate and what is not. Parents must protect their children from making immature, faulty decisions while at the same time teaching them how to make good decisions. That is what discipline is all about.

During the early years when one is carefully molding a child's behavior into good habit patterns, there may be a fine line between discipline and punishment. Parents must learn to distinguish the difference. A parent might react to a child's growing independence by yelling "no," and harshly slapping him whenever he makes a wrong decision. This may stop a child's misbehavior, but it does not teach him to make wise decisions and grow toward self-discipline. If a child doesn't learn *why* his behavior is inappropriate, he will view such parental admonitions as arbitrary and unjust.

Another parent might say "no" to the child in a firm, gentle way, might occasionally even emphasize the meaning with a little slap on his hand or bottom, and then *tell the child why his behavior is inappropriate*. This would be considered discipline. By explaining the reasons for limiting a child's behavior, a parent is laying the foundation for the development of decision-making skills.

A child can discipline himself and make his own decisions when he is able to:

1. *Seek* out the information pertinent to the decision.
2. *Evaluate* the possible alternatives.
3. *Accept* the consequences of his decision.

The acronym to remember is SEA: Seek, Evaluate, and

Accept. When a child is able to seek information, evaluate alternatives, and accept consequences in certain areas, then he should be given the responsibility of making choices in these areas.

You can help your child develop these skills by providing information and alternatives, and by allowing your child to experience the logical consequences of the decision he makes. For example, it would be inappropriate to expect a preschooler to decide when he should go to bed. He is not yet old enough to know how lack of sleep affects his body. A late bedtime would probably make him tired and cranky, so the consequences of his decision would affect the whole family.

At times, however, a preschooler should be allowed to make a *limited* choice about his bedtime—*if* his parents give him the necessary information to make a good decision; limit the alternatives; and allow him to accept the consequences of that decision. For example, you might give your child the necessary information by saying, "Eight o'clock is bedtime for four-year-olds. You'll need your sleep so you'll be wide-awake and happy when Jimmy comes tomorrow morning." You might limit the alternatives by stating, "You may go to bed anytime in the next forty-five minutes. If you go to bed earlier, I will be able to read a story to you." If your child then chooses to go to bed at eight, *don't* read a story to him. Let him accept the consequences of his decision.

For an older child who wants to attend a late-night party, you might make sure your child has the necessary information to make a good decision by asking, "Do you know where you are going; who will be there; what you will be doing; who will be driving; how late you will be?" Help him clarify alternatives. Perhaps he can attend for part of the time, have a party of his own, or find someone else to take his early morning paper route. Brainstorm. Write down all the ideas. Finally, consider the consequences of each alternative. Begin by asking, "If you choose to go (or not to go), how will it affect you?" If a late-night party means that your child will be too tired to get up when the alarm rings the next morning, he must decide if the party is worth it. You can help clarify the situation by asking, "Do you think you can get up when the alarm rings and cheerfully complete your paper route and your other household duties?" If your child honestly believes that he can, you might ask for a verbal commitment to that decision. *Then* encourage your child to decide whether or not to attend the party.

### Parental Challenges for the Early Years

If you accept the following challenges, your discipline will be more effective and your relationship with your children will be more rewarding.

Challenge #1: *Help your child develop self-confidence by building trust between you and creating a secure environment for him.*

In the very first days and months of life, a child begins to sense who he is and how other people feel about him. His own feelings of self-worth develop from this continual experience with others. A child's feelings of self-worth are determined by *his* perception of other people's feelings, *not* by their actual feelings.

Therefore, if that wet, dirty, hungry, crying baby is picked up lovingly at 2 A.M., cuddled, changed, and fed, he will begin to perceive that other people value him. But if that same child is ignored or is harshly thumped against someone's chest and shaken up and down a couple times while a bottle of cold milk is stuck into his mouth, he will have a different perception of his worth.

Self-confidence is a by-product of a sense of self-worth. And self-confidence is the vital ingredient that a child needs to be able to make wise decisions throughout his lifetime. This is how it works. When a child's needs are met, that child begins to trust the people he lives with and he begins to feel secure in his environment. If a parent or a trustworthy adult continues to mold his behavior in patient, loving, yet firm ways, he will continue to feel secure in his environment. This sense of security allows a child to feel confident enough to make his own decisions. If he is wrong, he knows that a trustworthy adult will be there to guide him. If he is in danger because of a poor decision, he knows that he will be protected. His confidence develops because he knows that the loving adults in his life will limit him, stop him, or help him change directions if his decisions are poor ones. Furthermore, he knows that he will only be allowed to make the decisions he is fully capable of making. And he knows that his parents will continue to love him no matter what he does! Therefore, an atmosphere of trust and security is essential for the development of effective self-discipline.

If a child's experiences do not convince him that he is a valuable person and that he can trust his environment, he will react to a growing sense of insecurity in either of two ways. He may protect himself by assuming an attitude of false superiority: "I can do things better," "I can beat you up," "My dad is better than your dad." And if he is challenged, he will downgrade others in an attempt to build himself up. This kind of attitude leads a child to make decisions arrogantly—before he is really capable of making wise decisions. He forces his choice, even though he doesn't have adequate information, and hasn't evaluated the alternatives. In addition, he is completely unconcerned about accepting responsibility.

Alternatively, an insecure child may develop a sense of inferiority: "I'm no good," "I can never do anything well," "Everybody is better than I am." This attitude makes decision-making almost impossible. A child who feels inferior will let others make decisions for him. Then, if a problem develops, he can blame someone else. He considers himself a victim of circumstances, and he feels unable to make any changes in his life.

If you want your child to become wisely self-disciplined, you must treat him in a way that affirms his value. He, in turn, will believe himself to be valuable and develop the confidence necessary to become a good decision-maker.

Challenge #2: *Convince your child of the wisdom of accepting parental authority.*

In the early months and years, parents must teach their children that "parents know best." Children must learn to trust their parents to make wise decisions for them. They must not be allowed to make a decision when they are too young to obtain the necessary information, evaluate the alternatives, and handle the consequences of their decision. This is the prime time for a parent to establish his credibility as an expert decision-maker—an authority.

For many people the word *authority* conjures up images of judges, rulers, or policemen—those with the power to enforce unpleasant rules and regulations. But an authority is also a specialist, a wise man, an expert. This is the kind of authority that parents must strive to develop. Children should obey because they trust their parents' wisdom and expertise, not because they fear their parents' superior power or strength.

The first few years of your child's life is the prime time to convey the message of parental authority. To do so, you must enforce your instructions and requests immediately. However, make sure that your instructions are enforceable. Don't begin by asking your child to be quiet, to go to sleep, to eat his dinner, to go to the potty in the proper place, to stop crying or pouting. These requests are almost impossible to enforce because a child has ultimate control over his body functions and his emotions. Make a request that will be easy for you to enforce. See the following chart for some examples.

When your child has learned that you mean what you say in a number of enforceable areas, it is more likely that he will follow your requests in unenforceable areas. Follow these procedures:

1. Make the request once, in such a way that you are sure your child has heard you and can understand the request.

2. If your child responds positively, reward him with a "feeling" statement of appreciation, such as, "I feel happy when you do what I ask," or with a demonstration of love, such as a hug or a smile.

3. If your child does not respond, repeat the request as you begin to enforce it. For example, "I asked you to take a bath. Take my hand and I'll turn on the water." Your

| Requests that can be enforced | Possible methods of enforcement |
| --- | --- |
| "Come inside." | Go out and bring the child in. |
| "Turn off the TV." | Take the child to the TV and turn it off yourself. |
| "Don't hit your brother." | Separate the children. |
| "Wash your face." | Lead the child to the sink and hand him the wet washcloth. |
| "Button your shirt." | Help him button it. |
| "Put your bike away." | Take the child by the hand and lead him to the bicycle. Help him put it away. |

words and actions should convey two important messages to your child—that you expect obedience when you speak and that you will stop whatever you are doing to enforce your request.

Children are often more willing to obey if they understand the reason for a request. Even if you think your child is too young to understand, try it; you might be surprised! Instead of only saying, "Put your crayons away," add, "They will melt if you leave them in the sun." When you say, "Please, pick up your mess," you might add, "It makes me feel good when the house is clean when Daddy comes home."

*Remember to keep the request simple.* When you make a request, you must always be aware of your child's ability to understand and remember that request. Even at three years of age, children are not yet able to follow instructions consistently. If your child complies with your request to shut the door, that does not mean that he will understand your request the next time you make it. Children learn (or guess) the meaning of your verbal requests by a combination of your words, the tone of your voice, your facial expressions, and your gestures. Therefore, the next time you ask your child to shut the door, your words may be the same, but the rest of your behavior may be so different that he cannot clearly understand your meaning.

Most parents make far too many requests of their children. "Kevin, brush your teeth and wash your face. Be sure to go to the bathroom before we leave. You forgot to clear your plate from the table. And have Kim run a comb through your hair." My seven-year-old can't even follow this string of requests. I know because we have tried it and it has never worked! Very few children will speak up and say, "Hold it. I can't remember everything you are telling me to do." Instead, they signal us silently by failing to follow all our instructions. And we respond by accusing them of disobedience! So, when you are trying to teach your child that you are an authority, remember this little jingle:

*Just ask the child one thing to do*
*And then make sure you follow through.*

Children differ widely in the persistence with which they challenge parental authority. The lesson of authority may be taught to one child in a relatively short period of time, but it may take another child months and sometimes years to learn. It takes a great deal of patience to discipline a persistent challenger in a way that will not be harsh and demeaning. If your child is particularly resistant to your authority, view his behavior as a challenge worthy of your time and effort. *Don't* dismiss him as stubborn and willful and allow him to get away with misbehavior. The consequences of such an attitude will be sizeable. Your child will continue to test each request with which he disagrees. As the years pass, it will become increasingly difficult to teach your child to respect your authority without resorting to your superior power and strength. But the lesson can be taught. If you have an older child who is a persistent challenger, don't feel guilty, anxious, or discouraged. Redouble your effort to avoid as much conflict as possible. Then concentrate on winning the battles that your child chooses to fight. (The following sections explain how to do this.) If your child continues to win a good share of the battles, he will continue to challenge authority. He will never learn to make his own wise decisions by using his parents as a valuable source of information.

Even if the message of parental authority is conveyed in the early years, children with a healthy sense of self-worth will occasionally challenge that authority. The way parents handle these little challenges will determine whether their child will continue to respect them or not. Effective discipline can lead to a resolution of the problem. Harsh punishment can result in willful defiance and rebellion. When these little challenges occur, parents should remember that, "Rearing children is like holding a very wet bar of soap—too firm a grasp and it shoots from your hand, too loose a grasp and it slides away. A gentle but firm grasp keeps it in your control."*

Challenge #3: *Mold the child's early behavior into acceptable habit patterns.*

Habits are established and most easily broken during the early years. During these years, parents have the size and the strength to impose their will upon a child if that becomes necessary in order to teach a child proper behavior. If these lessons are neglected and a child develops bad habits—whining for something he desires, pouting when he can't have his own way—it becomes increasingly difficult to correct his behavior. If a parent can bend the "little twig" in the right direction, the child's subsequent behavior is more likely to follow in this same general pattern.

Parents should seek help immediately if a child exhibits behavior problems that they cannot control. Sitting idly by and hoping that a child will outgrow obnoxious behavior may only intensify the problem. It is like a broken arm. If you don't treat it, it probably won't heal correctly by itself. And if you allow the arm to heal by itself and it turns out to be crooked, the arm must be rebroken and set properly in order to correct the error. The pain is far greater if the second course is followed. Similarly, if the problem behavior is not healed in the early years, the problem will have to be dealt with sometime in the future. And at that time the behavior may be so deeply ingrained that both the child and the family will experience intense pain.

How and where can you find the help your family may

* *Reader's Digest* (April 1979): 90. Credited to Elaine Hannagan.

need to make sure that problem behavior heals properly? You might try one or a number of the following.

1. Parenting classes—check the YMCA, YWCA, Red Cross, Public Health Department, local school district, community college, churches, or mental health clinics.

2. Professionally led parent discussion groups—check with the school district, the mental health service of the Public Health Department, guidance clinics, or a program like Parents Anonymous.

3. Family counseling—check with family counseling services, guidance clinics, psychiatric clinics, or licensed marriage and family counselors.

### The Qualities of an Effective Disciplinarian

There are four qualities that are essential for a disciplinarian who wants to avoid or resolve conflict and foster a child's self-discipline. An effective disciplinarian must: 1) keep open; 2) keep an even emotional temperature; 3) be consistent; and 4) balance tenderness and firmness.

#### *Keep open*

Dictatorial leadership in a family does not lead to quality time together, nor does it encourage self-discipline among family members. You cannot force your dreams of well-disciplined children to come true. Dreams come true when the groundwork has been well prepared and the children concerned begin dreaming the same dream.

Being closed is a defense mechanism learned in childhood. People don't like to be made fun of, so they hide their feelings; they don't like to be criticized, so they hide their talents; they don't like their position to be threatened, so they cut themselves off from anyone who might challenge them.

A dictatorial attitude may appear to be the easiest position to take as a disciplinarian, but this is not true. It is really the hardest, the saddest, and the loneliest. And it spells disaster where the family is concerned. When family leadership is closed, it leads to poor morale in the ranks; discontent can grow, and rebellion is often the result. Some parents feel that a closed form of family government is preferable during early childhood. But even young children feel resentful when their suggestions and wishes are ignored, and when they are not allowed to make the little decisions they are capable of making. Young children also resent parents who can't admit a mistake or change their ways, but require perfection from every family member under eighteen.

Being open doesn't mean that parents should surrender their authority. This would only lead to chaos. Being open means that parents are approachable; that they will listen. It means that they will seriously consider another person's (even a little person's) suggestions, criticism, needs, concerns, demands, and wishes before making a decision, rather than jealously guarding this function as their own parental right.

Honesty is the first step to becoming an open, approachable parent. An honest parent can admit mistakes, lack of knowledge, or embarrassment. When a child knows that his parents will be truthful and will listen without criticism or laughter, he feels that they are approachable.

Parents may be open in one area while closed in other. Children quickly learn when and how to approach a parent. They also learn the issues to avoid. In no area is parental openness more important than in the area of sex education. I want my children to be comfortable in coming to me with their questions or their problems. But this will only happen if I am open and honest; if I don't skirt the issue, act embarrassed, pretend that I don't know or that I'm too busy to explain something. The message of these maneuvers is a closed message. If it happens often enough, youngsters will stop trying to pry their parents open. It's easier to go elsewhere for the information and help they need.

### Keep an even emotional temperature

Lukewarm may be a distasteful temperature for milk or root beer, but it's just right for parents. When parents are emotionally too cold or too hot, they are not very much fun to be around. On the cold side, they are rejecting and neglecting. On the hot side, they are quick tempered and explosive. Many parents believe that anger is the only way to compel obedience, but this is not so. Children do not obey because of anger. They obey because they know that anger leads to swift and decisive action. And they want to avoid that action.

It is far better to take the time to handle misbehavior immediately, rather than letting your temperature continue to rise until you act emotionally and give your children a model of aggressive behavior.

When parents reach a boiling point, when emotions sour, their bodies are ready for immediate action—either to fight or to flee. And too many parents choose to fight! Thinking becomes irrational; demeaning words fly, and it is easy for parents to strike out physically at the object of their frustration. Child abuse, both verbal and physical, is too often the result of letting one's emotional temperature reach the breaking point. Therefore, I suggest that parents follow these two important principles.

1. Never discipline in anger. Wait until you cool down and can think clearly, or better yet, discipline before you get angry.

2. Keep an even temperature in front of your children. Angry words and aggressive actions are two of the easiest behaviors to model or imitate. You will have enough trouble

coping with your child's anger and aggression. Don't give him reasons to say that he learned this from you.

Of course, your temperature will—and should—fluctuate slightly at times. If you always bottle up your feelings, you're doing a disservice to your family. Be aware of your feelings. When you sense that your emotional temperature is beginning to rise, do something about it immediately.

Don't wait to reach the point of explosion before disciplining your child. If your child needs immediate attention, take a deep breath, think cool, and keep your voice low. If you're dangerously close to explosion, walk around the block, attack the dirty garage, yank out the weeds, play tennis, call your husband, or pray before interacting with your child. When you have brought your temperature under control, it is much easier to think of creative ways to solve the problem—ways that will not lead to further conflict.

### Be consistent

Let's pretend that you think it is very important for your child to make his bed each morning. Your child knows exactly how you feel—it is a rule that he should obey. But you are very busy during those morning hours and often forget to check his room. When you do check and find an unmade bed, you sometimes feel that it's easier to ignore the infraction than to exert the extra effort needed to get him to make his bed before the school bus arrives. So you decide to wait until after school. Then, by the time you both get home, the bed is forgotten.

Now, you still feel very strongly about the bed, and you have communicated this to your child in no uncertain terms. Shouldn't this be enough to get the job done? He clearly knows what he should do. Why doesn't he do it? The reason is that this requirement has not been *consistently* enforced.

When you enforce requirements—even very important

requirements—inconsistently, your child will become a "50/50" decision-maker. This is what happens. Junior wakes up in the morning and yawns. "Let's see," he says as he tumbles out of bed, "shall I make my bed this morning? Well, chances are 50/50 that Mom won't even notice, and I really don't feel like doing it. So . . . I think I'll take a chance and leave it unmade."

But if Mom consistently enforced and reinforced the type of behavior she expected from her child until this behavior became ingrained and habitual, the scenario would be different. Junior would wake up in the morning and say, "Let's see, shall I make my bed?" Then he would weigh the alternatives ("If I don't, Mom will make me do it before breakfast"), and make a wise decision ("I guess I'd better go ahead and get it over with").

Children will abide by reasonable requirements and limitations, but their tendency is to do as little as possible. Even a two-year-old will try to get away with as much as he can. He'll quickly learn that even though his parents *say* "no" frequently, the limits will come tumbling down if he kicks hard enough. When his persistent challenging meets with parental inconsistency, he'll be encouraged to kick at every limit he would just as soon do without.

Consistency in parental behavior checks this testing behavior in the young child before it becomes habitual behavior. After all, kicking against too many firm, solid rules takes a lot of energy and can cause pain. Therefore, a child becomes much more careful about the limits he chooses to test, and becomes better able to discipline himself.

It is particularly difficult to be consistent when Dad, Mom, Grandpa, Cousin Jim, Aunt Mildred, and the babysitter are all involved in parenting. When there are several parental figures, the child often becomes frustrated by conflicting messages.

As a child develops, it is important for him to learn to

relate to a wide number of adults, and to learn to cope with their differences of opinion. But he also needs consistency and order in his home life. It is very important that the adults responsible for a young child reach a consensus about their requirements, and support each other in this decision. Undermining an absent parent or another authority figure plants seeds of disrespect in a child's fertile mind.

If parents and/or parental figures are in conflict about disciplinary tactics, a child will take full advantage of this opportunity and play one adult against the other in order to get his own way. This only causes more family conflict. If parents have differences of opinion about rearing a child, these should be resolved privately. When a child is confronted, he should meet a united front. Otherwise, parents beware! A child does not have to take lessons to learn how to divide and conquer.

### Balance tenderness and firmness

Effective discipline depends upon a parent's ability to balance tenderness and firmness. It is fun to have a good time with children, to laugh over silly things, to play crazy games, but children can sometimes carry these activities to extremes. At that moment, a parent will have to say firmly, "Children, that is enough." At other times, parents must follow a strict admonition with a hug to show that all is forgotten.

One evening Jan told our daughters twice to settle down and go to sleep. But they continued talking, joking, and laughing. Finally, he sighed and nudged me, "Okay, Kay. It's your turn."

I marched into their room in military style and commanded, "That is enough. Be quiet this minute and go to sleep." Instantly the room was still. As I turned to march out again. I stopped and asked in a different tone, "Did you girls say your prayers?"

"No," they replied.

"Then you had better say them right now!" I said firmly.

Obediently, each girl knelt down and Kari earnestly prayed, "Dear Jesus, please help my mommy not to be so strict."

The irony of the situation was too much, and all three of us burst out laughing. After prayers, we hugged and kissed and parted friends.

A good disciplinarian constantly walks the tightrope between firmness and tenderness. Sometimes he may tip in one direction but he corrects the error with a little tip in the opposite direction. He is not afraid to be firm, but he is equally unafraid to be tender.

The balancing act works best when both tenderness and firmness are blended into a total approach—when a parent can say kindly but firmly, "Children, I mean what I say." Harsh, unreasonable demands have no place in the repertoire of a good disciplinarian. But if you do act harshly on occasion, an apology and a little love help to heal a multitude of sins.

## The Prevention of Disciplinary Problems

To prevent disciplinary problems, prime-time parents must be experts at defining limits, anticipating potential problems, and providing encouragement.

### Define limits

Many parents try to forestall misbehavior by presenting their children with a list of rules. Unfortunately, this tactic is often ineffective because children don't always remember all the rules. Furthermore, it is impossible for any parent to cover all possible bases and anticipate all a child's thoughts and activities.

To prevent children from making unreasonable decisions, teach them how to use their "child sense," by applying only *three* principles, rather than trying to remember 5,396 rules that won't begin to cover all minor infractions.

Principle 1: You may not hurt yourself.
Principle 2: You may not hurt others.
Principle 3: You may not hurt things.

Now, take a look at the effectiveness of this strategy. Step back into your childhood for a moment, and pretend that you want to play baseball in the living room. You can't remember a rule prohibiting the game, but just to make sure, you check your decision against the three principles. Principle 1: *You may not hurt yourself.* "How can playing baseball in the living room hurt me . . . unless Mom spanks me?" Principle 2: *You may not hurt others.* "That doesn't seem likely if we agree not to fight over strikes and balls." Principle 3: *You may not hurt things.* Oh, oh. Here is where the red light starts flashing. The picture window could get broken and Mom's $50 vase is on the table, and . . . "Hey, kids," you yell, "I guess we had better find someplace else for our baseball game."

On the other hand, consider what might happen if your parents only provided you with a series of rules. "Let's see," you say, "did Mom ever say that we couldn't play baseball in the living room?" Mentally, you run down your list of rules. #567. Don't play baseball in the flower garden. Well, that's close. #924. Don't throw the football in the house. Closer. But nothing about playing baseball in the living room, so "Okay, gang. Let's play ball!"

As an adult, you reason, "Any child with a little common sense could see that if it were wrong to play football in the house, baseball would surely fall in that same category." Maybe. The problem is that children sometimes lack that essential ingredient called common sense.

Start early, and help your child learn how to measure his decisions with these three principles. As you begin limiting your child's behavior, use these three principles to explain your decision. "No, you may not run out in the street, because *you may not hurt yourself.*" "No, you may not hit your little sister, because *you may not hurt others.*" "No, you may not throw books around the room, because *you may not hurt things.*"

You won't always be available to formulate for every new situation your child may face. Using these three principles will help him make a better decision when he can't seek your advice. Of course, this won't prevent every disciplinary problem. Children can make poor decisions even after applying these principles, because they do not always understand what might be harmful. But their errors in judgment will decrease with practice. The words, "Sorry, Mom, I forgot," will be heard less frequently as their "child sense" develops into good common sense based on principles that allow them to be effective decision-makers.

### Anticipate potential problems

"If only I had realized what he was up to . . ." "If only I had been there . . ." "If only . . ."—the two saddest words of Moms and Dads who haven't cultivated that all-important prevention technique of anticipating trouble. How can you do this? There is no foolproof method, but there are some useful techniques.

1. *Never take too much for granted.* If the playhouse seems awfully quiet, don't just thank your lucky stars and put another load in the washer. Take a moment to check out the situation. The kids may be painting the walls with catsup and mustard!

2. *Get to know your child—and his friends.* If you know that your child is a little bear when he doesn't get enough sleep, be sure he has a nap before you take him out

to a restaurant for dinner. If you know that your child and his buddy can get into a lot of trouble together, don't just idly sit by waiting for the inevitable. Give them careful and clear instructions about their behavior and limit their play space to an area that you can supervise adequately.

3. *Be observant.* If you see that your child's face is turning red, don't wait for the explosion before moving into action. Watch for the first sign that all is not well, and begin preventive treatment immediately. If your four-year-old is building a fancy block structure across the main traffic pattern in your home, help him move it to a safer location *before* some careless person knocks it down.

4. *Stay close at hand.* If your six-year-old is building with Daddy's tools, don't choose this time for your beauty rest. If your teenagers are having a Saturday night shindig at your home, don't go out to eat. There are times when children need parents close at hand, in order to assist them if they need it, or to protect them from situations that could get out of control.

The following techniques can be used to forestall developing problems. Remember, these work best when used as *preventive* measures.

1. *Touch control.* Nursery school teachers are masters at touch control. When they notice a child who is disturbing another, they move closer to the situation. Close proximity has a positive effect on a child's behavior. As a last resort, a teacher might sit next to the disturbing child and, if this closeness isn't enough, might put a gentle hand on his knee—or place him on her lap for a while. This gentle touch control seems to work miracles. A soft touch is the key. It's not accusing or derogatory. It says to the child, "I like you and I'll stay close by as long as you need me."

2. *Diversion.* Some people feel that a good parent must deal directly with every problem. But it is often easier to divert a child's attention, especially a very young child with a short attention span. Diversion can be useful in other situ-

ations as well. If your children are crabbing about the injustice of a teacher and a discussion has not helped, it might be appropriate to divert their attention. For example, you might say, "Hey, let's get that model boat out. You have been wanting me to help you with it. I think I have time right now." Later, when tempers have cooled, you can return to the teacher problem and help the children find a solution.

3. *Play-act problems away.* Play-acting is a creative technique that is useful with young children who enjoy make-believe. When you have to get a brush through a child's tangled hair and you know you can anticipate a battle, play beauty salon. "Good morning, Ms. Adams. I'm so glad you came to my beauty shop. How would you like your hair fixed today? Let's see, I think you would look nice with your hair combed like this. . . ." You'll be surprised how much more cooperative a "beauty shop customer" is than a little girl who hates to have Mommy comb her tangled hair.

Have you ever had difficulty getting your child dressed? "Hello, Sir. I'm glad you came to my men's store. How would you like a new shirt and pants? I think we have just the thing for you. Please step into this dressing room and try on our bargain for the day."

Try playing restaurant if your child balks at eating dinner. "Here is the food you ordered. It's the specialty of the house. The cook has been busy all afternoon preparing this just for you. And what would you like to drink?" To be really effective, add candlelight and drape a towel over your arm. Eating can become much more interesting when you add a little make-believe.

When you meet obstinacy head on, don't buck it; try a role reversal. "You be the mommy and pretend that I'm your little boy. Grab my hand and take me carefully to the other side of the street." "This room is a mess. Pretend that you are my daddy, and help me clean my room because you feel sorry for your little girl who has to clean it all by herself."

If your child is running through the house like an escaping fire engine, say, "Remember, Doctor, this is a hospital. The patients are trying to sleep. You will just have to be more quiet as you walk down the halls."

4. *Send a telegram.* A written message can often be more effective in forestalling problems than personal involvement. Kari and Kevin were out watering the garden one afternoon and Kari had the hose. I overheard an argument and a threat about a water fight, so I quickly penned a note. "Dear Kari. Please do not water Kevin. He is not a flower. Love, Mommy (from Africa)." I put the note in an envelope and sent it "special delivery" with Kim. By the time Kari put down the hose and read the note, tempers had cooled and Kevin had escaped to the safety of the house.

If your teenager seems to be heading for problems, take the time to write a loving message, and see if this new form of communication doesn't have a special meaning. Children would much rather read a note two or three times than hear their parents tell them the same thing over and over again.

5. *Play a game.* Kevin never left for school with a clean face until we stopped saying, "Kevin, wash your face," and started playing the game, "Whoever-walks-outside-the-house-with-a-dirty-face-gets-to-empty-the-wastebaskets." Now, I'm having a hard time finding anyone to empty the trash! But faces are clean. Nine thousand, three hundred and forty-two reminders did not get through to Kevin, but one simple game made the difference.

When you initiate a game to teach children self-discipline and responsibility, it's important that the rules apply to the entire family. Our family uses an electric toothbrush, and Jan and Kevin are constantly reminding me to take my toothbrush off the appliance when I'm finished. Kevin finally decided that the family should play the game, "Whoever-forgets-to-take-his-toothbrush-off-has-to-go-to-his-bedroom-and-count-to-twenty-five." And the first night, Kevin was the one who had to count to twenty-five! Surprisingly, the game has actually helped me remember this simple task.

If you decide to try this technique, make sure that *every* family member agrees to play and has a say in setting the rules. Games lose their value if they cease to be fun or if the consequences of losing are not consistently carried out.

6. *Offer an incentive.* When you anticipate a stubborn reaction to one of your requests, encourage and motivate your child into the appropriate action by providing an incentive. A child may be ready to argue about cleaning his room, but if he knows that a Popsicle waits at the end, the job might seem more attractive. Your car needs a washing, but you don't have the time to take it to the car wash. Why not offer your reluctant teenager the same amount you would have paid someone else to do the job? A small incentive may be all he needs to tackle the task enthusiastically.

Chore charts are effective incentives for some children. These charts list a child's daily chores and activities. When a child completes a chore he places a check (or a star) next to the listing. Some parents offer a reward at the end of the day or week if all chores have been completed. Chore charts are a particularly useful method of providing meaningful activity for schoolchildren who come home to an empty house. They also help children establish positive work habits.

Positive attitudes and behavior can also be encouraged with incentives. John had a nine-year history of teasing his younger siblings. When he was twelve his parents felt he was old enough to change if he wanted to. As an incentive they bought him a present, wrapped it, and placed it on the refrigerator. He could open it when he convinced the family that teasing was no longer a part of his life-style. Immediately his attitude and behavior changed. For ten weeks the wrapped package was a constant and effective reminder. Now he has learned more positive ways of interacting with his siblings. He no longer teases. It was the incentive that made the difference.

7. *Point out reality.* Children often protest against restraints because they don't understand the full picture. They rebel when they are unable to comprehend the reality of a situation. And parents often give hasty orders and ultimatums without explaining their reasons. This can lead to a great deal of resentment.

Whenever possible, trust your child's capacity for understanding, and take the time to explain the reality of the situation. For example, our family had been looking forward to a Hawaiian trip, which we had to cancel. Jan and I knew that the children would be disappointed. But when we explained that the airline strike meant that Jan and I had to take two extra days off to get alternate reservations, which neither of us could afford to do, the children surprised us by replying, "Well, we'd just as soon go to Grandma's house this summer and wait to go to Hawaii when we have more time."

Pointing out the reality of a situation is useful when warning children of impending disaster. "If you continue screaming, you will have to go outside." "If you pull her hair, she is likely to pull your hair." "If you do not come immediately, you will have to stay home."

### Provide encouragement

This can be a wonderfully effective way of preventing potential problems. Inspire your child with a sense of hope; assure him of your support and your trust in his capabilities.

Between the plunking of the typewriter keys, I thought I

heard a whimper. I left the study to investigate. Kari was sitting on the piano bench, her eyes brimming with tears. "What's wrong, Kari?" I asked.

"I can't do it. It's too hard. I'll never get a gold star at my next lesson," she cried.

"Oh, I don't know about that," I said. "What is the first note of your piece?" Step by step I began encouraging her to pick her way through the difficult music. I sat beside her as she played it over and over again until it was mastered.

That night Kari hugged and kissed me with extra feeling and bounced off to her bed joyfully. The next day the joy of encouragement buoyed her again when her teacher rewarded her with a gold star.

Encouragement. What a tranquilizer! What a stimulant! What an antidepressant! What a tonic for whatever ails a child! I don't think there is ever a time when encouragement and hope are inappropriate. A disobedient child is often a discouraged child. He reasons, "When I don't feel good about myself and nothing I do seems to work out, it really doesn't matter how I act. Why even try to be good?" Discouragement can lead to despair, moodiness, even apathy. All these emotions severely restrict a child's ability to cope and to make wise decisions.

Don't risk discouragement; give your child an injection of "hypodermic affection" every three hours, or as often as needed. This quick injection of love can be a hug, a wink, a smile, or a playful nibble on a baby's tummy. These little attentions can give a child a new outlook on life. It's a great way to boost a child over a difficult situation and send him on his way with a large dose of courage and hope. "After all, if all the special people in my life love me, what else matters?" This subtle encouragement is a powerful incentive for a child—he'll want to do his best.

Each child is the architect of his own behavior and personality. If it were in my power, children would be neat, polite, obedient, and happy all the time. But as much as I plan and scheme, I can't do it. I can't choose the characteristics that my children will ultimately develop—that choice is theirs. But parents can encourage a child to move in the right direction, encourage him to have high expectations for himself, and encourage him to see that he has the potential of reaching those expectations by the daily decisions he makes.

Imagine that your eleven-year-old wants to attend a slumber party (so named because of the significant lack of slumber that occurs at such gatherings). The following day she has a piano recital. You know that she needs a good night's sleep, and should start practicing early in the morning. Should you make the decision for her?

It's easy to say "no," put up with a little fussing and fuming, and make sure that she is in bed by 8 P.M. You can even wake her up at eight the next morning and tell her to start practicing. But you can't make her go to sleep, nor can you make her practice, nor can you make her happy while she is complying with your rules. She must make these decisions on her own.

Instead of forcing the issue, why not encourage her to make a wise decision? Tell her exactly how you feel about attending the slumber party, and what you think a wise decision would be and why. Then encourage her to decide whether it is a good idea to attend a "slumberless" party the night before her big recital. Encourage her to weigh the alternatives and the consequences of each possible choice. When the decision has been made, encourage her to live with her decision and accept the consequences.

Let's assume that she attends the slumber party and stumbles through her piece at the recital because she's tired. Obviously, now is the time to say, "I told you so!" Right? Wrong! She is old enough and smart enough to know that it would have been better if she had gotten more sleep and more practice. Parental criticism at this point may only elicit a defiant reaction such as, "I don't care how I did at the recital, anyway!" When your child makes a poor decision, be especially encouraging. Let her know that even though the consequences are difficult to bear, she will benefit from this experience in the long run.

Many parents believe that if they teach their children an appropriate set of rules, the children will do what is right. But this is not necessarily so. One study reported that children nine to fourteen years of age who had a good opinion of adults retained their sense of right and wrong and managed to monitor their own behavior. But those who had little regard for the credibility of adults tended to show their cynicism by rejecting moral tenets and going along with the crowd.* It would seem that children who view their parents as encouraging rather than dictatorial would be more prone to respect them. This respect for adults appears to be an important factor in preventing later problems.

### The Methods of Discipline that Foster Self-discipline

Even if you have mastered all of the prevention techniques, there will still be times (many times) when you will have to deal with unacceptable behavior. Your skill in this area depends on knowledge and practice. Skillful prime-time disciplinarians should master the following four methods: 1) positive power; 2) consequences; 3) contracting; and 4) shock therapy.

### Positive power

To discipline effectively, you must be positive in dealing with your child and accentuate your child's positive behavior. It is all too easy to be negative when disciplining a child. "Don't do that," "No," and "Stop it," are familiar

* Edwin and Barton Bixenstine and Margaret DeCorte, *Today's Child* (January 1977).

phrases in most homes. Although it is important to limit a child's behavior with these commands at times, a steady diet of negative requests does not help a child feel good about himself. Negative statements limit behavior, but they don't tell a child what he *can* do. For example, a phrase like, "Don't push your brother," only tells a child not to do what he is doing. However, a positive statement—"Take your brother's hand and lead him"—offers the child a guideline, a direction in which to move.

Whenever possible, limit your child's behavior with a positive statement, or follow a negative command with a positive direction.

Accentuating the positive is important because it prevents the reinforcement of negative behavior. A parent's time and attention are rewarding to a child. Therefore, if you devote a great deal of time and attention to a child when he is misbehaving, that behavior is rewarded. The child soon learns that his obnoxious behavior will bring attention. To stop rewarding negative behavior, give your child time and attention when he is behaving well, and limit your time and attention when he isn't.

Some experts believe that parents should reward the positive and ignore the negative. However, if you completely ignore obnoxious behavior, your child may view this as indifference or as passive approval. It is possible to let him know in a positive way that you do not approve of his behavior and will help him learn how to behave in an acceptable way.

To encourage acceptable behavior, especially with young children, use the behavior modification technique of "time-out." Send your child to a designated room or area for a short period of time—not more than five minutes—after he has done something inappropriate. The amount of time spent in the room is not the significant factor. To use this technique effectively, let your child know that you expect his attitude and behavior to change when he comes out of the room or he is destined to return. This method should not be considered punishment. It is a logical consequence of misbehaving—and children will accept it without resentment if their parents carry out this method matter-of-factly, without force or anger. You can successfully apply the behavior modification technique with your child if you follow these guidelines.

1. Choose *one* behavior that you would like to modify.

2. Count the number of times this behavior occurs during a particular time period—one hour, an afternoon, an entire day. It is best if you do this for three different time periods and obtain an average.

3. When your child misbehaves, calmly say, "Time-out for_____(given reason)_____," and take the child to the room you have selected. Be sure to tell the child how long he will have to stay, or allow him to make that decision by saying, "You may come out when you are ready."

4. When your child emerges and acts appropriately, *give him your time and attention.*

My friend Mary tried this technique on her four-year-old son, Jack, who was hitting thirty-three times a day. Every time Jack hit another child she took him by the hand and said, "Five minutes time-out for hitting." When the time was up, she gave him attention for his good behavior. His hitting behavior steadily declined, and in three weeks it had decreased to three times per day.

Mary then decided to use this positive approach with her twenty-two-month-old daughter, who was climbing on the kitchen counter approximately seventeen times per day. One week went by. No change. Two weeks. No change. (Most people would have given up and concluded that it works for boys and not for girls, or for hitting and not for climbing, or for four-year-olds and not two-year-olds, but Mary was determined to continue.) Approximately seventeen times per day Mary took her daughter down from the counter and to her room for a five-minute time-out period.

Then one day, three weeks after she had started the program, the problem was solved. Her daughter stopped climbing up on the counter, and Mary has never had a problem with this behavior since.

Positive power does work, but it is not an easy method to use. You must be observant, and willing to stop whatever you are doing at the time to take your child to the time-out room, and you must have enough determination to continue the program until your child finally gets the message.

Try positive power with your child. Select the behavior you would like to change. Count the number of times the behavior is occurring, then record the average number of times per day. Put the time-out plan into action and chart your results. Use the plan for a three-week period. Chart your success on the following graph.

If you get the kind of results that I think you will, you will be sold on positive power.

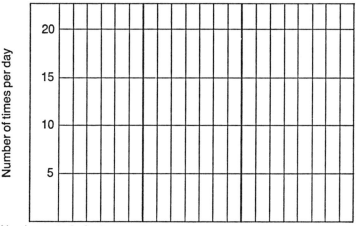

### Consequences

Billy slept late, "dawdled" over his breakfast, and refused to get dressed when his mother asked him to, so he missed the school bus and arrived at school late because he had to walk. Sue planted a garden for her school project and forgot to water it. Everything died and she received an F on the project. Jim left his bike outside the garage one night, even though he knew better. The bike was stolen and his parents refused to purchase another bike for him until he earned at least half of the money. Jim was not able to join his scout troop bike trip the following week.

Consequences. They often seem so harsh. Why didn't Mom take Billy to school? It was a long way to walk. Why didn't Dad water Sue's garden when he saw the radishes drooping? What a lot of work was wasted. Why didn't Jim's parents ask him every night if his bike was safe? What an expensive loss.

Why? Because these parents had wisely learned that one of the best techniques for modifying a child's behavior is to let him suffer the consequences of his inappropriate behavior—to learn a lesson from his mistakes. Consequences are especially effective when milder measures, such as reminding or warning a child, have failed to produce behavior changes. Letting a child suffer the consequences is the quickest, and, in the long run, the most painless way to encourage a child to make wise decisions about disciplining himself.

This method is equally effective with very young children. In fact, it is during the first three to five years that prime-time disciplinarians must teach a child that misbehavior will result in both natural and parent-imposed logical consequences.

Natural consequences are the actions that will naturally occur if a child continues on his own path of "destruction." For example, if the child grabs a toy away from another child, he is likely to receive a kick or a bash on the nose. However, if there is no natural consequence, or the natural consequence is harmful, parents must impose a consequence that will help the child see the folly of his behavior and learn a lesson from the experience. For example, you can't allow a two-year-old to run out in the street. The natural consequence is that he might get killed. You can't allow a ten-year-old to steal your neighbor's apples. The neighbor might verbally rip the child apart or send for the police. Furthermore, getting away with a theft might encourage this behavior in the future.

Instead, in such cases, you must teach a child what is inappropriate by using a parent-imposed logical consequence. For example, "If you can't stay out of the street, you'll have to play in the fenced backyard." "If you don't stop picking our neighbor's apples, I will have to take $10 from your allowance, and together we will tell Mr. Jones that this money is your payment for the apples you are stealing from his orchard."

Some parents say, "I use parent-imposed consequences all the time. If my child breaks a window, I spank him. If he gets into a fight, I spank him. If he spills his milk, I spank him." These are parent-imposed consequences, but they are *not* logical consequences that are related to a child's specific behavior. To be most effective, a parent-imposed consequence must be logical. It must be clearly linked to a child's behavior. If a child breaks a window, let him clean up the mess (if he is old enough not to get cut), apologize to the owner, and pay for the damages. If a child gets into a fight, a logical consequence might be, "If you can't get along, you two will have to be separated or sit in the talk-it-over chairs (two facing chairs) where children must sit until they have settled their dispute." Even a young child can wipe up spilled milk and learn a lesson about the consequences of carelessness.

The beauty of using natural and logical consequences

is that a child can never truthfully shout, "Unfair." He begins to learn that the discipline fits the act, and that he deserves to suffer the consequences.

Here are some important instructions to follow when using consequences as a disciplinary method.

1. Don't shield your child from consequences that would be, in the long run, beneficial to him.

2. Don't allow your child to blame others for the predicament he got himself into. *Neither* should you cast blame on your child. It is enough that he is suffering from the consequences of his act.

3. If the natural consequence is too harmful, or if there is no immediate consequence, impose a logical consequence on your child, one that is linked to his unacceptable behavior.

4. Support your child in accepting a consequence as a beneficial experience. Encourage him to keep a positive attitude about the experience. Help him develop the attitude that a valuable lesson can be learned from each mistake.

5. Don't let your child face a major consequence that he may be unable to handle, without your support. Stay close to him if possible, and let him know that you care. Otherwise, he may become discouraged, and discouragement often leads to misbehavior.

6. Decide in advance what logical consequences you would impose on your child for the following acts.

Screaming and yelling, when you have asked him to be quiet.
Breaking a toy carelessly.
Eating a candy bar before lunch.
Playing with matches.
Scribbling on the wall.
Hammering dents in the table.
Telling a lie.
Being disrespectful to an adult.

Forgetting to notify you when he will be late.
Going someplace without permission.

It is always easier to think of logical consequences at your leisure instead of on the spot, so prepare yourself in advance.

7. Let the child select the consequence. Self-imposed consequences are effective in changing behavior. Rather than risking the child's resentment of what he considers unjust discipline, allow him to choose. After Kent had been caught whittling holes in his desk, the teacher asked that he talk to his parents about what should be done. Rather than face them, Kent lied to his teacher, saying he talked to his parents and they were too busy to fix the desk. Later, his parents learned of the situation and after talking with Kent decided that, in addition to fixing the desk, the lesson of truthfulness should be emphasized. Kent was allowed to choose one of three consequences; not play games with the family that day, forfeit his night with Dad, or receive a spanking. Willingly he chose to be spanked.

Life is full of natural and logical consequences. It is better for your child to learn this lesson from you than to leave home thinking that he can do whatever he wishes without taking any responsibility for his actions.

### Contracting

The third method of disciplining is contracting. Nobody likes to be ordered about. I would be very resentful if Jan *told* me, "Pick up the laundry, mail this package, and invite these people over for Saturday night." I'd much rather hear him say, "Honey, I'm very busy today, but I think I can be home for dinner if you can pick up the laundry, mail this package, and invite the guests for Saturday night."

Children feel the same way. If we involve them in decision-making that concerns them, they will be much more willing to comply with our requests. Contracting is one way we can do this.

In order for contracting to be effective, a child must be: 1) verbal enough to discuss possible solutions; 2) smart enough to understand what he is contracting for; and 3) mature enough to keep a bargain that he has made.

How does contracting work? Follow these steps.

Step 1: *Define the problem with your child.* For example, John has not been brushing his teeth regularly and he rebels at every reminder, so you approach him about his behavior. "John, I have to pay the dentist bills and when you don't brush your teeth, the bills can increase. What can we do together to make sure that this important job gets done?"

Step 2: *Brainstorm together about possible solutions.* Working together you might come up with the following list: "Put a reminder note on the table; no dessert until John brushes regularly; buy an electric toothbrush; get better-tasting toothpaste; have a special code as a reminder; give John a nickel every time he brushes; John returns the nickel if he forgets.

Step 3: *Decide together which possibility is most acceptable.* John thinks that he would remember if he receives an electric toothbrush. If he forgets, John promises that he won't get angry if he is reminded with the code words, "Billy Goat." When he hears the code, he will brush his teeth immediately.

Step 4: *Decide when the contract will be put into effect.* "I think I'll have a chance to go shopping on Wednesday. What about starting our contract then?"

Step 5: *Indicate in some manner that you both agree on the contract.* Write it down, sign it, shake hands, or seal it with a kiss!

Step 6: *Evaluate the effectiveness of the contract periodically.* If the contract is not working, go back to the bargaining table and draw up a new contract.

Contracting involves a child in the decision-making process. It is excellent training for a child's inner control system—a necessity for self-discipline. The following guidelines will help you use this method most effectively.

1. Don't approach a problem by placing blame solely on your child. This will only antagonize him and prevent a successful resolution. Use the "I message" to avoid this mistake. For example, "I get upset and angry when I hear so much quarreling." This is much less offensive to a child than an accusing "You message," such as "You kids quit quarreling right now. All you do is fight with each other."

2. Be willing to bargain. Don't come to the bargaining table with a rigid solution in mind. Be flexible.

3. Be supportive—not antagonistic. Show your child by your behavior and attitude that you are the ally, not the enemy!

The older your children are, the more you will both enjoy contracting as a preventive disciplinary method. Master the technique early so you'll be able to get as much use out of it as possible. Start today by writing down an offensive behavior that your child might be willing to change with an attractive contract. Don't delay. Head to the bargaining table. Use the following form to record the contract that you and your child agree on.

### Shock therapy

Centuries ago a French philosopher, Jean Rousseau, said, "Do the opposite of what is usually done and you will almost always be right." Shock therapy is based on this concept of doing the unexpected. Furthermore, it is a disciplinary technique that is only effective when used *very infrequently*.

I have heard parents say, "When my child threw a temper tantrum, I gave him a good hard spanking immediately, and he never did it again." Other parents argue, "I tried

I _____ and my child _____
   parent's name                              child's name

do hereby agree to the following:

What I will do: _____

_____

What my child will do: _____

_____

Date effective _____    _____

                                   Signed:

                                   _____
                                   parent's name

                                   _____
                                   child's name

                                   _____
                                   witness

spanking and it didn't work. But I gave my child a cold shower, and he never threw another tantrum." Still other parents have said, "When my child threw a tantrum, I ignored it and walked off and left him. That cured him instantly, and before I knew it he was walking like an angel by my side."

Testimonies like these have always surprised me. Why do so many different techniques seem to work? I'm convinced that it is not the technique itself but the fact that the parent's reaction *shocked* the child. It was completely unexpected. Indeed, it was the very opposite of what the child expected. The very fact that these techniques were *not* the parent's common way of responding was what made them so effective.

This concept should have a strong cautionary effect on

a parent's use of some methods of discipline. Although you might effectively cold shower a child once, it would soon cease to be effective if it were used for every inappropriate act. If a method is effective once, twice, or even twenty times, that does not mean that it will continue to be effective. Nor does it mean that it is the best technique to use, if your final goal is to rear a child with a healthy sense of self-worth. The end (whether or not a method is effective in producing behavior changes) should never justify the means, if a child's feelings of self-worth are damaged in the process. This would be termed psychological abuse. Nor should the end justify the means if it results in physical child abuse. Sticking a child's hand in boiling water may be an effective way to change a child's behavior, but it is clearly child abuse!

Spanking is a shock therapy technique. It can be an effective method of discipline. But the more frequently a spanking is used, the less effective it becomes. In fact, I'm convinced that parents who use spanking successfully to stop a temper tantrum have not spanked their child for every minor infraction. Therefore, it surprises the child and shocks him out of his negative behavior. Before spanking a child, consider the following suggestions carefully.

1. Only spank your child when he is willfully defying your authority and milder measures have failed. Avoid this method when your child has acted inappropriately because he is too young or immature to know better. Don't automatically spank a child for challenging a request you have made. Willful defiance is not the only reason for disobedience. *Do not overuse this method.*

2. Never spank your child when you are angry. It is too easy to spank too hard or too long. There is a very fine line between a hard spanking and child abuse.

3. Tell your child beforehand whether the spanking is a one-strike, two-strike, or three-strike spanking. There should never be a reason for more than three strikes.

4. Spank immediately after the misdeed. If you wait too long to administer a spanking, it won't be shock therapy.

5. Make sure your child clearly understands the reason for the spanking. A child should be able to feel that "his punishment fits the crime." If he can understand the reason for this discipline, you won't have to contend with feelings of resentment or injustice.

6. Spank your child in private. It is demeaning and embarrassing to discipline a child in front of an audience.

7. Your child should experience enough discomfort to change his rebellious attitude. If, after the spanking, he slams doors, calls you names, or stares you in the eye and says defiantly, "That didn't hurt," the spanking was ineffective. Calmly repeat the spanking *once,* or use a more effective disciplinary technique immediately.

8. Plan a love experience after the spanking. If your child is young, take him in your lap and rock him. If he's older, go to him in five or ten minutes. If he is not yet ready to talk, return in another five minutes. Talk about pleasant things. Offering your time and tenderness after such an experience will convince him of your love.

9. Consider your child's age. In order for this technique to be effective your child must be old enough to realize that this isn't your usual method of disciplining. He must be able to reason from cause to effect to see the justice of this type of discipline. An older child's self-worth can be shattered by a spanking. It can be a demeaning experience. Therefore, I would caution you to avoid spanking before your child is two and after he is eight or nine.

10. Finally, the rapport you have with your child will determine whether or not you can safely use spanking as a method of shock therapy. Diana Baumrind, a psychologist, has found that spanking produces passivity, timidity, and fearful conformity when it is used automatically by repressive restrictive parents. But when parents are warm, responsive, and flexible, and have a good rapport with their

children, an occasional spanking as fair discipline is linked to self-reliant, independent, and confident behavior in children.*

Positive techniques of shock therapy can also be quite effective. Surprise your child. When he expects you to be angry, smile and willingly forgive. When he expects a spanking, take him in your lap and cuddle him instead. When he expects you to send him to his room in sackcloth and ashes, ask him if he could use your help in picking up the mess he made. You'll be pleasantly surprised by the effect of such unexpected parental behavior.

### Common Mistakes of Parents

All parents make mistakes. But the number of mistakes you make is *not* important; the fact that you are making them less and less often *is*. The following list of common parental mistakes offers some guidelines to help you err less frequently.

1. *Living too close to the problem to view it objectively*. One day a frustrated mother lamented to her child's teacher, "I have no idea what I am going to do with my boy. I can't cope with his behavior. He is constantly on my nerves and in my hair and under foot. He is always doing things that annoy me."

"Well," replied the teacher, "have you ever thought of getting him a bicycle?"

"A bicycle!" the parent exclaimed. "Now, how is that going to change his behavior?"

"Well, it may not change his behavior," replied the teacher, "but it would spread it over a wider area."

Sometimes, problems are magnified because we view them at such close range. We tend to notice our children's misbehavior and forget how many good things they do. Gain a new perspective by stepping away from the situation occa-

* Reported in *Today's Child* (November 1978).

sionally. Talk to other parents with children of similar ages. Learn to view your child from the perspective of others. Don't err by being overly critical, nor should you err by viewing your child's problems through rose-colored glasses. Don't hesitate to ask another person's advice, especially if that person has dealt with your child. He or she may have some insights that will help you understand your child better. In this way you will be more objective. Remember, a child's behavior is not nearly so irritating if it is spread over a wider area and viewed from a healthy perspective!

2. *Being too restrictive or too permissive.* Parents who feel insecure about their children's behavior tend to restrict that behavior to such an extent that the child has little room to think creatively and misbehave. When a child's behavior is severely restricted, he cannot learn to make decisions and experience the consequences of those decisions. Overly restricted children are followers; they are overly compliant, shy, and hesitant to reach out to others. These children can surprise parents by suddenly going to the opposite extreme during the teenage years and rebelling against parental values and standards.

When you trust your child to do his best, and give him the opportunity to make the decisions that he is capable of making, you can avoid being overly restrictive.

The opposite extreme, being too permissive, is equally detrimental to a child's development. If you allow your child to do whatever he pleases, you are heading for conflict throughout the child-rearing years. Overpermissiveness may seem like a good way to avoid conflict, but without parental guidance, children tend to pack together and run wild until their aggressive, noncompliant behavior gets them into trouble.

Children need limitations to make them feel secure. They need to feel that their parents are strong and able to protect them. They need the security of knowing that their parents will help them when they need help. Without this feeling of security, children tend to act upon their environment impulsively. They often strike out first to get the upper hand, and attempt to control as many situations as possible. They feel that control will reduce the number of surprises in their lives and make their world less threatening.

If you are not sure how to handle a situation, it is best to shun these extremes. You should not throw up your hands and abandon your decision-making responsibility. Nor should you slip to the other extreme and attempt to control every movement your child makes. Avoid the overly restrictive and the overly permissive parenting styles.

3. *Expecting misbehavior.* When asked the question, "How is your child's behavior?" one father quipped, "I don't know. He has never behaved!"

Children tend to fulfill the expectations of others. If you expect them to be bad, they will usually reward you with this very behavior. In fact, they may even outdo your expectations. On the other hand, if they know that you trust them to make good decisions (unless they are rebelling against you in some way), they will usually do everything in their power to fulfill those expectations.

Schoolchildren often get pegged as the bully, the clown, or the shy one, and it is very difficult for them to change their image. Report cards follow children for years, documenting their successes as well as their failures. In addition, each teacher records his perception of a child's behavior and personality. If these grades and perceptions are negative, and are read by the teacher who inherits that child the following year, the new teacher's perception of this child is colored by these comments. And the child will again be compelled to live out these expectations.

Dr. Robert Rosenthal, an educational psychologist, has done a number of studies concerning this phenomenon—the self-fulfilling prophecy, as he calls it. In a classic study, all of the children in a school were tested with a standard intelligence test. The researchers told the teachers that the test was a special test that would predict those children who could be expected to make tremendous intellectual advances during the school year. Then the researchers randomly selected a number of children from each class, without any reference whatsoever to the test results, and told the teachers that these children would be intellectual bloomers. At the end of the year all the children were retested. The results were impressive. Those randomly selected "intellectual bloomers" had indeed made tremendous progress during the school year, more so on the average than other children. The younger the children, the more impact these expectations had on their performance.* If this is evident in school, you can be sure that this same self-fulfilling prophecy operates at home.

Children should not be reminded of their past errors and failures. Shred the record and begin today to see them in the best possible light. Honestly communicate the high, yet realistic, expectations that you have for them. See their infinite possibilities—what they can become with your encouragement and support. The sooner you begin to expect them to do their best, the sooner they will be able to begin rewarding your expectations.

4. *Being too busy to discipline.* It takes time to lay the proper groundwork for effective discipline. The first time a child misbehaves, he must be corrected and taught a more acceptable mode of behavior. If he does it again, he must be corrected again. Surprisingly, however, parents are often too busy to follow through on their instructions to a child. Your arms may be elbow deep in the dishwater; you may be talking on the phone to a business associate; you may be entertaining the boss and his wife. Too often, parents allow the dishes, a caller, or a guest to absorb their full attention, so they ignore misbehavior and neglect to discipline their

---

* Robert Rosenthal and Lenore Jacobson, *Pygmalion in the Classroom: Teacher Expectation and Pupil's Intellectual Development* (N.Y.: Holt, Rinehart and Winston, 1968).

children at the teachable moment. Disciplining a child after the company has departed is not as effective as immediate disciplinary action. Imagine the impact on your child if you excuse yourself from your company for a few minutes to talk privately with your child about the inappropriateness of his behavior. Your child will never forget that Mom and Dad *will leave whatever they are doing in order to teach their children appropriate behavior,* even though they may be *very* busy at that time.

A busy doctor that I know once left a waiting room full of patients to drive the thirty miles home to discipline his teenage son, who had been unusually disrespectful to his mother. What an impression that made on the boy about his parent's care and concern for him! A child feels very important in his parent's eyes when that parent takes time away from whatever seems important at the moment in order to discipline the child.

5. *Not trusting the child's capability for self-discipline.* I learned a valuable lesson about a child's capability for self-discipline one day when I was driving home from work with my three-and-a-half-year-old daughter in the back seat of the car. We had just begun our trip of approximately eight miles when Kim discovered a box of cookies in the grocery bag beside her.

"Mommy, may I have a cookie?" she asked in a pleading voice.

"Kim, it's only four in the afternoon and it's not good to eat between meals."

"Mommy, I'm hungry. . . . *I'm starved.* Mommy, I need a cookie."

"I'm sorry, Kim. Not now. You may have one after supper," I said.

"But Mommy, p-l-e-a-s-e can't I have a cookie now?"

"No, you may not," I replied a little more firmly.

"But why not?"

I began to realize that I would never make it home with

Kim's self-esteem and the bag of cookies still intact, if I didn't change my strategy. "Kim," I spoke authoritatively, "a mommy is not supposed to let any bad things happen to her child. One of the things that is bad for you is to eat between meals. So, I told you not to eat a cookie because I love you and want only good things for you. But I really think that you are old enough to make good decisions. You know how I feel about eating between meals. Now, I will let you decide what you think is good for you."

I knew the box of cookies would be devoured before we got home. But I had taken a position. I continued driving and I didn't hear another word from the back seat. As we drove into the driveway, I couldn't believe it. There was the box of cookies, untouched. She had made the decision and, at three-and-a-half, she had the self-control to follow through on her decision.

That experience convinced me that children can make their own wise decisions, even at a very early age, if parents set the stage properly. They can then use their will-power to stick to their own decisions, rather than using that energy to fight Mom's and Dad's decisions.

How can you set the stage properly? If I had just told Kim, "Okay, Kim, I don't care. Go ahead and eat a cookie," you can be sure that the box would have been empty eight miles later. Instead, I told her what I thought was best. Then I gave her the information that she needed to know in order to make a good decision.

If you have established a good rapport with your child during the early years, and have taught him that you are a wise decision-maker, then you can trust him to make more and more of his own decisions as he grows older and more independent. The type of decisions you allow a child to make depends on your child's maturity—his ability to *seek* information, *evaluate* alternatives, and *accept* the responsibility for his decision. (Remember the acronym SEA.) Although you would not allow a two-year-old to choose what he wanted to eat without limitations, you can allow him to choose between a peanut butter or cheese sandwich. When a child is allowed to make as many decisions as he can under the watchful and instructive eyes of his parents, he will gain invaluable experience in the methodology (SEA) of good decision-making.

The following chart illustrates the relationship between parental responses and the degree of trust a parent places in a child's ability to be self-disciplined.

Parents should not tell a child, year after year, that he will be able to make his own decisions when he is older, and then wait passively for that future time. Children cannot learn and prepare for that "unknown" time unless proper training occurs along the way. Since there is no clear emancipation time in most modern families, children need to know *when* they can make their own decisions. If parents do not plan for a child's eventual independence, a teenager may become impatient—and rebellious—when his parents continue to make decisions that he feels he could and should make.

Charlie Shedd had a fantastic idea when he gave his son Peter these three goals for his independence:

"Goal 1: By your senior year in high school you will be making all your own rules.

"Goal 2: By your junior year in high school we want you to totally manage yourself financially.

"Goal 3: By driver's license age we want you in your own car."*

You may not agree with these goals, but that is beside the point. The important thing is that Peter knew when he would be given the responsibility for making his own decisions, *and* his parents knew exactly how long they had to prepare Peter for this responsibility.

Individuals who know they are trusted are able to exert

* Charlie Shedd, *Promises to Peter* (Waco, Texas: Word Books, 1970), pp. 22–25.

**No trust**

Parent decision

↓

Appeal to the
child to make the
decision to let the
parent decide.

↓

Give the child all
the information
necessary to make
a good decision.
Then trust him to
make the deci-
sion.

↓

Child decision
**Complete trust**

1. *I will make this decision for you* because you don't have all the information; because you are not capable of weighing the alternatives; and because you are too young to accept the full responsibility for the decision, especially if the decision is a poor one.

2. *Trust me to make this decision for you.* Look at my record. In similar situations in the past you were happy with the decisions that I made for you, so trust me now.

3. *I will make sure you have all the information you need to make this decision.* I feel that _____ would be the best decision. My reasons are a) _____, b) _____, and c) _____. I know that you are able to understand all of the issues involved and that you are aware of the consequences. Furthermore, I believe that you are capable of accepting the responsibility for your decision. Therefore, I will allow you to make this choice.

4. *You may choose what you think is best.*

a great deal of self-control and willpower. In college, I had a dormitory dean who trusted each one of her girls implicitly. Even though I had many opportunities to break dormitory rules, or sneak in late, I never did because I did not want to lose that trust.

A good psychologist friend once told me, "I had plenty of opportunity to take advantage of ready and willing girl friends, but I would not. The reason was not because of my own willpower. It was because I knew my mom and dad trusted me to live an honorable life. Even though they no longer had direct control over what I did, their trust influenced my ability to discipline myself."

Of course, parents should not blindly trust in a child's ability to discipline himself. However, if parents have laid the necessary foundation and taught their child to make good decisions, they will be able to trust both their child and his decisions. This means that parents must provide their child with a wide variety of opportunities to practice decision-making and to prove himself. Good decision-makers are not impulsive decision-makers. Good decision-makers have been taught how to be good decision-makers. This is what discipline for self-discipline is all about.

# 8

## Solving Job and Family Conflicts

I love working and I love parenting. I feel I have the best of both worlds and I want to enjoy them both to the fullest. But this is not always easy—or possible. The demands of one do not always dovetail with the other. But the dual roles can be compatible and satisfying when you learn the secret to success: you must become indispensable to the job and dispensable to the family. Consider the following illustrations.

Crystal was a skilled secretary—no doubt about that, as she typed letter-perfect memos at 140 words per minute. But she worked mechanically. It was her job—nothing more. She did only what was necessary. When work was slow she pulled out her needlepoint. When work piled up and a crisis demanded overtime, she politely excused herself. "My job description says my hours are from eight to five," she told her boss. She was frequently late because of babysitting problems. When her child became ill, pediatrician appointments interfered with office hours. Crystal made no attempt to make up this time. When a mother-daughter day was planned at her daughter's school, Crystal asked her boss for time off. Her boss, a kind, understanding person, was clearly not happy about the request. He suggested that she look for another job that would allow her a more flexible work schedule.

Lenore was not as good a typist, but from her first hour on the job, her boss was aware of her enthusiasm for her work and her dedication. Lenore was a working mother with preschool and school-age children. Her family/job conflicts exceeded Crystal's. But when it came to the job, she was 100 percent there, ready and willing to go the extra mile. When the volume of work piled up, she came in early and worked late. And her dedication paid off. She was liked, she was needed, and she was considered an indispensable employee. Once her track record was established —and it didn't take long—Lenore did not hesitate to ask for small benefits. "I'd like to take the afternoon off. My son's class has a field trip and he wants me to go along. The statements have been mailed and your latest tape has been transcribed. I'll be happy to come in early tomorrow morning if anything comes up that needs immediate attention."

"Sure, take the afternoon off," her boss replied, "And don't worry about coming in early. You deserve a break."

Why did Crystal's boss and Lenore's boss respond as they did? What made the difference? It was the indispensability. Lenore had become indispensable on the job. Her boss viewed her as a valuable asset to the business; one he did not want to lose. It was to his advantage and to the company's advantage to make the job as attractive as possible in order to keep employees like Lenore. When an employer has a valuable employee, he is often willing to help that employee reduce family/job conflicts. Employers are aware that most working mothers will favor the family when conflicts arise. Indeed, if conflicts cannot be resolved, many working mothers will either quit or opt for a less challenging job in order to meet their families' needs. But if an employee can prove that she or he is indispensable to the job, most employers are willing to make concessions to keep the employee happy and satisfied.

However, this is only one half of the secret. The second half is to become dispensable to the family. If a working mother feels that her family cannot survive without her, she will always be torn between her home duties and her job responsibilities when conflicts arise. Let's see how Crystal and Lenore handled this part of their lives.

Although Crystal worked, she wasn't able to shake the age-old idea that a woman's place is at home, caring for her children full-time. This drove her to overcompensate for the hours spent at her job by taking on many more home responsibilities than her husband, and doing things for her children that they should have learned to do for themselves. She believed that a good mother should be able to care for her children without calling on her husband, friends, or relatives for help. When doctors' appointments had to be made or when her babysitter was ill, she felt that it was her responsibility to take the day off to care for her children. Consequently, her children and her husband grew increasingly dependent on her, and this reinforced her belief that the whole family would fall apart if she weren't around. Her family also began to feel that she was shirking her responsibility if she wasn't home on time.

Lenore, on the other hand, viewed her relationship with her husband as a co-partnership. She had encouraged him to care for the children since birth, and she did not hesitate to call on friends and neighbors to help out in a pinch. So when she went to work she had confidence in a number of adults who could step in and care for the children when her job demanded extra time and effort. She was also willing to give this same support to her friends when she was available. Her children and husband valued her work, and they never felt deprived, because she was always with them for the really important times. She also encouraged her children to take over home responsibilities. She taught them to prepare simple foods, to wash and dry their clothes, to mend and sew on buttons. She prepared her family for her absence, and in this way she became dispensable to her family when her job demanded it.

### Becoming Indispensable to the Job

Although very few of us are ever completely indispensable, it is certainly possible to become so valuable to your employer that he or she will be willing to make small concessions when necessary. How can you accomplish this? Obviously, ability is a number-one prerequisite, but it's not everything. You may lose your job to a less capable person because you lack four essential qualities that require no special training—only the right mental attitude. These qualities are: responsibility; enthusiasm; loyalty; and cooperation. If you can bring these qualities to your work, you can become an extremely valuable employee. Just follow these guidelines.

1. Follow directions. Do what you are asked to do, but use common sense. If you see a more efficient way of handling some task, don't hesitate to discuss your idea with your boss.

2. Remember what you are told to do. If you are given a number of instructions at one time, write them down immediately. If you interrupt your boss later with a constant stream of questions, he'll find it easier to do the work himself or hire someone else.

3. Clarify the importance of various tasks and finish them in order of priority. If you can't meet a deadline, give your boss enough notice so he can devise a substitute plan. Don't wait until the last minute.

4. Keep your employer or supervisor apprised of your progress and accomplishments. Unless you are closely supervised, your boss may not be aware of your achievements,

especially if they are the less than tangible kind. At first, this might seem like bragging, but if it is done with a proper attitude, it won't be interpreted that way. Jill Frazier, a professor at a large university, learned this lesson the hard way. She met her class assignments and kept her office hours, but other than that, she came and went as she pleased. She was dedicated to her job, and her students felt that she was a real friend and counselor. Jill spent all her extra time preparing teaching aids and devising programmed learning materials that she hoped to publish. She balked at accepting committee assignments or joining departmental social activities because it took precious time away from her major interests—teaching and counseling. Her departmental chairman was too busy with his own research to observe her teaching skills or materials, or inquire about her effectiveness with students. He only noticed the obvious—she did not attend departmental functions and she was not in the office eight hours a day! Jill's promotion request was denied, primarily because her departmental chairman was unable to justify it. When Jill realized the problem, she made an appointment with her chairman to show him the programmed learning materials she had been preparing and to explain her heavy involvement with the students. As a result she received her promotion, and was officially appointed as the student adviser for the department. Since then, Jill has kept a written record of her activities, and periodically advises her chairman of her accomplishments. In turn, he is more supportive of her efforts.

5. Plan for emergencies. Realistically, emergencies will crop up from time to time. Prepare for these occasions in advance, and devise a back-up plan that can be put into operation when you need time off. It's much easier to ask for time off when you can assure your boss that the work will be completed. Take work home if necessary, put in

some extra time the next day, or ask another employee to help you out, and return the favor when he or she needs it. If you plan ahead, you won't feel guilty and your boss will appreciate your dependability.

6. Maintain an enthusiastic attitude. Put your heart, as well as your mind, into your work. A spirit of enthusiasm stimulates others to give their all to a job, and creates a pleasant office atmosphere. No one likes to work with an individual who complains. When you're given an unpleasant task, do it as quickly and cheerfully as possible. Don't bring your personal problems to your job.

7. Be cooperative and willing to work with others to accomplish a task. Listen to other people's points of view, and compromise when necessary. Stubborn, willful, and egocentric people do not make pleasant co-workers. If you're willing to work with others cheerfully, your boss will be appreciative.

8. Give your company or employer the same loyalty you give your family. If you discuss company "secrets," gossip about your boss or other employees behind their back, or take advantage of company policies, you're not likely to keep your job.

### Becoming Dispensable to the Family

Becoming dispensable to your family does not mean that you are no longer important to them. It simply means that your family can survive without disruption and pain when your job becomes particularly demanding. This is possible if you follow these guidelines.

1. Make sure your family knows that they are more important than your job. When children feel that something else holds first place in your life they will constantly strive for that valued position. They will test your love, argue, fight, complain, and resent whatever fills that number-one

place. To alleviate these feelings, you must convince your children of their prime importance. This is only possible if you follow the second guideline.

2. Be with your family when it really counts. Every family has special times when togetherness is particularly important—mealtimes, worship times, after-school times, bedtime, birthdays, holidays, special school activities, performance times, and so on. Select the priority times for your family and BE THERE! It might entail some inconvenience—coming home for supper, for example, and then returning to work—but this will convince your family that they do indeed come first.

3. Include your family in your job. When family members feel excluded from a major and important part of your life, they tend to resent it. Be willing to share. Even if aspects of your job are confidential, you can still share the tensions and deadlines with your family. You can still say, "I'm facing an important deadline right now. I need your encouragement and support for the next three days and then we'll celebrate."

If possible, let your children help with small projects at work. For example, alphabetizing files, folding letters, or stapling papers. When I'm facing a deadline on the preparation of a manuscript, my children enjoy pushing the button on the copy machine and collating the pages. At other times, they can help by being good—and quiet—so I can concentrate. When they know that they are helping me with a project, they feel involved, and they also feel a sense of pride in having contributed in some small way.

4. Be willing to share child-care and home responsibilities. Contrary to a widely held notion, the best mothers aren't necessarily those who handle all the child-care and home responsibilities alone. Quality and diversity can be compatible. This is certainly true when a father is encouraged to share these responsibilities. Relatives and

friends can also make an important contribution.

5. Teach your children self-sufficiency. If you teach your children to handle various chores on their own, you'll be able to spend your free time with your children in enjoyable ways, rather than tying up that time in a constant round of necessary and routine activities. If your children can prepare simple meals, you won't feel guilty if the boss asks you to come in early or work overtime. You can feel confident that they can pack their own lunches, get themselves off to school on time, or prepare supper for the family.

6. Don't expect perfection from others. Many working parents who try to share child-care and home responsibilities with others expect perfection. This creates dissatisfaction for the parents, and discouragement and frustration on the part of those who are trying to help. Working mothers, especially, must guard against this tendency, and accept and appreciate whatever help they receive from others. When Junior washes a tub of clothing, don't criticize the amount of soap he used. Just say thanks, and casually mention that a half cup will suffice the next time. When your daughter fixes supper and burns the beans, tell her you appreciate her hard work, and explain how easy it is for food to stick to the bottom of the pan and burn if it isn't stirred. Don't kill their willingness by expecting perfection. Instead, encourage them to learn from their mistakes. It's the effort and the motives that count. With practice, their products and skills will improve.

### Finding the Right Job for Your Family's Stage of Life

Parents of infants, toddlers, and preschoolers often face particularly difficult family/job conflicts. Although older children still require parental time and attention, they are much more self-sufficient, and other people can fill many of their needs. But there is no magic solution that will turn dependent infants into less dependent schoolchildren. Therefore, becoming indispensable to your job and dispensable to your family may only be possible to a limited extent, depending on the job and the ages of your children. To minimize conflicts, you must focus on the changes that can be made in your work situation.

Consider these questions: Is your job the right one for this stage of your family life? Is it flexible? Is it demanding? How much overtime is required? Are the hours regular? Can your children visit your office occasionally? Is your job taxing and tension producing? Is it fulfilling? Can you make changes within your job or change jobs?

Martha, a pastor's wife who attended one of my seminars, had just moved into the area and had to choose one of three possible nursing jobs. Each job held different advantages. "If I didn't have school-age children, I'd take the teaching appointment at the junior college," she told me. "But it requires teaching night classes, and I just can't depend upon my husband to be home. Private nursing pays the best—but the hours aren't regular or dependable. So I've decided on the seven A.M. to three P.M. hospital nursing job. My husband can easily get the kids off to school, and I'll be there when they get home. It's ideal for me now while my children are young."

"I bet you're glad you took nursing," I commented. "It seems to allow you a considerable amount of flexibility."

"Well, the interesting thing is, I didn't take nursing at first. I was an elementary education major and taught for five years before we had children. I loved it. In fact, it's still my first love."

"Then why did you change?" I asked, confused over this apparent contradiction.

"It wasn't easy to change. I had three preschool children when I decided to go back and take nursing. I knew

I needed to work to supplement the family income, and teaching took up too much of my time: seven hours at school and the constant preparation at home. I could never take my mind off my teaching responsibilities. In addition, the job was too similar to my role as a parent—nurturing, caring for, and teaching children. It was too much for me. I needed to do something different at work so I could return to my children with enthusiasm and energy. I enjoy my nursing work, but someday when the children are grown, I wouldn't be surprised if I went back into teaching."

Similar conversations with parents across the country indicate that many parents avoid family/job conflicts by seeking a job that fits their stage of family life. Since this period is a relatively short one, they can return to more demanding jobs as soon as their children are old enough to be more self-sufficient.

As you seek the type of work that will minimize job/ family conflicts, follow these steps.

Step 1: *Set your priorities.* What do you really want from a job—high wages, flexible hours, job security and satisfaction, an understanding and supportive boss, or a convenient location?

Consider the items on the following chart, and rank them in their order of importance to you. Top-priority items receive a #1; second-priority items receive a #2; unimportant items receive a #3.

## Pay

_____ High wages.
_____ Salaried position, rather than being paid by the hour.
_____ Production incentives (commissioned work, paid by the rate of production).
_____ Good benefits (sick leave, paid vacations, retirement).
_____ Other: List _____

## Hours

_____ Regular hours.
_____ Flexible hours.
_____ Part-time possibilities.
_____ Seasonal work that allows summers and vacations to be spent with the children (i.e., nine-month appointment instead of twelve).
_____ Other: List _____

## Job security

_____ Tenure possibilities.
_____ Low possibility of being laid off.
_____ Job availability (always needed, regardless of economic conditions or future automated and computerized advances.
_____ Ease of drop-out and reentry (if necessary).
_____ Other: List _____

## Job satisfaction

_____ Challenging work.
_____ Creative possibilities.
_____ Job advancement possibilities.
_____ Maximum decision-making (freedom to be your own boss).
_____ Other: List _____

## Location

_____ Close to home.
_____ Close to the day-care facility or school.
_____ Other: List _____

## Type of work

_____ Clerical (receptionist, typist, file clerk, etc.).
_____ Service-type (social work, beauty shop, restaurant worker, newspaper reporter, police or security work, etc.).
_____ Teaching.
_____ Manager or administrator.

_____ Professional and technical (nursing, occupational thera-
pist, computer programmer, artist, musician, etc.).
_____ Salesperson (sales clerk, home product salesman, etc.).
_____ Other: List _____

## Miscellaneous

_____ Minimum travel during the job.
_____ Possibility to work at home.
_____ Low mental or physical fatigue.
_____ Requires *no* additional training or education.
_____ Makes maximum use of previous education and training.
_____ Prefer to work with people.
_____ Prefer to work alone.
_____ Other: List _____

Next, list all your number one priorities on one sheet and rank them in the order of their importance. Use this list as a guide when you begin searching for a job or making changes in your current job.

For long-term job satisfaction, try to imagine what your priorities might be in five or ten years and add those items to your list. An ideal job should meet your current needs, and offer the potential of meeting your future needs. But finding such a job is not easy. You may have to compromise on some of your future requirements and take a job that best fits your immediate priorities if you are interested in minimizing family/job conflict.

Step 2: *Check careers that seem to mesh with your stage of life.* Seek advice from career counselors or from the personnel departments of large organizations that offer a wide variety of job opportunities. Talk to people whose jobs or careers seem to present the least conflict. Consider the possibility of further education or training. For example, skilled typists often contract for work they can do at home, such as typing grant proposals, reports, or invoices. Because of my advanced professional degree, I can teach on a flexible university schedule, rather than being tied down to classroom teaching in a day-care center or an elementary school.

Step 3: *Pace your career.* Women who have established themselves in a job or career before their children were born often face fewer frustrations when they return to work. But for many women, this is impossible. Don't fall into the trap of feeling sorry for yourself, or feeling cheated because your children arrived before you had a chance to begin the career of your choice. Be realistic. You may have to give up some of your hopes for job recognition and advancement for the first few years. Be patient and plan ahead for the time when your children will not need you as much as they do now.

If you decide to quit your job for a while or work part-time while your children are small, establish and maintain contacts with other people working in your chosen field. Keep abreast of changes, innovations, and problems. If you gave up teaching temporarily, only to discover that teaching jobs have become scarce, use your time at home to prepare for another job. Use this time creatively. Even if you're not working, you don't have to spend all your time with your children. Go back to school part-time, take some night courses, read books and professional journals, learn a new skill at home, write an article. Prepare yourself for your eventual return to work. Because our society still expects women to assume primary responsibility for child rearing, many employers will not question a resume with several blank or low-achievement years. And as roles become more flexible, this attitude may be extended to fathers as well.

The following stories illustrate how some parents have solved family/job conflicts by fitting their jobs to their family's stage of life.

Jeanette Peterson was a very popular junior high school teacher, but she accepted a job as the educational director for a local church. The job allowed her to plan and prepare curricular materials at home while she cared for her one-year-old. On weekends, she taught in the church program while her husband cared for their baby.

Bill Owens loved trucking, but he sold his big rig to buy into a local business so he could spend more time with his two preschool boys.

After medical school and an internship, Janice Kline decided to work only two afternoons a week in a family planning clinic until her children were in school. During the next three years, her husband, also a physician, cut down considerably on his practice in order to take over primary family responsibilities while Janice finished a hectic obstetric-gynecology residency. Now, as the children approach high school and college, both Janice and her husband are doing exactly what they want to be doing in their careers.

Marilyn Cramer, a librarian, quit her job when her two girls were small. At first she devoted her talents to developing the church library. Now that both girls are in school, she has become the school librarian. Her girls enjoy going to school with Mommy, and they proudly announce, "That's my mommy," every time they pass the library door.

Kathy Lyn, a teacher, converted her garage into a very lucrative home nursery school for her own children and others. Now that her children have graduated from nursery school she has sold the preschool equipment, turned the room into a game room, and returned to her teaching position.

Bill Turner sold his law practice, which required many hours away from home, and took an eight-to-five corporate job. He is helping his children build an addition to their house on evenings and weekends.

James Dobson, a well-known child psychologist and lecturer, put his most popular lectures to parents on film. Now, he can continue his work and spend more time with his own children at home.

Connie Blue loved her position as a receptionist in a dental office, but she is now selling Tupperware and Avon products. This allows her maximum flexibility in dovetailing her working hours with her husband's.

Lisa Miller enjoyed her position as chef for a large restaurant. But she took a year's leave-of-absence to care for her new baby and write the cookbook she had always wanted to write.

Mary Brown was a French major who had difficulty finding a job in the field. When her children were young, Mary volunteered for various types of hospital work, trying to decide what she would eventually like to do. When her youngest child began nursery school, she was ready to go back and take the chaplin's program.

Betty Taylor was a literary agent who worked overtime for five years, making as many sales as possible. She was planning ahead. When her first child was born, she had enough money to go into "semiretirement" for a few years.

Charlene Casper was in the fast changing field of electronics. She quit when her first child was three years old and she was expecting a second. To remain active in the field, she took small consulting jobs, read technical journals, and dabbled on the side with her own research project.

Stephanie Jones, an assembly-line worker, asked her supervisor if she could work at home on piecemeal work. She took a year's leave-of-absence from the company. Although she lost company benefits, she maintains a profitable relationship with the company and has gained valuable time for her children.

Whatever your position, if you feel overwhelmed by family/job conflicts, you can minimize these conflicts with planning and determination. Parents are making changes. Parents are accepting temporary setbacks in their career aspirations. Parents are pacing their careers to benefit their families. Don't be afraid to voice your priorities to your employer. Think creatively about the changes you could make in your current job. Carefully explain that these are temporary, a result of your current stage of family life. You may be surprised by the respect you will gain when you take such a stand.

Family/job conflicts are usually minimized when a job is highly satisfying; when its schedule matches your own; when it is close to home, child-care facilities, or school; and when the administrators or supervisors understand your family obligation. Finding such a job may not be easy, but it is worth the effort.

### The Importance of a Supportive Family

Your success in minimizing family/job conflicts will be determined in part by the support you receive from your family. The negative attitude of relatives, especially your parents, can undermine your effectiveness. Family members tend to blame all problems on the fact that you are working, and this attitude only increases guilt and makes it more difficult to find an acceptable solution. *Spouse support is crucial.* Major problems can develop if a husband does not appreciate his wife's need to get out of the house or if he expects his wife to assume full responsibility for the children and the house while working full-time.

Every working parent needs help occasionally. When your husband or wife responds to a desperate phone call with a cheerful, "Sure, I'll be glad to pick up the children, stop at the grocery store, and fix supper," conflicts won't develop. But what can you do when you don't have this type of support system? The answer is to develop it.

Many parents find it difficult to communicate their need for spouse support. The following list highlights some common causes of misunderstandings.

1. The wife feels that her husband disapproves of her job.

2. The husband (wife) feels that he (she) is fulfilling his (her) fair share; the wife (husband) does not agree.

3. The husband (wife) thinks things are fine because the wife (husband) has never openly discussed her (his) feelings.

4. One spouse feels that the other is taking advantage of him/her.

5. The husband (wife) feels that the wife (husband) is so absorbed in the job that he (she) and the children are being neglected.

All of these problems can be solved by effective communication and compromise. The first step is to establish some ground rules for communication. Study the following rules with your spouse and start using them today.

Rule 1: Agree to talk. Silence is a subtle method of manipulation that can cause bitterness and increase conflict.

Rule 2: Agree not to get angry. Anger only clouds the issues and creates resentment. Words spoken in anger often become weapons. Conflict cannot be resolved when either spouse is angry.

Rule 3: Listen to your spouse's position respectfully. Don't make snap judgments or hasty statements of self-justification such as, "You're being overly sensitive," or "I can't help it if my boss called me in at the last minute." These statements cut off communication prematurely before the issue is clearly understood.

Rule 4: Clarify your spouse's position. "Are you saying that you feel I care more about the job than the family?"

Rule 5: Be honest and specific. If you resent your wife's constant references to her boss, tell her. Issues can only be solved when they are out in the open. Don't allow resentments to grow out of proportion and affect family relationships.

Rule 6: Be willing to compromise. Never say, "It's impossible!" Brainstorm for possible solutions, then go back and evaluate each one. List its pros and cons. Don't discard a possibility until you both agree that it's impractical. Don't argue about these ideas! Accept a wise, practical solution whether or not you proposed that option. Don't keep score of who wins. Consider the final solution as a joint solution.

Rule 7: When you reach an agreement, set up a specific timetable for its implementation.

Rule 8: Evaluate your solution on a weekly basis. Don't be afraid to discard it if it's not working. Go back to the bargaining table and find another compromise.

Encourage your spouse to be supportive through praise and appreciation rather than criticism. People are much more likely to repeat behavior patterns that win them praise and appreciation. This behavior modification technique works for grown-ups as well as children! But your praise must be sincere; don't use praise to manipulate or change your spouse, or to get what you want.

Criticism often hardens a person's determination to maintain the status quo. If something bothers you, wait until you and your spouse have the time for a quiet talk, and then follow the ground rules for effective communication. Don't lash out impulsively; it's too easy to lose your cool.

Don't allow your job to interfere with your family time. Leave your job worries at your place of employment. If you are preoccupied with business dealings and worries when you're with your family, you might as well be at work. In fact, children feel most rejected when a parent is physically available, but psychologically absent. Avoid this family/job conflict. Devote your time at home to the family. Bring work home only when it is absolutely necessary. When your job cuts into time that your family formerly enjoyed together, resentments will surface. When you're too tired to play with your children or go out for an evening with your spouse, your job is interfering with your family.

Share benefits with your family. Let them see that your interest and enthusiasm for your job spills over into your life at home. List all the benefits that your job contributes to the family, and start a subtle public relations-promotion campaign to make sure that your family realizes these benefits too.

It is impossible to avoid all family/job conflicts, but they can be minimized by facing problems squarely and working on solutions. Be creative and flexible, and don't be ashamed to ask for help. Develop as many support systems as possible. You *can* work and be a good parent.

# 9

## Shortcuts to Prime-Time Parenting

I must get this chapter written. Writing, who's got time for writing? It's final exam time. Students need help! Papers to grade. Why did they have to have an administrative shift right now—new department—new courses—and bulletin copy due yesterday—or not later than 5 P.M. today. Must fly to San Jose tomorrow for three days of taping. Poor timing. Only seventeen days till Christmas. Christmas letters to send out. Shopping; should take advantage of the 10 percent sale at the market—keep forgetting the coupon! Kids' Christmas program tonight. Kevin's got the croup. Should we risk taking him? Girls will be disappointed if Jan doesn't go too. Kim is Mary in the shadow play—may never happen again. We'll all go! Must get chapter off to editor and order a cake for Kim's birthday. The office party is Saturday night—got to get supplies. Who's taking care of the kids? Faculty retreat this weekend. Must get Kari to music lesson. Ought to fix food for the family while I'm away . . . ought to. Must clean off the desk and surprise Jan. I received a letter the other day, a working mom with two, and a third on the way. "Dear Dr. Kuzma, I know you are a working mother. You have a full-time job and three children, and even find time to write! How do you do it? I need every suggestion I can get."

Every working parent I know is searching for shortcuts. Parents, whether they are working or not, are busy because children have a way of generating a lot of extra housework. In fact, it has been estimated that by the time children are eighteen, a mother of three will probably spend more than 18,000 hours doing child-generated housework. Add a heavy working schedule to these hours and it is easy to see the time-problem that working parents face. Since prime-time parents want to spend as much time as possible with their children, shortcutting household duties is essential. Furthermore, when you are burdened down with too many responsibilities, you don't have the time to do the things that matter most in your life. And when you are constantly behind in your chores, your family interactions are less satisfying. The solution is to structure your home and your life to make time for everything that you really want to do. To make this a reality, follow these four principles:

1. Carefully organize and budget the time you have.

2. Learn to delegate; seek other people's help—including your children's—whenever possible.

3. Cut out all unnecessary activities. Ask yourself the question, "What difference will it make if I don't do it?"

4. Become an efficiency expert. Find shortcuts for essential tasks.

Housework has a way of expanding to fill all your available time. To avoid this tendency, compress housework into your schedule and master it; don't let it get out of hand and master you.

Working parents who are most successful at shortcutting tasks are confident that they can control their environment; that they can become more efficient housekeepers. It is not easy to be organized, nor to organize your family into a cooperative team, but with the proper attitude you can do it. And if you do, you'll find life much more rewarding.

Your first task is to organize yourself and your home. Some important time-saving suggestions follow.

### Organize Yourself and Your Home

1. Write down everything that you have to do.
2. Sort these chores into time categories, such as,
   a. Things that must be done today.
   b. Things that must be done this week.
   c. Things to be done this month.
   d. Things that can wait for a more convenient time.

3. Subdivide daily and weekly lists by type of chore, such as telephone calls to be made, appointments, pickup and deliveries, housecleaning tasks, time with children, yard work and office work—writing letters, paying bills.

4. Select priorities. Start with the most urgent item that appears on the list of things that must be done today. Then go to the second and so on.

5. Update your list of things to do daily, by transferring these items to your appointment schedule. A number of chores can be sandwiched into your work schedule by using breaks or the lunch hour efficiently, if you keep your list with you.

6. Plan your week's activities at one time. Check these with your spouse and children. Plan menus, after-work appointments, after-school activities, birthdays, and so on.

7. Schedule routine weekly, monthly, and quarterly activities in advance.
   a. Once-a-week activities might include marketing, washing, mending, baking, or washing the car.
   b. Monthly activities might include writing a family newsletter, inviting guests for dinner, dusting

baseboards, wiping off fingerprints, or cleaning the oven.

   c. Quarterly activities might include cleaning under the beds, cleaning out closets, washing windows, shampooing carpets, or cleaning the garage.

  8. Schedule a quarterly family clean-up day in advance. Ask your family to contribute to a list of things that need to be done. Let them bid on the jobs that they want to perform. You may want to make the day more interesting by drawing lots for activities, working against time, or letting the children take turns supervising.

  9. Organize your day into habit patterns. A sample daily routine might include the following:

Mornings:
>Make beds and put away clothes.
>Make breakfast.
>Wash dishes.
>Take food out of the freezer for dinner.
>Empty garbage and trash.
>Straighten bathrooms.

Evenings:
>Spend first thirty minutes at home with the children.
>Set table.
>Prepare dinner.
>Wash dishes.
>Wipe off appliances and cabinets.
>Sweep kitchen floor.
>Make sack lunches for the next day.
>Set the table for breakfast.
>Help children with homework.
>Tackle one cleaning project.

Before bed:
>Straighten rooms.
>Put out clothes for tomorrow.

10. Take a break every hour on the hour no matter what you are doing. You will feel refreshed and more energetic.

11. Try the twenty minute plan. Allow yourself only twenty minutes to accomplish any given task. If necessary, break large tasks into smaller units. This is a good way to create a sense of accomplishment. Projects that might be done in twenty minutes include washing dishes, cleaning out a drawer, making beds, or cleaning the bathroom.

12. Have minute projects that you can sandwich in between other projects. For example, straighten books on the shelf; put a child in the bath and clean the basin or polish the mirror at the same time; wipe fingerprints off the doorway.

13. Take minute breaks. Stop what you are doing and lie down, do sit-ups, glance through an interesting article, jump rope, breathe deeply.

14. Don't forget to schedule activities that add to your own personal fulfillment. Don't tie yourself to a schedule that doesn't give you time for yourself and your children.

*Time-saving tips*

1. Organize tasks into the following categories: what the kids can do; what I can hire out; what I have to do. Then, concentrate on those tasks that only you can do.

2. Hire outside help if it's financially feasible. Tasks that can be handled by others include carpet cleaning, laundry, housecleaning, gardening, catering, and auto maintenance.

3. Make time-saving substitutions. For example:
   a. Cook from scratch only once a week, not every day.
   b. If you enjoy sewing as a hobby, take up crewel or some other form of stitchery that can be carried with you to fill empty pockets of time.

    c. Encourage company to drop in, so you don't have to worry about elaborate plans, invitations, and a clean house.

4. Use as many labor-saving appliances as you can afford, such as a washer and dryer, a microwave oven, a dishwasher, a blender, a pressure cooker, and a steam iron.

5. Eliminate unnecessary, time-consuming activities. For example:

    a. Give up drying dishes; doing dishes more than once a day; ironing sheets, towels, pajamas, or undergarments.

    b. Give up window shopping.

    c. Give up giant cleaning projects that don't fit into your working schedule. Break them down into manageable parts.

6. Stick to a specific job until finished—but don't take on more than you can handle in a short time. It is depressing to spend an entire day cleaning one closet and wake up to the leftover mess the next morning.

7. Double-up on activities. For example:

    a. Exercise by riding your bicycle to appointments.

    b. Keep stationery, a book, or other projects in your purse or briefcase for an unexpected spare moment.

    c. As you iron or wash dishes, listen to your child read or tell him a story.

    d. Listen to a cassette tape while you fix dinner.

    e. Clean the kitchen while you are on the phone.

8. Plan ahead. Decide what you will wear the night before; plan menus in advance; plan chores for the children.

9. Avoid getting caught in urban rush hours. Avoid shopping during the busiest times, such as the week before Christmas or the day before holidays.

10. Ban television. TV viewing reduces productivity significantly. Time yourself and you'll notice that you get

more done without TV, even if you listen as you work on other projects.

11. Set up a communications center in a central location. Include a telephone, a large bulletin board for messages, a monthly calendar suitable for recording appointments, a notebook, a shopping list, and a pencil.

12. If you are not easily available by phone during the day, use a telephone-answering service to keep track of your family. The children (especially teenagers) can call in and leave messages.

13. Write everything down. Buy a notebook that you can carry with you at all times and organize your notebook into the following sections: appointments, things to do today, long-term projects, shopping lists, addresses, notes, lists of presents to purchase, sizes of clothing for family members, and gift ideas.

14. Streamline communications and letter writing.
    a. Preaddress envelopes to family members or individuals whom you write to on a regular basis.
    b. Xerox monthly family letters and add a short personal note to each letter. If you dislike form letters, start a family letter that circulates among relatives on a regular basis. When it gets back to you, pull out your old letter, file it away for a diary of family happenings, write a new one, and send it on.
    c. Telephone rather than write whenever possible.
    d. Answer letters and memos by replying on the bottom of the page and returning the whole letter if you don't need a copy.
    e. Plan a regular monthly session to write all checks and pay all bills.

15. Organize your paperwork. Read your mail immediately and file it appropriately.
    a. Throw out what you don't want.
    b. Set up a file for important papers.

    c. Keep a special box or file for items that need further attention. Include all correspondence that must be answered.

    d. Set up a drawer or file for your spouse's mail.

    e. Organize tidbits of information on 3 x 5 cards rather than on scraps of paper.

16. Organize family papers:

    a. A family record book should include family names, Social Security numbers, dates of innoculations, guardians of children, and names and addresses of relatives.

    b. A safe deposit box is a good place for important papers such as birth or adoption certificates, marriage license, stock certificates and other securities, military discharge papers, automobile titles, and real estate papers (deeds, title, insurance, closing statements, title abstract, copy of mortgage and other insurance papers).

    c. Keep a file or record book for pet's licenses, shots, birthdates, pedigrees, care manuals, and vet's phone number.

17. Organize a pool of working mothers who are willing to help one another when difficulties arise. This is especially important for single parents. Exchange services might include babysitting, car pools, shopping trips, or the sharing of problem-solving ideas.

18. Have a work area that can be closed off from the rest of the house so you don't feel compelled to pick up half-completed projects every time you leave the house.

19. Take action to eliminate the following time-wasting activities.

    a. Inefficiency: do things right the first time; set up work areas that are close together; place telephone extensions in convenient places and use a long cord to save steps.

b. Indecision: weigh alternatives and make decisions immediately.

c. Disorder: have a place for everything and keep it in its place.

d. Waiting for others: carry small projects so you can spend your time wisely even while waiting.

e. Television: control its use.

f. Telephone: make all your calls at one time; keep projects close to the telephone; place a time limit on your conversations.

*Meal preparation*

1. Presort groceries and have them bagged in categories for easy storage. For example, put all frozen products in one bag, all refrigerated products in another, all canned goods in a third, and so on.

2. Prepare food before putting it away. Slice meat, grate cheese, wash fruits and vegetables that will keep after being washed.

3. Blend a breakfast. Try a combination of milk, fruit, and yogurt.

4. Specialize in one dish dinners such as soup or casseroles.

5. Premix as many basics as possible. (See *Make a Mix Cookery* by Karine Eliason, Nevada Harward, and Madeline Westover, H.P. Books, Tucson, Arizona, 1978.)

6. Seal-a-meal in plastic Ziploc bags and freeze. Immerse the bag in boiling water to reheat.

7. Freeze leftovers. Cooked dishes freeze better than uncooked, but don't overcook. (Rice and potatoes go mushy after being frozen.)

8. Use the freezer to store staples such as chopped nuts, onions and peppers, grated cheese, or cookie dough.

9. Prepare co-op meals—various family members each prepare a part of the meal.

10. Plan dinner menus ahead of time. Another family member can start dinner if you are late.

11. Plan Monday through Thursday menus at one time. Later in the week plan the weekend meals to coincide with weekend plans.

### Preparing box lunches

1. Prepare sandwiches for a week and freeze. (Spread bread with softened margarine. Bread may go soggy with mayonnaise, salad dressing, or jelly. Don't freeze lettuce or tomatoes.) Form a family assembly line. Make a week's supply of sandwiches for each family member. Bag each person's separately and put one day's supply in a large plastic bag. Freeze until needed.

2. Encourage each child to clean out his lunch box at school after eating. As soon as he gets home, he should finish the job and immediately fill the lunch box with staples (napkin, cookie, apple, nuts, raisins, or chips).

3. Use small plastic screw-on-top containers for cold drinks. Ask the children to rinse out the containers after school, immediately fill them with a drink for the next day, and put them in the freezer overnight. By tomorrow's lunch time, the drinks will be just right.

### Laundry

1. Buy only wash-and-wear clothing and resist the urge to touch up garments with an iron.

2. Don't buy clothing that requires extra laundry instructions.

3. To streamline the sorting process, purchase one basic color of clothing (especially socks) for each child.

4. Place a sink-sized plastic container in each child's room for dirty laundry. (Children often have difficulty putting their dirty laundry in the main hamper every day.)

5. Keep two hampers—one for dark clothing and one for light. On wash day (or the day before), ask the children to empty their own laundry containers and place dark and light clothes in the appropriate hampers. Have them put their containers beside the hampers so you will know whose clothes are there.

6. Wash once a week on a regular schedule. Let the family know that you will wash only what they have placed in the hampers.

7. When the clean clothes are folded, put them in each child's laundry container. Children should carry their containers back to their rooms and put the clothes away. When their containers are emptied, they're ready for another week's worth of dirty laundry.

8. Older children can fold and put away their own laundry.

9. Have children pin dirty socks together to eliminate sorting and folding.

10. To identify clothing of two or more similar-sized children, put indelible colored marks or the child's initials on the neck label or the waistband of each garment.

11. Place all garments that need mending in one pile, and garments that need ironing in another. Don't put anything away that is not wearable.

12. Encourage family members to do their own mending or ironing.

13. Use laundry products wisely. For example, presoaking products require a presoaking time to be effective.

14. Keep a stain removal guide handy.

15. Use a diaper service if you can afford it.

16. If you hang out diapers and fold them in pairs, hang two together. After they have dried, take them down by placing them over your arm in a way that will prevent wrinkling and make folding easy. Avoid folding prefolded diapers by storing them in an attractive covered basket.

17. Encourage children to help hang up clothing by placing a clothesline at a child's level.

18. Reduce wrinkles by using a final cold rinse and a cool-down cycle on the dryer.

19. Use the correct setting on your dryer to prevent unnecessary wrinkling. Use "permanent press" for permanent press clothing.

20. Don't overload the washer or dryer.

21. Remove clothes from the washer as soon as the cycle is finished. Shake out as many wrinkles as possible and hang the clothes up immediately.

22. If you use a dryer, take out the clothes immediately and hang them up or fold them. This prevents unnecessary wrinkles. Don't stuff dry laundry into a basket.

23. If you must iron, remove garments while they are damp and iron them immediately or place them in a plastic bag.

24. Let the children learn to iron napkins and handkerchiefs.

25. Purchase clothing that does not soil easily.

26. Use paper napkins and plastic place mats. It cuts down on laundry.

27. Make tablecloths from polyester doubleknit. They look great and need no ironing.

28. Pay a teenager to do your laundry.

29. Find someone to do your laundry in exchange for the use of your machines.

*Housecleaning tips*

1. Do the daily routine activities first.

2. Plan a daily time for regular cleaning above and beyond the daily activities. For example, vacuuming, dusting, cleaning the refrigerator, or mopping the floor.

3. Take a five minute trip through the house, pick up all books, toys, games, and put them in an easy-to-carry

container. Unload items in appropriate rooms. Place these items in a special box in each child's room. Ask the children to empty the box every day and put the items away in the appropriate place.

4. Maintain your daily schedule at all costs. Don't let cleaning jobs pile up.

5. Don't tackle a major job that will throw you off your daily schedule.

6. Do one type of housework at a time.

7. Rest before you get tired.

8. Clean up after each activity and encourage each family member to do the same. Don't let small messes accumulate into huge jobs.

9. Give each family member a room assignment. He or she must straighten that room by mealtime or bedtime each evening.

10. Don't use sheets and blankets on the children's beds. Replace these with quilts or decorative sleeping bags that are easy for a child to smooth out.

11. Get rid of possessions you don't need or haven't used in five years. Too many possessions cause clutter and need dusting.

12. Don't overdecorate. Remove everything that doesn't add to the decorative scheme of a room.

13. Assign a place for everything and put everything in its place—immediately.

14. Set aside a special place for things that need mending or repairing.

15. Organize storage facilities for maximum use. Keep out clutter. Label each container. Keep everything in its place.

16. Set up a hobby area, a shelf for books, a place for new and old magazines, a closet for art, a drawer for tools, and so on.

17. Keep all cleaning supplies in one easy-to-carry-around-the-house container.

18. Keep basic cleaning equipment on every floor of the house.

19. Keep bathroom cleaning supplies in each bathroom.

20. Hallway fingerprints can be eliminated by hanging children's pictures at hand level in the hallway.

21. Use paper plates and cups once a week and have a picnic.

22. As you unload the dishwasher, immediately set the table for the next meal.

23. Clean appliances and wash or soak dishes and utensils immediately, before food sticks.

24. Wipe off items before storing them or putting them in the refrigerator.

25. Wipe up spilled food immediately.

*Shopping*

1. Compile a giant shopping list that contains every possible product or food that you regularly purchase. Xerox this list and keep it on the bulletin board or inside a cupboard door. When you need an item, simply check it off on the list.

2. Sort and file coupons in envelopes by categories, such as hair products, margarine, canned goods, cakes and cookies, and so on.

3. If possible, redeem coupons immediately. Don't waste time searching for filed coupons.

4. Before a shopping trip, check the coupon envelopes and clip appropriate coupons directly onto the giant shopping list.

5. Before discarding an empty container or can, note the item on the shopping list.

6. Do all your shopping in one grocery or department store. Choose a market near other stores to save travel time.

7. Shop on a regular schedule. Resist impulse shopping.

8. Buy staples in large quantities when they are on sale.

9. Cluster shopping and errands.

10. Don't waste time shopping for sales. Choose a store that has the best prices on most common items.

11. Read the newspaper ads, but call first to see if an item is still in stock.

12. Shop with a mail order catalog.

13. Shop with the Yellow Pages.

14. Don't buy presents for special occasions at the last minute. Whenever you find the item you want, buy it immediately.

15. Buy family gifts rather than individual gifts. It eliminates extra shopping and wrapping.

16. If possible, have the store giftwrap presents while you finish your shopping.

17. Buy all the birthday and anniversary cards for the year at one time. Address these ahead of time. Put the mailing date on the envelope where the stamp will be placed. Write that date on your calendar as well.

18. Older children can shop for their own clothes. Leave them for a designated time to make their selections and try them on. Have the clerk hold their choices. Meet at the designated time and examine, approve, and purchase or disapprove and help locate something better. Hours and arguments can be saved this way.

### Teaching Children How to Save Time

You must become an effective leader if you want your children to work for you, rather than against you, in maintaining order and effective organization.

Most parents fail in this area because they use the push

technique. They push children to hurry, to pick up their clothes, to finish their homework, and do all the other tasks that a growing child is capable of doing. The push technique has only one sure effect and that is resistance. The harder parents push, the more determined children are to resist. However, leading has an entirely different effect. When you lead an object gently in the direction you want it to go, it will follow without resistance. Parents must learn to lead and not push if they want to harness each family member's ability and determination to save time.

Effective leaders are good decision-makers. They know what needs to be done; they are able to break tasks into small, manageable components and decide on a plan of attack. Good leaders must be able to communicate their decision to the rest of the family, and encourage group participation. Finally, they must learn how to inspire the family with a spirit of willingness to perform the necessary tasks efficiently.

Cooperation is more easily gained when the family feels they have had a part in the decision-making process; when they are praised and thanked rather than criticized or belittled for their participation; and when the leader is willing to listen wholeheartedly and remain sensitive to their desires and needs.

Children need good leadership to help them assume appropriate responsibilities and develop skills that will allow them to perform efficiently. Often, children do not understand what a specific task entails. Generalized statements such as, "Help me," or "Clean your room," are far too broad for most children. When tasks are broken down into little pieces, children are more willing to help because they understand what's expected of them and they can anticipate completion of the task. A four-year-old may resist cleaning his room, but responds readily to the direction, "Put your socks in this box." This is a specific instruction.

He knows that he'll be finished when all the socks are in the box. But when is the room clean? That is a very abstract concept for a child. On Monday, that may mean putting all the toys away. On Friday, it may mean vacuuming and dusting.

A child may not be capable of completing an entire task by himself. Analyze each part. He may be able to lick the stamps for you, even though he is too small to address the envelopes. Remember, every little bit of help from others will mean more time for you.

Here are some ways to encourage children to be more helpful.

### Help children keep organized

1. Do away with a toy box. Organize toys in plastic containers, decorated boxes, or large painted coffee cans. Label each container.

2. Store toys and materials that children use regularly on shelves or in a closet that's easily accessible for them. (If a child is at the stage of pulling down and emptying containers, put only a few toys at his level.)

3. Hang a shoe bag in the closet and put small trinkets, games, balls, cars, marbles, and other small toys and collections in its pockets.

4. Hang children's clothing on pegs. Children usually resist using regular hangers.

5. Hang a shoe bag in the entrance-way closet for mittens, scarves, ear muffs, and other small items.

6. Use a clothes rack in the entrance way for the coats and sweaters that usually end up on the furniture or the closet floor.

7. Use large clear plastic boxes in the entrance-way closet for each child's belongings. Then a child won't have to sort through the whole closet to find what he wants.

8. If your children aren't at the reading stage, draw

pictures on the outside of containers or next to hooks so they can return items to their proper place.

### Teach children efficiency

1. When children do a job, reward them for speed and efficiency. For example, give them a nickel for a job completed in a certain amount of time. If it takes them longer, decrease the reward.

2. Children enjoy breaking records. Post official family records for various chores on the bulletin board. Encourage the children to beat their own records.

3. Reward children by playing games with them. Say, "If you make your lunches by 7 P.M. I'll play a game with you."

4. Set completion deadlines for certain jobs. Encourage a child to meet this schedule by offering an incentive. For example, if a child finishes five minutes behind schedule, he must go to bed five minutes earlier that night.

5. When clearing the table after meals, announce a two-hand takeoff. Every family member uses two hands to remove as much as possible to see if the table can be cleared with only one trip per person.

6. To wake children in the morning and get them off to a good start, play rousing marching music.

7. Let your child listen to a story record while tackling certain tasks. Encourage him to finish before the record is over.

8. Ban TV when work must be done. It destroys a child's efficiency. Have them listen to story records or cassette tapes instead.

### Encourage responsibility in children

1. When a child balks at doing a regular task, offer to exchange his chore with one of yours.

2. Contract with the children. For example, "I'll make the beds if you'll make the lunches."

3. Make children's work pleasant by giving them unexpected rewards—bring them a cold drink or read to them as they work.

4. Don't nag your children; write chore reminders on the bulletin board instead. And when they forget to pick up their things, place the items in a "nag-bag," and insist that they perform a chore in order to redeem their things.

5. Draw a duty. List chores on cards and set up a daily random drawing. Always include several pleasant treats, such as "relax," "read a book," or "one half hour of free time." A child must draw one duty when he comes home from school each day.

6. Write each child's daily chores on a separate piece of paper. Give children the list a day before the deadline. Children enjoy knowing everything that will be required of them and crossing off the jobs when they are done.

7. Construct a daily duty box with two slots for each child. One slot holds duty cards, such as brush teeth, make beds, and so forth. As soon as these duties are completed, the child takes the card and places it in the second slot. At the end of the day, rewards are given if all the child's daily duties have been completed. Rewards are subtracted for the number of duties that haven't been done or are only half finished because of misuse of time.

8. Occasionally hide pennies under doilies, knickknacks, pictures, and magazines in rooms that need dusting. If the child dusting finds all the pennies, thus doing a good job, give him a bonus. For small children, a penny under each wastebasket emptied is a nice surprise.

9. Solicit bids for routine housework and room assignments. Scale the pay to fit the work load. For example, cleaning the hall might pay 50¢ per week, the living room would be worth $2, and emptying the wastebaskets would pay 25¢. At the end of the week, a child should be paid for

the job *if* he has kept his part of the bargain.

10. When the children borrow your things, require a deposit of their favorite toy and they will not forget to return the borrowed item.

11. If the children constantly seek your help, gear the task to their level. For example, make bathroom paper cups easily reachable, put a pitcher of water in the child's room, keep the toothbrushes and toothpaste at your child's level, or provide a stool so he can reach the sink.

12. If your child has trouble keeping his face clean, hang a mirror at his level in the bathroom. Be innovative. Encourage him to put shaving lather on his face and wash it.

13. If children have trouble reaching a light switch, cut a hole in one side of a cardboard tube from a roll of paper towels. Place the hole over the switch, and the child can push the light switch on and off.

14. To encourage a child to dress himself, lay out his clothing for the next day.

15. Help children keep slippers on by sewing the top half of a sock onto the slipper.

16. For children who are too young to tie their shoes, replace laces with 1/8 inch elastic. It stretches so the child can get into his shoe without untying it, and untied laces will not drag on the ground.

17. For children who have a difficult time pulling on their galoshes, cover their shoes with a plastic bag or a sock. Their feet will also stay warmer this way.

18. If your child has a tendency to forget the sweater he wore under his coat, sew an old sweater into his coat.

19. If mittens get lost, crochet mittens directly onto an old sweater.

20. If your child has difficulty telling the right shoe from the left, make a pattern on the floor that he can place his shoes in before putting them on, or make an *X* on each

instep and let him match up the marks.

21. To cut down on lost clothing, stamp the child's name on each piece. (This is easier than sewing on name tags.)

22. If your child has trouble with buttons, sew them on with elastic thread. The thread stretches, making it easier for little fingers to get the button through a button hole.

23. If boot zippers are too hard for small fingers to grasp, attach metal rings to the zipper.

24. Purchase clothes with fasteners that children can handle.

25. Let your child work beside you and learn how to do household tasks. Make chores fun and interesting, and you will find that your children will be more helpful.

*Miscellaneous time-savers*

1. Read to the children while they are eating.

2. Take a warm bath with a young child or baby. It's a relaxing time for both of you and an easy way to bathe a child.

3. For fussy eaters who enjoy a novel change, fill ice cream cones with mashed potatoes, yogurt, cottage cheese, sandwich filling, or fruit. There will be no dishes to wash.

4. Instead of nagging a child to finish his food, have each member of the family guess how many bites are left. Everyone counts while the child eats to see who was closest.

5. Spillproof a young child's plate and cup by attaching a rubber suction cup under the plate and placing wide rubber bands around a slippery glass.

6. Reduce poorly timed visits from neighborhood children by hanging a do-not-disturb picture on the door knob, showing the family's activity. For example, at nap time draw a sleeping child; at dinner time, a family eating, and so on.

7. Place a canteen beside a child's bed in case he wants a bedtime drink.

8. If your child has trouble falling asleep, put perfume on his hand and tell him to smell it until the odor disappears. Deep breathing encourages sleep.

9. When a tiny baby has trouble falling asleep, strap him in an infant seat and place him on the vibrating dryer. Gentle motion also encourages sleep. Stay close by and hum a lullabye as you work.

10. If your children wake you up too early, prepare a surprise bag and place it beside their pillow. Include items such as a purse-sized mirror, baby doll, decorative stamps and paper, or small cars and trucks that will keep little hands busy until it is time for you to get up.

11. Instead of picking up toys thrown out of the high chair or playpen, attach them with elastic. Encourage your child to retrieve his own toy.

12. If you have an active, curious toddler, put all breakables beyond his reach.

13. Use the local library as a babysitting service for school-age children when you must do errands that they're not interested in, or shopping that you can do more quickly if they're not tagging along. Be sure they know proper library behavior.

14. Keep an emergency survival kit handy and use it when your child gets on your nerves. Include fascinating toys that are sure to capture your child's interest. This will free your time to do what you need to do.

15. If your child needs a work space in the kitchen, open a low drawer and cover it with a bread board, rather than dragging in a small table from another room.

16. Store children's wet bath toys in a fish net that can be hung on a hook above the tub. They can drip dry and they're easily accessible for the next bath time.

17. To keep toys organized and readily available in the car, fill a shoe bag with interesting travel toys and hang

it over the front seat. Make sure all toys are replaced before the children leave the car.

18. Keep a canteen in the car so you don't have to stop for drinks.

19. Keep a container of "Wet Ones" in the car for last-minute cleaning of dirty faces and hands.

20. Use travel time to listen to stories on cassettes.

21. Use travel time to teach your children. Prepare cards with questions for the children to answer, such as, "If you were lost what would you do?" "How are an apple and an orange alike and how are they different?" Keep a small dictionary in the car and teach new vocabulary words, or teach foreign words or phrases. Teach new songs and enjoy singing together.

Organize and budget your time, delegate whenever possible, delete the unnecessary, become an efficiency expert, and teach your children how to be responsible. If you do, you'll find more time for those things that matter most in your life.

# 10

## Making Your Family
## a Winning Team

Everyone wants to be on a winning team. Defeat is depressing; failure can be humiliating. But success is exhilarating. A successful family team works together to achieve goals. Every member has a unique role to play. Each contributes his share. Each is essential to the final outcome. But the whole—the concerted team effort—is stronger than the sum of its parts. And as a result, each family member shares in the gratifying joy of meaningful relationships, a growing sense of self-worth, and the satisfaction of fulfilled ambitions.

A good coach is the key to building a winning team. It is your spirit, your drive, your enthusiasm, and your expertise that will ultimately make the difference between success or failure. Creating a winning team requires a plan and a rich investment of time.

First, you must define exactly who is on your team. In sports, team members are selected. In families, team members are *accepted*. Families do not come in neat little packages, so it is impossible to define a standardized team structure that can be applied to all. With divorce, widowhood, remarriage, adoption, desertion, and death, many prime-time parents are no longer sure who is part of the family team.

I define a family as two or more people who have a mutual relationship of care and concern. They form an intertwined system, and events that affect one member have some effect on all members. Within families, no individual can live in complete isolation. Even if one member cuts himself off from the family (which often happens in the case of divorce), this separation has some effect on other family members, even after it has existed for years.

A family, broadly defined, is made up of individuals related to each other, either biologically or legally—through marriage or adoption. Extended family members may or may not live together. But in order for a family to be molded into a team, the members must interact on a regular basis. Therefore, a simple way to define your team is to include those individuals living together—regardless of relationship.

Once your team has been defined, you are ready to start building it into a winning team. The following suggestions have been drawn from the success stories of some of the greatest coaches in history: Red Auerbach of the Boston Celtics; John Wooden, who put UCLA's basketball team on the map; football's memorable Vince Lombardi, and others.

### A Team Purpose

Every team needs a purpose to keep it going. A mutual enjoyment of hockey is not enough to hold a team together and build unity, but winning the national championship is worth the struggle, the self-discipline, and the time it takes to mold individuals into a team. Every family needs a goal that is worth striving for.

Why do we need families? A family purpose might include any or all of the following:

1. To provide emotional support and physical care to other family members.

2. To help each person realize his personal goals and aspirations, and reach his potential.

3. To pass on values and wholesome character traits to the new generation.

4. To contribute to the well-being of others and the community.

These are long-term general guidelines. But what does this mean to your family in particular? Are these goals meaningful enough to ignite the spirit and enthusiasm that it takes to mold a winning team? Probably not. The answer is to break these general purposes into smaller objectives that each family member can identify with. A concentrated focus enables family members to analyze their team's track record—are they winning or losing?

Why is your team unique? What is your purpose in living together? Consider the following list of broad family goals: excellence; family unity; cooperation; aesthetic enrichment; wisdom (good judgment); intellectual attainment; service to others and the community; economic sustenance; fulfilling creative potential; rearing happy, healthy children; being loved and wanted; having fun together.

These goals should be broad enough to permit each family member to set a specific objective that supports the overall family goal. For example, if your family goal is service to others, Dad may decide to donate some spare time to a worthy cause, Mom may choose to build a better relationship with a difficult co-worker, and the children may decide to help Mom, Dad, and the babysitter by taking on some extra home chores.

Specific goals can be time-related. For example, a family may work together to put Dad through medical school, or pay for Mary's orthodontic work. However, if family goals relate only to one family member for too long a time, jealousy and dissatisfaction may arise.

One of the Kuzma family goals is excellence; we all strive to reach the highest level that each of us is capable of attaining. On occasion, I've told the children, "Every day, your daddy is trying to be the best biostatistician he can be. That's why he isn't home tonight. He has a deadline coming up for a paper he is preparing and it must be out by tomorrow. How do you think we can help him?" The children come up with various ideas to help Jan accomplish his immediate goal, which they view as part of the ultimate family goal of excellence. Sometimes the children decide that we should fix a nice supper and take it to him so he won't have to waste time going out to buy something. At other times, they may decide to feed the dog, clean the garage, or wash the car to lighten some of their father's home responsibilities. I'm always surprised by the willingness the children exhibit when they consider their efforts essential to reaching a family goal.

Kim wants to be the best flute player she can become. Knowing this, it is much easier for the rest of us to remain quiet and stay out of her way while she is practicing. At times, Kari has even offered to make Kim's bed or fix her sack lunch when time is running short and Kim is preparing for a lesson.

In order to have a successful team, children must feel that they are ultimately contributing to family goals. One of our short-term family goals has been to help Mommy finish her book. The children have curtailed boisterous play outside the study door and have taken on a number of Mom's home responsibilities. Each finished chapter is cause for a family celebration. And now the watchword is "only one chapter to go!" Just this morning as I was taking the children to school, I asked if one of them had a good thought to guide us through the day. Kim quoted something that she was learning at school. "Remember that you will never reach a higher standard than you yourself set. Then set your mark high, and step by step, even though it be by painful effort, by self-denial and sacrifice, ascend the whole length of the ladder of progress."

"Oh, Kim!" I exclaimed. "That's beautiful! That is just the thought I need today, for me—*and* for my book. In fact, I think I'll include it in the last chapter." Looking very pleased, she gave me the reference. The moment I got home I looked it up. What a message for every prime-time parent!

The passage continues, "Let nothing hinder you. Fate has not woven its meshes about any human being so firmly that he need remain helpless and in uncertainty. Opposing circumstances should create a firm determination to overcome them. The breaking down of one barrier will give greater ability and courage to go forward. Press with determination in the right direction, and circumstances will be your helpers, not your hindrances."*

A common purpose binds the family together in a cooperative working relationship that encourages them to overcome obstacles and progress toward the standard—their team goal.

### Create a Team Identity

Every team needs an identity. Team members need to know who they are so they can better assess where they are going or where they *should* be going. Every family has a unique history. Draw on that history to create a strong family identity; to make family members feel that they are part of a special group.

Is there a special meaning in your family name or in the names of family members? Are there meaningful stories that have been handed down from generation to generation? Are there incidents from your childhood that would help your child identify with the values and ideals you hold

* Ellen G. White, *Messages to Young People* (Nashville, Tenn.: Southern Publishing Association, 1930), pp. 99–100.

dear? Does your family have some unusual characters with remarkable personalities? Are there interesting facts about your family background that you can share?

I remember how impressed I was when I first learned that my great-grandfather was a U.S. Marshal, and was such a good shot that William Cody (Buffalo Bill) asked him to be a sharpshooter in his entourage that performed in Europe. I identified with this man in my distant past. He achieved excellence. What a meaningful example for the children to identify with!

To foster a sense of heritage in our children, Jan and I have told them: "You are special children. God has a plan for each one of your lives—just as He has a plan for Daddy's and Mommy's life. The purpose of our family is to help each other grow and develop so these plans can be realized.

"You have a special heritage. Oma and Opa Kuzma showed tremendous courage, spirit, and determination to share their religious faith in a country where faith was practically unknown. They were constantly serving others, even when their own lives were in danger. This same dedication led them to leave loved ones and friends behind to come to a land where they felt their children could have more freedom to achieve their full potential and could better prepare themselves to serve others.

"Grandma and Grandpa Humpal worked very hard to give their children advantages they didn't have and they expected their children to do the same for others. Excellence and beauty were also important to them. Grandpa loved mountain land and became so good at selling it that the slogan, "For mountain land, see Humpal, the Mountain Man," became well-known around his hometown. And both Grandma and Grandpa have spent hours beautifying the homes and yards of others.

"Both Daddy and Mommy have a responsibility to fulfill our parents' dreams for us to reach our highest potential so we can be of greater service to others—to help make the lives of others more meaningful. That's why Daddy works so hard doing studies on life-style to see why some people are healthier than others. And that's why Mommy writes books and teaches classes so other people will understand children better and have happier homes. Each of you also has a responsibility to do your best in whatever you choose to do so that you can ultimately be of service to others."

In addition to telling your children about their heritage, what can you do to establish your family's identity? You might try some of the following:

1. Tell stories about your family—about you, your relatives, and the children. Write these down. Read them at special occasions.

2. Design a family tree. Place pictures of all the relatives in their appropriate place. Hang it in the hallway, study, or family room.

3. Research and write your family's history.

4. Collect items that symbolize your family name. For example, if your name is Crane, Behr (bear), Bird, Robin, or another animal, collect these things.

5. Make a family symbol or coat of arms. My sister married an Affolter. The original meaning of the name had something to do with apples, so a simple drawing of an apple has become their family's trademark.

We made our own Kuzma coat of arms. At the bottom is the Polish national bird—the eagle that symbolizes Jan's heritage. At the top is a mountain and butterfly symbolizing my background. In the center are the symbols of nature that the children chose to represent themselves. Kim is a tall, graceful evergreen tree, Kari is a daisy, and Kevin— well, Kevin decided that he wanted to be a pickle! He loves them, and after all, he is the spice of life for our family! We put this design on a large banner which hangs in our family room.

6. Develop "family" talent. Plan a program where each person can participate. Sing or play instruments together. Put on a talent show, a skit, a puppet show, a pantomime, or an art exhibit. Print a book with contributions of stories, poems, or drawings from each family member. Set up a family business making doll houses, growing house plants, or raising puppies.*

7. Write a family motto. Make bumper stickers or design a wall plaque that embodies your family purpose.

8. Start a family chain letter to keep in touch with different family members on a more regular basis.

9. Make a family birthday and anniversary calendar. Remember each occasion with a card, letter, or telephone call.

10. Hold a family reunion on a regular basis. Some of the following ideas may make your family reunion more meaningful.

a. Set a regular time—annually, every three years, or whatever is most meaningful and possible for your particular extended family.

b. Plan it a year in advance. Decide who is in charge and who will be responsible for various tasks; choose the date and the location; send out invitations; plan the program, the menu, and the housing arrangements.

c. Plan "memory" food—family favorites.

d. Have a talent show with at least one representative from each nuclear family.

e. Stage contests and give a trophy for such feats as spitting out the most watermelon seeds or shooting out the flame of a candle with a water gun.

f. Plan to participate in some old traditions, such as baking bread, making soap, dripping candles, or churning butter.

* For more ideas, see: *The Family Creative Workshop,* available from Time-Life Books, Time-Life Building, Chicago, Illinois 60611.

g. Print T-shirts or bumper stickers with a motto such as, "I'm a Kuzma," or "I was there for the 1980 Kuzma reunion."

h. Plan a skit or a charade depicting a favorite family happening.

i. Plan a seminar day and ask various family members to prepare "papers" on a certain topic for presentation. Topics might include, "Why our family is important," or "What our combined family purpose should be for the next five years."

## A Code of Behavior

Every successful coach establishes behavior standards for team members. A successful family must do the same. Your team's record of wins and losses will be determined by the willingness of family members to live up to the standards that you have set. Each individual's personality and character, as exhibited in their behavior inside as well as outside the home, is the foundation upon which team success is based. Your challenge is to help each member of the team see the relationship between his behavior and the success of the team.

It is important that you, the coach, set an example by meeting your own standards. If you want others to be self-disciplined, loyal, and cooperative, you must be this way first. You must inspire your family with the fact that winning or losing is really dependent upon each one's willingness to reach the standard of excellence. Finally, it is your responsibility to discipline those who do not uphold the ideals.

John Wooden was a master coach in this regard. The UCLA basketball team won eight consecutive NCAA championships and had thirty-two consecutive victories in tournament play under his leadership. This coaching record clearly indicates that John Wooden knew how to build a winning team. He believed that the foundation for winning was his code of behavior called the "Pyramid of Success." As coach, he presented this model as the base for building the team at the beginning of each season and at all of his summer camps. In his opinion, "Success is peace of mind which is a direct result of self-satisfaction in knowing you did your best to become the best that you are capable of becoming." To reach this standard he developed a model incorporating the following character traits: industriousness, friendship, loyalty, cooperation, enthusiasm, self-control, alertness, initiative, intentness, condition, skill, team spirit, poise, confidence, ambition, adaptability, resourcefulness, fight, faith, sincerity, honesty, integrity, reliability, and patience, all culminating in competitive greatness and success.

Using John Wooden's Pyramid of Success as a basis, I have developed a similar pyramid that can be used as a model for a family team. Although it is organized in a slightly different manner, the intent is the same. It is to serve as a code of behavior for individual family members; an ideal for which to strive if you really want to be part of a winning team.

*Level 1—Individual Behaviors:* These behaviors primarily affect your own life. In a sense, if you exhibit these qualities you will be true to yourself. They form the basis for relationships with others. You must be honorable and upright in your relations with yourself and your ideals *before* you can find success in other relationships.

1. Integrity: Possessing sound moral principles—upright, honest, and sincere.

2. Self-discipline: Control of one's thoughts and behavior.

3. Responsibility: Dependable; accountable for one's behavior.

4. Enthusiasm: Intense eager interest; zeal to reach a goal.

## Model for a Winning Family

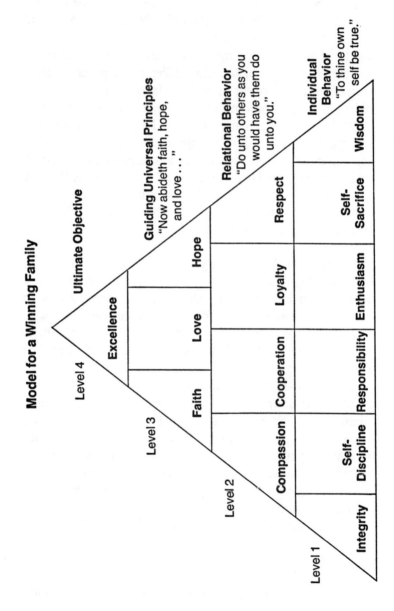

Level 4 — **Ultimate Objective**

Excellence

**Guiding Universal Principles**
"Now abideth faith, hope, and love . . ."

Level 3

Faith    Love    Hope

**Relational Behavior**
"Do unto others as you would have them do unto you."

Level 2

Compassion    Cooperation    Loyalty    Respect

**Individual Behavior**
"To thine own self be true."

Level 1

Integrity    Self-Discipline    Responsibility    Enthusiasm    Self-Sacrifice    Wisdom

5. Self-sacrifice: Willingness to sacrifice oneself or one's interests to help others or to achieve the team's objectives.

6. Wisdom: Good judgment based on knowledge, experience, and understanding. The process of following the soundest course of action.

*Level 2—Relational Behaviors:* These behaviors primarily affect your relationship with others. The guiding motto for these behaviors is the Golden Rule, "Do unto others as you would have them do unto you."

7. Compassion: The ability to empathize with others and to help them when needed.

8. Cooperation: To work together with others for a common purpose. A willingness to compromise.

9. Loyalty: An obligation to defend and support others. Dedication to principles.

10. Respect: Showing admiration, regard, honor, and esteem for others.

*Level 3—Guiding Universal Principles:* These principles should permeate every aspect of your life, making it possible to reach the ultimate goal of excellence.

11. Faith: Confidence in what you believe. Steadfast adherence to your principles.

12. Love: A deep attachment and devotion to ideals, to one's God, to humanity, and to your family.

13. Hope: Belief in your ability to conquer obstacles and reach your goal. The knowledge that nothing is impossible.

*Level 4—The Ultimate Objective—Excellence:* The process of reaching the highest level that one is capable of attaining. Doing your very best at all times, under any conditions, in whatever you attempt.

To be meaningful, a model must reflect your own values and those behaviors that are important in your religious affiliation and culture. Therefore, you must take the time to develop a model that fits your family. If your children are old enough, enlist their participation in building a model. They will be more likely to support your code of behavior if they've helped create it.

Begin by choosing an ultimate objective. This will probably reflect the basic family purpose or purposes that you have already established. Once the highest level has been determined, list the character traits or behaviors that will contribute to the ultimate objective. Organize these under three headings:

Level 1—Individual Behaviors.
Level 2—Relational Behaviors.
Level 3—Guiding Universal Principles.

Then form your own Pyramid of Success, defining each behavior trait in writing. In order to keep these standards before the family, do as John Wooden did and put your model on a large sheet of paper and hang it in a place where it can be a constant reminder to the whole team.

Talk about these traits and evaluate the family's progress toward the ultimate objective on a regular basis. My model has thirteen behaviors, one for every week of the quarter. In this way, each behavior can be emphasized regularly four weeks out of the year.

When you meet to discuss these traits on a weekly basis, the agenda might include the following:

1. *Inspirational presentation.* Include a story about the importance of the trait you have selected. Show how it can help each individual reach the ultimate objective. This is a good time to tell stories about your family's heritage to strengthen the family identity.

2. *Interaction based on the trait.* This might be a discussion question, such as, "How can we be more loyal to the family this week?" Or it might be a project such as writing a motto, making a bumper sticker, or composing a poem or a song that will reinforce the trait during that week.

3. *Specific ideas and plans for a week.* Ask each person, "How can family members better put the behavioral trait into practice during the next week?" It might be fun if each person devised some ideas for every other person on the team. Sometimes teammates are more aware of improvements that need to be made than you are! To keep these suggestions honest, they should not be read to the entire family. Every constructive suggestion should be couched in the spirit and language of love. Discouragement leads to failure! It might also be constructive for each person to write a specific objective for himself and then each teammate plan how he can help that person to achieve his goal. This fosters the spirit of team cooperation and support.

When team members are striving toward the same behavior standards, the quality of family life will be enhanced. The results will be seen in each team member's personal life and his relational life as a teammate.

### The Game Plan

Planning is an essential part of a winning formula. In addition to a general plan that includes the family purpose and a code of behavior, the family must have a game plan for each new day. A successful game plan should provide a step-by-step scheme that will help you achieve your goals without being sidetracked. Game plans should consist of bite-sized objectives—what you want to accomplish on a weekly or daily basis—and have balance in a variety of activities, as well as an appropriate sense of timing. To be a winning team, the family must also consider what problems they are likely to encounter and provide an adequate plan of defense. For example, if Mom is late getting home from work, someone should start dinner. Or if Dad gets out early, he should phone Mom and see if there is anything she needs to have him pick up on his way home.

The game plan should consist of a daily schedule as well as a long-term schedule for meeting family objectives. When making long-term plans or schedules consider these guidelines:

1. Do the activities planned promote family objectives?

2. Is there a balance and variety in the activities planned?

3. Are there too many outside activities to effectively keep the home fires burning?

4. Is there a time for parents to be alone with one child and with each other?

5. Are there too many individual activities planned and not enough family activities?

6. Is there enough flexibility in the schedule to do the unexpected? To handle emergencies? To take advantage of an unanticipated treat?

Long-term plans are important, but the real key to winning is an effective daily game plan—a detailed schedule of how the family plans to make it through the day. The daily plan should be workable if the following questions are considered.

1. What is going to happen during the day?

2. What does each individual have to accomplish?

3. What does each individual *want* to do?

4. Are there any deviations from the usual routine such as a TV special or an after-school football practice that must be considered?

5. Does anything have to be done today in order to get ready for tomorrow?

Anticipate problems by thinking yourself through the day's schedule. Ask yourself these questions:

1. Do I have time to get from one appointment to the next?

2. Should I really try to do everything that I have planned?

3. How can I dovetail activities to save time and energy?

4. By doing something special for one child, is this going to handicap or inconvenience another?

Avoid impulsive decision-making. Good thoughtful decisions usually take time to make. Conflicts occur when you haven't taken time to check with the whole family about a decision that will affect them or when the family was not prepared for an unexpected turn of events. This might happen when a parent accepts an evening business appointment and then later finds that the children have a social program that night, or when unexpectedly Dad decides to take the family out for dinner and Mom has a beauty shop appointment. Conflicts like these can be avoided if the family has a game plan based on these policies.

1. Confirm plans *after* consulting with the other family members.

2. Don't overschedule outside activities.

3. Don't make hasty decisions that the family isn't prepared for.

4. Follow as closely as possible the daily game plan. If deviations must be made, be sure to communicate these as far in advance as possible to every person affected.

5. Don't be so tied to a schedule that you can't take advantage of unexpected, fun activities that could benefit the entire family.

### Communicating the Game Plan

Effective communication is an essential quality for a successful coach. You must know *what* to say and *when* to say it. Your goals for the team, your winning strategies, your standards, even your expertise and enthusiasm, won't make a winning team if you fail to communicate these things.

Coaches plan a variety of team meetings to get their message across to their players and listen to the players' feedback. They hold weekly *rallies* to encourage the team, they give pep talks, they ask the players to evaluate the team's progress and make suggestions, and they develop long-range plans. Then, before the team hits the field, they hold *chalk talks* to plan strategies for specific games or solve specific problems. Once the play begins, communication does not cease; rather, it increases in the form of a *huddle.* Huddles are called whenever necessary in order to make immediate plans or give the necessary encouragement that may ultimately make the difference between winning or losing.

Winning family teams need this same form of communication. You will be a more successful family leader if you plan (or encourage your family to help plan) a weekly family rally, a daily chalk talk, and family huddles whenever needed. Use the following list to plan objectives for these team meetings.

*A weekly family rally (the family STAFF meeting):* 1–2 hours

1. To establish the team's identity as a *winning team.*
2. To establish and identify the family purpose.
3. To inspire the family with the importance of standards or a code of behavior.
4. To discuss team strategies; how the family can meet its goals.
5. To discuss long-range plans—appointments for the month, vacations, special occasions, paying off the bills, planning projects and hobbies.
6. To encourage participation and discussion.
7. To bring up problems and discuss solutions.
8. To work on a family project together.
9. To listen to others and learn more about them.

10. To encourage leadership skills by asking the children to take the lead in some aspects of the rally.

11. To have fun and enjoy each other.

*A daily chalk talk* (morning or evening): 20 minutes

1. To give an inspirational thought for the day.

2. To make immediate plans for the day—review schedules, appointments, and other things that must be done.

3. To work out last minute snags in previous planning.

4. To encourage the family to play a winning game that day.

5. To communicate your love.

*Family huddles* (*as needed*): 1–5 minutes usually

1. To be willing to meet individual needs as they occur.

2. To solve sudden crises before they get out of hand, such as a discipline problem.

3. To reorganize the game plan when something unanticipated occurs.

4. To communicate any changes in plans.

5. To fill the little pockets of time with a heaping dose of love.

Team meetings should be meaningful and viewed as a necessary part of family life. Every member should be present, but no one should be forced to come. A team functions best with willing participants. Here are some ideas for making team meetings more attractive to your family.

1. Make the meetings so interesting, informative, warm, and enjoyable that everyone will want to join the fun.

2. Ask each person to put suggestions for a rally or chalk talk in a suggestion box, and use them.

3. Make sure each person feels that his contributions are important to the family.

4. Plan something special that everyone enjoys.

5. Serve dessert or a special treat at a family rally.

6. Allow disagreement but ban put-downs.

7. Listen to each other carefully. Don't cut a person off prematurely.

8. Be interested in everyone's views.

9. Allow plenty of time to discuss issues in depth. If there is a time constraint, set up another session to discuss the matter.

10. Vote on decisions.

11. Handle problems that require an immediate solution.

12. Make sure that everyone has a chance to express himself.

13. Present topics in a democratic way so that everyone feels free to contribute.

14. Defuse controversial or emotionally heated topics by active listening rather than direct confrontation.

15. When the children are old enough, have them take turns leading a session.

## Establish and Maintain Team Spirit

A superstar is not the key to a winning team. The key is one's ability to mold an aggregate of individuals with different interests, personalities, and needs into a body that functions as one. A winning team is a group of people who believe that team glory is more important than individual glory. They will not jeopardize the team in order to make a name for themselves. Each member of the family must feel vitally important and essential, but the family must come first. This is not a popular philosophy in a society that believes the most important thing is to look out for yourself. But it is a winning team philosophy.

For example: how did the Boston Celtics achieve the outstanding record of winning the National Basketball Association Championship eleven times out of thirteen? They were not a rich team, they did not have the fans (Boston's big winter sport is hockey), nor did they have the superstars (no Celtic ever led the league in scoring). The Celtics became a winning team primarily because Red Auerbach, their coach, insisted that the team was more important than a superstar. He knew how to mold team effort and team spirit so the team became greater than the sum of its parts.

The spirit of the team and its morale are closely linked. You can protect this spirit in several ways. Encourage each family member to understand his own importance *and* the primary importance of the family. Make sure that every family member feels needed. Establish a buddy system in which each person is responsible for another. Finally, inspire your children to conduct themselves as champions.

*Everyone is important, but the team comes first.* Superstars seldom make it to the top by themselves. In team sports, the outstanding player owes much of his success to the support of his teammates, just as every individual owes much of his success to his family.

The superstar of a family might be a parent who is a famous scientist, or an outstanding musician, or president of a company. It may be a child who is a born athlete or intellectually gifted. If these individuals overshadow other family members or receive attention and recognition at the others' expense, there will be a breakdown in family morale. Each superstar must learn to accept recognition and praise graciously, and honestly credit the family when credit is due.

Children who are not superstars sometimes feel neglected, worthless, and unloved because they do not receive the attention that another is receiving. The family cannot always prevent this if the attention comes from outsiders.

But within the family they can make sure that all of their children receive recognition for their skills and abilities, even if the outside world has not crowned that child with superstar status. Each team member should be challenged to do his best, and when he does, superstar status should be granted by the family!

Even with precautions, family members may be overshadowed by the family superstar at times. When one member of the family has achieved status and recognition, it's easy for the rest of the family to be known as so-and-so's son, brother, or sister. These individuals may find it difficult to establish their own identity because they can never hope to match or surpass the superstar. In such cases, parents must make it very clear that striving to become a superstar is not necessary. Children do not have to match or exceed another sibling's accomplishments. They must simply try to do their best at all times. The scope of your achievements is less important than the spirit with which you tackle them. Borrow a phrase from Winston Churchill as your family motto. "Success is never final. Failure is never fatal. It's courage that counts." Neither children nor any other family member should feel that the family revolves around them—that they are the center of their universe and that their wants, wishes, and needs will always preempt everyone elses. One woman told me a sad story about her own childhood: "I saw my mother give *everything* to her girls. Dad was excluded altogether too much. I got smothered. Dad was starved. I would have liked to see my parents enjoy each other more in such things as play, sports, entertainment, and friends. I came to marriage unequipped to have fun with my husband. Unless a child can receive a warm happy feeling from seeing his parents enjoy themselves together with and without him, he may be crippled in adulthood."

Children must realize that parents have needs too—that Mom and Dad need time alone; that appointments must be met; that out-of-town travel is sometimes necessary; that business crises do arise which require time away from the family. If a family has a team spirit, these occasional inconveniences can be viewed as opportunities rather than handicaps. For example, when Mom is sick, Junior won't feel cheated because no one has prepared his dinner. Instead, he can turn the situation into a challenge and prepare the family meal.

A winning team cannot function effectively when one or two members always get their way at the expense of others. It destroys the team spirit of those who are neglected.

In my opinion, the breakdown of the family in today's society is primarily a result of losing the team spirit. Too many people have the mistaken sense that "I can do it by myself," or "With enough self-assertiveness I can make it to the top without anyone else." When one has this attitude, there is little need for a family. The family only hampers progress because it demands time and attention. Too often, children are pushed into the background by achievement-oriented parents who don't realize the importance of a family team.

To build an effective team, every member must feel that he can contribute to the overall team goal or purpose. In this way, every family member can feel important—a superstar on a winning team.

*Everyone is needed.* It is not much fun to play on a team when you don't feel needed. Parents sometimes err when they try to be so self-sufficient that their children come to believe that their contributions to the family are really not worth very much.

Kelley appeared to be a self-sufficient mother. Even when her children were young, her house sparkled, dinner was on time, and she looked like a fashion plate. When the children started school she volunteered as the fund raiser of the local children's hospital. This led to a full-time job in public relations. However, the stress of combining job responsibilities with her home responsibilities was almost overwhelming. But she kept this to herself. One day she was asked to represent the hospital at an out-of-state conference. She would be gone a week. How would the family manage without her? Despite her misgivings, her husband and the children persuaded her to go. And they managed quite well. Father roasted hot dogs in the fireplace and cooked things that his wife had never heard of and the children did the cleaning. Kelly returned home to a healthy, happy family and an orderly home. She was surprised. "Well," she said sadly, "it looks as if you don't need me anymore."

"On the contrary," her husband replied. "At last we feel that you need us. I think we'll be a happier family because of this."

Children are much more willing to cooperate in household tasks when they know that they are needed. A child's willingness to cooperate is also affected by other factors. For example, it has often been observed that children of widowed parents are more cooperative and helpful than the children of divorced parents. Team spirit has something to do with this. In the case of a widowed parent, the family team has not really been broken. They have lost one member, which means that the remaining family members must work even harder. However, in the case of divorce, the team has been broken. A child's allegiance must span two separate teams, and this weakens his team spirit. Consequently, he is less willing to help the parent he now lives with. In such a case, the answer is not to nag and criticize, but to concentrate on building a new team where the child feels vitally needed.

*Establish a buddy system in which each person is responsible for another.* One of the family's major purposes is to be an emotional support system for family members. How often do children come home with a poor report card and get chewed out? When a neighbor calls to report some mischief that your child was into, how often do you tear into him before he has a chance to explain? How often do parents avoid telling the family that vacation plans have to be changed or that a raise didn't come through because they fear criticism. In many families, home is no longer a safe place to let your hair down and be yourself. If you show your failures or voice your true opinions, you might be verbally, if not physically, assaulted.

If home doesn't meet a person's emotional needs for belonging and for safety, where else can these be found? A child has no other place to go to find a full-time support system. And divorce—the way out that parents too often choose—destroys the team that prime-time parents are hoping to build.

Therefore, it is very important that families support one another. Don't permit verbal hostility. Don't allow character assassinations. Don't allow one person to be taken advantage of by another. Make your family responsible for the emotional (as well as the physical) well-being of each member. This is not easy because differences can easily lead to hostile conflicts when emotions flare out of hand. To discourage such conflicts, set up a buddy system in which each individual is responsible for supporting one other person. You might assign responsibility according to age, letting each child care for the sibling directly below him in age. This system will not diminish team support, but it will ensure that at least one person will support and encourage another family member.

It is a mistake for families to be so involved in building their little teams into winning teams that they forget about people and families beyond their door. Your family team will increase in team spirit when it breaks out of its shell and becomes a team buddy for another family, or another individual. It would be mutually beneficial if families with older children would adopt families with younger ones. In this way the older children could babysit and learn about child development and responsibility; and the younger children could have a big brother or sister that they could admire and respect. Every family needs friends. Every family needs emotional support. And every family at times needs to be bailed out of difficult circumstances. Start your search today and you will not have to look far for a family who needs you. And remember, to keep your own family's spirit high—you need them.

*Champions act like champions.* This is perhaps the coach's easiest task. For if you have established a family purpose and identity; if you have inspired your children to live by a code of behavior that will ultimately bring them success; if you have established a good communication system so the children have no doubt about the family's game plan and feel free to contribute to it; and if you have made it clear to the children that they are loved even though they make mistakes, then the result will be children who will act with the assurance and spirit of champions. When children know they are an essential member of a winning team, they don't have to go through life putting other people down in order to make themselves feel more successful.

The story is told of a young man who became enthralled with the wisdom of a certain philosopher. He begged the philosopher to teach him so he too could achieve excellence. The philosopher questioned him concerning the strength of his desire and finally bade him to follow wherever he went. Day after day the young man attended the philosopher. Then one day the philosopher came to the edge of a river and waded in until the water was swirling around his waist. The young man hesitantly followed. The philosopher went deeper and deeper and then suddenly turned around, grabbed the young man, and held his head under the water. Minutes went by. The young man frantically struggled to get free. At last he was able to push his head from the water and gasp a life-saving breath of air. Then the philosopher let go.

"Why did you do that?" the young man breathlessly questioned.

The philosopher replied, "You will never achieve excellence until it becomes as dear to you as that breath of air, and until you struggle for it with the same determination."

And so it is with parents. Becoming a prime-time parent, who is the "coach" of a winning team, is not easy. Until you value winning as Vince Lombardi did, and say as he said, "Winning isn't everything; it's the only thing," will you give your family the leadership that they need to win and achieve excellence.

Prime-time parents can't spend every minute every day with their children. But by developing a prime-time parenting personality, by anticipating and creatively solving problems, and by effectively using their time, they can provide a supportive emotional base from which each individual family member can emerge with the competence to continue growing toward excellence.

# Index